Stanton in Her Own Time

WRITERS IN THEIR OWN TIME

Joel Myerson, *series editor*

STANTON

in Her Own Time

A BIOGRAPHICAL
CHRONICLE OF HER LIFE,
DRAWN FROM RECOLLECTIONS,
INTERVIEWS, AND
MEMOIRS BY FAMILY,
FRIENDS, AND
ASSOCIATES

EDITED BY

Noelle A. Baker

University of Iowa Press,
Iowa City

University of Iowa Press, Iowa City 52242
Copyright © 2016 by the University of Iowa Press
www.uiowapress.org
Printed in the United States of America

The University of Iowa Press is a member of Green Press Initiative
and is committed to preserving natural resources.

Printed on acid-free paper

Library of Congress Cataloging-in-Publication Data
Names: Baker, Noelle A. (Noelle Annette), 1964– editor.
Title: Stanton in her own time : a biographical chronicle of her life, drawn from recollections, interviews, and memoirs by family, friends, and associates / Noelle A. Baker, ed.
Description: Iowa City : University of Iowa Press, 2016. | Series: Writers in their own time
Identifiers: LCCN 2016004608 | ISBN 978-1-60938-433-3 (pbk) | ISBN 978-1-60938-434-0 (ebk)
Subjects: LCSH: Stanton, Elizabeth Cady, 1815–1902. | Suffragists—United States—Biography. | Social reformers—United States—Biography. | Feminists—United States—Biography. | Women—Suffrage—United States. | Women's rights—United States.
Classification: LCC HQ1413.S67 S73 2016 | DDC 305.42092 [B] —dc23
LC record available at https://lccn.loc.gov/2016004608

For Kay Baker, and in loving memory of Bob Baker (1937–2013)

Contents

Introduction

"COME, COME, MY CONSERVATIVE FRIEND, wipe the dew off your spectacles, and see that the world is moving." With these words, at once inviting and patronizing, Elizabeth Cady Stanton introduced the two-volume *Woman's Bible* (1895, 1898), critical commentaries on the bible's treatment of women, compiled and penned by Stanton and a committee of female collaborators.[1] With this publication and other late-career critiques of religion Stanton intended to illuminate her contemporaries' perspective on what she regarded as the fundamental barrier to women's social, medical, economic, sexual, legal, and political independence; further, she hoped to energize her younger suffrage colleagues.[2] In this case, she badly misjudged their reaction. Both her loyal but determined partner of nearly half a century, Susan Brownell Anthony, and the majority of second-generation suffrage reformers had targeted their sights on the single goal of enfranchisement.[3] They considered Stanton's greater interest in the cultural underpinnings of women's subordination anathema: concerns and demands that repelled the public and obscured the path to the ballot box.

While in earlier years Stanton fired verbal bombs at the church and advocated women's reproductive and sexual rights, fertility limitation, and liberal divorce laws with relative impunity, after the publication of *The Woman's Bible*, the National American Woman Suffrage Association, whose ranks she had led for many years, publicly disavowed Stanton, even while freethinkers and socialists granted her heroic stature.[4] Her late publications identify religion as the primary source of women's unequal stature. As she suggested to freethinker Benjamin Underwood in November 1885—a full decade before the publication of *The Woman's Bible*—"I have passed from the political to the religious phase of this question, for I now see more clearly than ever, that the arch enemy to women's freedom skulks behind the altar."[5] Primary among her concerns was the clergy's role in upholding divorce laws that oppressed women and deprived them of their children.

These anticlerical analyses triggered a backlash that would nearly efface Stanton's standing as a suffrage activist and as the primary philosopher of the woman's movement; only in 1940 would her reputation begin to revive.[6] *Stanton in Her Own Time* documents this trajectory, highlighting the ways in which Stanton's different roles and conscious self-representations—among them, impish youth, woman's suffrage activist, lyceum lecturer, wife and mother of seven, writer, and freethinker—influenced her contemporary reception. In so doing, it also illustrates another trajectory: Stanton's evolution as an activist—from early woman's rights organization and oratory, beginning in Seneca Falls in 1848, to a post–Civil War lyceum career of widespread popularity, to her conscious distancing from NAWSA and final, complex engagement with a host of radical reforms that assumed, for her, a level of importance equal to, if not greater than, the goal of women's enfranchisement.

Examined in terms of this full scope of her long career, Stanton's reformist causes were extraordinarily diverse and at times conflicting: a short list includes prison reform, public street cleaning, bicycles, universal suffrage, educated suffrage, divorce, free love, coeducation, instruction in cooking for men and in needlework for boys, children's rights, eugenics, prenatal care and fertility limitation, dress reform, the separation of church and state, and homeopathic medicine. She embraced them all enthusiastically. Interviewed in 1895 by a journalist from the *American Wheelman* and reprinted in the *Free Thought Magazine*, for example, the eighty-year-old Stanton championed the bicycle as the medium to inspire the construction of bike paths across the country; to encourage women to exercise and develop "more courage, self-respect, and self-reliance"; and to democratize society as a relatively inexpensive mode of travel. In short, she concluded, "The wheel is a missionary of peace and good-will, teaching democracy in politics, charity in religion, an equality in social relations without distinction as to color or previous conditions of servitude."[7] As might be intuited from the breadth of her interests, Stanton was also a person of frustrating contradictions. An intellectual powerhouse, fierce chess competitor, highly entertaining lecturer, and principled advocate for women, she was also selfish, unscrupulous, and despite her occasional abolitionist work and long-term interest in associationism and then socialism, often painfully biased against laborers, African Americans of both sexes, immigrants, and devout individuals of any religion. Always supremely confident of her own opinion and smug about her nearly perpetual good health, Stanton was impatient with illness and free with advice about the best way to eliminate it. Almost invariably optimistic, Stanton charmed with her sparkling blue eyes and her witty and self-deprecating jokes. For instance, in a letter written around 1870, she commented on a recent mass meeting speech in which she demanded liberal divorce legislation, remarking laconically, "The entire press of the country are howling at me but as I weigh lbs 175, I think I can stand it."[8]

Because I consider the dual trajectories of her activist career and its contemporary reception important contexts for understanding Stanton's relevance in the nineteenth-century cultures of authorship and reform as well as in our own time, I have selected aspects of her life that adumbrate those stories and that feature Stanton at different ages. Hoping to capture some sense of the "girth" of Stanton—at "lbs 175" and more—*Stanton in Her Own Time* represents moments in her life that indicate the range of her contradictions and the tensions that shaped them. In addition to portraits of a rebellious and playful student during her time at Troy Female Seminary in "'She Always Played to Win': The Young Elizabeth Cady," I have compiled selections by multiple figures and grouped them in thematic chapters entitled "Seneca Falls and Early Reform Days," "Marriage and Maternity: The Public 'Mother of the Gracchi,'" "Partnership of Elizabeth Cady Stanton and Susan B. Anthony," "Schism," "The *Woman's Bible* Controversy," "Not 'A Person of One Idea': The Aging Radical," and "Death and Legacy of Elizabeth Cady Stanton." As this introduction details, some of these chapters require more historical and cultural context than others.[9]

According to her contemporaries, Stanton was widely considered an accomplished writer, gifted raconteur, and "inimitable" speaker. In this regard, Stanton, who was frequently compared to peerless abolitionist orators Wendell Phillips and Charles Sumner, might extemporaneously narrate an amusing anecdote, but she typically composed her orations in advance; and she prepared many of Anthony's addresses, as well as their joint publications.[10] Of her lectures Grace Greenwood, herself a talented writer, remarked in 1869, "Her speeches are models of composition—clear, compact, elegant, and logical. She makes her points with peculiar sharpness and certainty, and there is no denying or dodging her conclusions."[11] In addition to producing myriad published addresses and discourses, Stanton wrote countless newspaper and periodical pieces, literary reviews, an autobiography, *Eighty Years and More* (1898), and with Anthony and Matilda Joslyn Gage composed and edited three of the ultimately six volumes in *History of Woman Suffrage* (1881, 1882, 1886).[12] In her final years when nearly blind, Stanton dictated to a secretary. Her last political appeals for women's enfranchisement—letters to President Theodore Roosevelt and his wife, Edith—are dated 22 and 25 October, the last a mere twenty-four hours before her death on 26 October 1902. So prolific were these closing days that posthumous articles appeared for weeks.[13] Stanton recalled in old age that she had composed over one hundred speeches, but Lori D. Ginzberg, emphasizing "the sheer volume of her words," adds that this assessment "does not begin to account for the paper trail she left behind. Even with culling by her and her children, the written documentation is daunting."[14]

What changes in the *Woman's Bible*-era writings from her earlier critiques of religion elicited such a dramatic shift in mainstream perceptions of Stanton? On the surface, not a lot. These publications, like those of earlier years, reveal her ongoing penchant for provocation, her insistent posturing as an intellectual enfant terrible, her contradictory and often inflammatory rhetoric. Elitist and racist discourse mars her writings early and late.[15] More positively, Stanton's masterful deployment of narrative anecdote, humor, and intellectual rigor is also consistent over time. Nonetheless, her insistent targeting of religion in her last decades, a decision that infuriated Anthony, certainly accounts for much of the hostile tone of her late reception.

In addition, however, beginning in the 1880s—for practical reasons that ranged beyond her increasing interest in the cultural roots of women's subordination—Stanton slowly withdrew from the lecture circuit and from the organizational work of NWSA and NAWSA. In 1880, she terminated a lucrative career as a popular lyceum lecturer; at age sixty-five and overweight, she could no longer physically tolerate the rigorous eight months on the road she had managed ably over the previous decade. Never one to suppress her sensual enjoyments, she grew morbidly obese; as a result, more than occasional public addresses were impossible, but she remained the titular head or figurehead of NWSA and then NAWSA until she resigned the presidency in 1892.[16] Moreover, as early as 1882, lengthy trips to Europe, where two of her adult children lived, removed her from the American public scene. In her absence, "Aunt Susan" and her deputy "nieces," the next generational leadership of NAWSA, filled the political void in public perception despite the fact that Stanton continued to work behind the scenes, writing and sending ideas to be presented by her supporters, occasionally to force a controversial conversation into the public minutes. Writing to Anthony and Clara Bewick Colby from England in February 1891, for example, Stanton urged them to produce some "decent resolutions" (unlike the "trash" the two had formulated alone the previous year) for the upcoming meeting. "I will try & grind out some good resolutions but do not let it be known that they are mine," she advised sternly.[17]

Notably, by the mid-1880s, Stanton was still presenting her ideas and publications to the public eye at rapid fire, but she was less and less a tangible physical presence in America. In truth, Stanton's heyday as a beloved and respected public figure coincided with her career as a lyceum lecturer, between 1869 and 1880. During that time, the stories others tell about Stanton demonstrate the effective ways in which she crafted her public persona as a maternal figure, a self-presentation that allowed her to domesticate her radical commentary and to protect herself from controversy. Characterizing this period, Elisabeth Griffith emphasizes that Stanton used this calculated maternal image "to legitimize her public activities," adding that she "shrewdly chose to appear matronly, respectable, charming, and genial."[18] Intriguingly, many of the posthumous tributes written by her supporters consciously or unconsciously replicate this strategy. Many—perhaps adapting the language of her grandchildren[19] in denominating her their "Queen Mother" or perhaps responding to her own public self-crafting—called her their "Mother Superior"† or described her in various other ways as the motherly head of the movement (see fig. 8).

This maternal persona was more than a PR tool, however; it was firmly grounded in fact, and her political interest in motherhood evolved later in her life into philosophical speculations and writings about the "Matriarchate," an ancient period then deemed to be a time of feminine civic and religious authority. Maternity looms large in Stanton's actual biography and played a role in the trajectory of her legacy and her evolving interests as an activist. After her marriage in 1840 to the abolitionist Henry Brewster Stanton, Elizabeth Cady Stanton gave birth to seven children and suffered at least one and perhaps two miscarriages over a span of seventeen years, a period during which her public reform activities were severely curtailed as a result.[20] In 1860, the year after the birth of her last child, Robert, she gave her first public address in six years (see fig. 9). Moreover, Stanton spent ten years on the lyceum circuit in part to pay for the college degrees of her children; further, because of her increasingly limited mobility from 1887 to the end of her life in 1902, Stanton's adult children served as caregivers.[21] For much of her adult life, then, the prolific Stanton was engaged in caring for or being assisted by her children.[22] In this regard, she is not unlike her own mother, Margaret Livingston Cady, who delivered eleven infants, of whom six survived. Elizabeth Cady, born in Johnstown, New York, on 12 November 1815, was her mother's eighth.

Father Daniel Cady, a lawyer and later a New York Supreme Court judge, provided a privileged lifestyle and educational opportunities for his children; and Margaret Livingston descended from old, wealthy New York families—advantages that set Stanton apart from many other abolitionist and woman suffrage reformers and that may yield some insight into her biases as well as her reception.[23] Stanton attended Johnstown Academy, learned Greek, and from 1830 to 1833 received additional education at Emma Willard's well-respected Troy Female Seminary. Before and after graduation, Stanton also benefited from her father's flourishing legal practice. His household, teeming with young men clerking for Cady, promoted stimulating legal conversations, access to his law books and library, and an opportunity to clerk for her father, as rheumatism made writing increasingly difficult for him.[24] This legal education would serve her well as a woman suffrage advocate: throughout her career Stanton brought to bear the full force of her canny legal acumen onto her attempts to change Constitutional and state laws in regard to women's right to obtain a divorce, gain custody of their children, vote, and own property. Moreover, Daniel Cady not only opened his home to his daughter and new son-in-law but later provided domiciles for the couple in Boston in 1844 and then again in 1847 in Seneca Falls, New York, where, even before the passage of the New York Married Women's Property Act in 1848—granting married women the right to own property—he placed the deed in Elizabeth Cady Stanton's name. After his death in 1860, his daughter's inheritance stabilized the Stantons' uncertain finances.

The financial difficulties plaguing Henry and Elizabeth Cady Stanton in their first eight years of marriage also reflected a dynamic that likely fed the initial attraction between the couple but then contributed to their increasingly distanced relationship over time. The two met in the fall of 1839 at the home of her cousin, the abolitionist and philanthropist Gerrit Smith. Finding the perpetually impecunious Henry Stanton an unfavorable prospect as a husband, Daniel Cady successfully demanded that his daughter break their engagement, resistance that may ultimately have enhanced Stanton's appeal. Henry Stanton was then at the peak of his career as an abolitionist: a dynamic speaker, outsized personality, and fascinating conversationalist, traits Elizabeth Cady shared and valued. Their sexual attraction was undeniable then and in the first fifteen to twenty years of the relationship. Of the couple, however, abolitionist Sarah Grimké observed, "Henry greatly needs a humble, holy companion, and she needs the same."[25]

Elizabeth ultimately married her suitor, but her father's concerns proved astute. As an abolitionist, New York legislator and Custom House appointee, and journalist, Henry Brewster Stanton was never able to fully harness his considerable ambition. By contrast, in 1848, even in the midst of childbirth and child-rearing, his wife collaborated with more experienced reformers to organize one of the earliest woman suffrage conventions in Seneca Falls; national conventions would follow.[26] Because of her partnership with Anthony, even during the years when she could not attend conventions, Stanton wrote and published prolifically, and Anthony delivered her political addresses. After the birth of her last child, Elizabeth assumed a woman suffrage leadership role. Then a decade later, during the first two months of her popular and lucrative lyceum career, she generated two thousand dollars after covering expenses—approximately thirty-seven thousand in 2014 dollars. Lisa Tetrault, arguing that the "central site of activity" for the woman's rights movement between the mid-1860s and early 1880s was the lecture circuit, suggests that Stanton may have earned ten thousand dollars or more each season.[27] "There were few models in the 1850s for a marriage in which the wife's fame eclipsed the husband's," notes Lori D. Ginzberg. "Finding himself with a wife whose outspokenness, accomplishments, and public acclaim outstripped his own, Henry Stanton probably never quite knew what hit him" (see fig. 7). When Henry died in 1887, he left no will, but his entire estate amounted to $1,100, approximately $28,200 in 2014 dollars.[28]

In 1868, when Elizabeth purchased land for a country house in Tenafly, New Jersey, the marriage had deteriorated to the point that the couple ultimately resided in separate households. Describing a Christmas Eve dinner at Tenafly she enjoyed with Stanton and her children in 1876, Anthony wrote, "no husband & Father out to enjoy it with them—& no seeming care that there is not."[29] Henry, then a journalist for the *New York Sun*, a position he would hold until his death, rented rooms in New York City and occasionally commuted an hour by train to the country, while his wife remained primarily in Tenafly. Confiding in her dear friend and second cousin Elizabeth Smith Miller in a letter dated approximately 1880, Elizabeth mourned the absence of a "deep soul love" such as the British novelist George Eliot found in life. "The older I grow," she mused, "the deeper my sorrow that I have no son of Adam to reverance [*sic*] and worship as a God."[30] One could argue that her deep and sustaining partnerships with women, such as those with Miller, as well as with Susan B. Anthony, Lucretia Mott, Helen Hamilton Gardener, and Clara Bewick Colby—whose voices are reflected in this volume—provided the intellectual and spiritual relationship she fruitlessly sought in a "son of Adam."

Perhaps the most important—and certainly the best-known of Stanton's political associates—was her friendship of over half a century with Susan B. Anthony (1820–1906); so often were they fused in the public imagination that I include a chapter on the reception of their partnership (see fig. 3). As an example of this pervasive understanding of their collaboration, after Stanton resigned her presidency of NAWSA in 1892, newspaper reports claimed that their relationship was dissolving. Stanton wrote her old ally wittily, "Have you been getting a *divorce* out in Chicago without notifying me? . . . I shall not allow any such proceedings. I consider our relation for *life*, so make the best of it."[31] More than a public perception, however, as collaborators their differing strengths and weaknesses promoted their activism, and the two friends accomplished together landmarks they could never have achieved alone. A Quaker, Anthony was raised in a culture of reform and abolition, and as was more typical of nineteenth-century reformers than was Stanton's advantaged upbringing, she withdrew from boarding school and then supported herself as a schoolteacher after the 1837 financial crisis decimated the Anthony family's finances. When Stanton and her Quaker allies organized the Seneca Falls convention, Anthony was involved in temperance and abolitionist reform.

The women met sometime in 1851, on or about May 13, and despite internal disagreements, such as the necessity for Stanton's numerous pregnancies and their differing, late-century priorities—religion for Stanton and organizational methodology and enfranchisement for Anthony—they labored shoulder to shoulder, always presenting a unified public face to the world, until Stanton's death in 1902.[32] As Theodore Tilton depicted with comic power, the two were perceived as a singular entity—or at least an indissoluble pair. "Elizabeth Cady Stanton, or, as she is sometimes called, Susan B. Anthony, is a celebrated lady with snow-white and auburn hair, plump and slender figure, Grecian and Roman nose, and lives simultaneously in two houses—one at Tenafly, N.J., and the other at Rochester, N.Y." He opined,

> Indeed, Mrs. Stanton, or, to call her by her maiden name, Miss Anthony, is a ubiquitous personage, and not only attends all the woman's meetings wherever they are held, but also has been known on certain occasions to be writing the resolutions, and at the self-same moment to be delivering the speech, in their support. It has been sometimes suspected that Mrs. Stanton and Miss Anthony are two distinct persons, united by a cartilage like the Siamese twins, but in the absence of any medical or other scientific proof of this hypothesis, I remain of the opinion that, like Liberty and Union, they are "one and inseparable."[33]

Importantly, in terms of a conjoined Stanton/Anthony public reception, Tilton understood their union to be "inseparable" from "Liberty," a popular and foundational Revolutionary-era sentiment both women, but particularly Stanton, fostered in addresses. Such natural rights liberalism likewise informs the Declaration of Sentiments.[34] Until Frederick Douglass championed its successful passage along with the rest of the declaration's petitions, Stanton's radical call for women's enfranchisement electrified and divided attendees; and years later Stanton and Anthony came to understand that the convention's symbolic moment of unity between the famous abolitionist leader and emerging woman suffrage activist would play well as history. Not surprisingly, then, when seeking to establish both the Seneca Falls convention and NWSA as the "origins" of a singular woman's rights movement in America, Anthony adroitly perpetuated these connecting threads and connected them to herself in the late nineteenth and early twentieth centuries.[35]

With Anthony, Stanton undertook a long and multifaceted career in reform. She presided over annual woman suffrage conventions, presented addresses before state and national judiciary committees, traveled across the burgeoning western territories to speak to audiences of men and women, presented petitions to the Senate for women's and African American men's enfranchisement, campaigned in states and territories for women's enfranchisement, attempted to vote, and ran for Congress (receiving 24 votes).[36]

Exuding humor, self-confidence, and dismissive bias by turn, Elizabeth Cady Stanton provoked and weathered execration, at times gleefully; and as previously suggested, the tenor of that reception reveals a distinct trajectory, one that over time contributed to her legacy, both in the nineteenth century and today. No longer is her name automatically associated with her conjoined twin, Susan B. Anthony; her features grace no silver dollar, and she is an unlikely candidate for new currency designs that will celebrate female civil rights leaders in 2020, the one hundredth anniversary of the Nineteenth Amendment to the Constitution. "Given her tendency to utter the most radical conclusion she could imagine at any given time," observes Lori D. Ginzberg, "it is not surprising that her legacy has remained slippery, or that the next generation of activists saw in Susan B. Anthony a more appropriate icon for the march to woman suffrage."[37]

"'She Always Played to Win'" illustrates the origins of that radicalism. Much of the readily available information about Stanton's youth and young adulthood derives from Stanton's autobiography and narratives written by her children and may be of uncertain validity. Many nineteenth- and early twentieth-century commentaries relied on these anecdotes, and in the main I have tried to avoid them. Stanton's eldest daughter, Margaret Livingston Stanton Lawrence, however, sketched a "pen picture" of Elizabeth Cady that resembles later descriptions and holds the ring of truth: she was "a plump little girl with very fair skin, rosy cheeks, good features, dark brown curly hair, laughing blue eyes, and beautiful teeth."[38] This youthful portrait captures the physical and personal characteristics that critics and friends of the adult Stanton reiterate—a joyous sense of humor that rarely failed her, sparkling blue eyes, and a healthy head of curly hair. As a mature public figure, those attributes, and in particular the white locks, became her PR weapons; and in later selections Theodore Tilton, May Wright Sewall, and Laura Curtis Bullard pointedly remark upon the relationship between her vibrant "animal spirits,"[†] her mischievous humor, and her activism. Selections from Stanton's two reformist children and Thirza Lee similarly anticipate the ways in which devious and competitive youthful traits enriched the determined activist of later years (see fig. 1).

"Seneca Falls and Early Reform Days" depicts the Stanton who was in the process of "becoming" a reformer. As her biographers have revealed, the events that propelled her toward woman's rights were several. Among them were—and as will be prominent herein—her own experiences as a young mother and wife and her engagement with other wives and mothers in Seneca Falls. Stanton was, effectively, a single parent for months at a time (see fig. 2).[39] As Anthony wrote to Antoinette Brown Blackwell in September 1858, Henry Brewster Stanton, "full of *Political Air Castles*," would be out of town throughout the fall: "he was gone 7 *months* last winter," she complained; "the whole burden of home & children, therefore, falls to her."[40] Stanton likewise heard the complaints of other women and dispensed advice, in Seneca Falls and also later in her career when she lectured to exclusively female audiences about motherhood and marriage.[41] These related topics propelled an important facet of her feminism and her reformist vision, and she understood them experientially as well as theoretically. In this chapter we witness Stanton's Seneca Falls home life and parenting decisions from the perspective of her children's piano teacher, Anna Elizabeth Henion.

In a selection written by Mary S. Bull, a young attendee of the 1848 Seneca Falls convention, we also observe the "public" Stanton as she appeared within her community as a fledgling writer for the temperance journal the *Lily*, as a passionate advocate of dress reform, as a sounding board for local wives and mothers, and as the organizing spirit of the Seneca Falls meeting. Intriguingly, Bull is clearly a "resisting" witness to Stanton's reformist platforms, so her perspective also indicates that Stanton could charm and repel simultaneously. Bull published her reminiscence of midcentury Seneca Falls in 1880—including an unflattering description of the portly Stanton in Bloomer attire—and although Stanton read its occasionally sharp critique with her typical equanimity, she protested with an equally characteristic convenient memory. "The only point that vexed me was the suggestion that I was not well formed," she complained. "If I remember aright in those days I was not beyond the becoming point of plumpness."[42]

Other glimpses of Stanton as an early reformer include Lucretia Russell Gray Smith's depiction of Stanton attending, rather than speaking before, a Quaker reform meeting; significant here is an early example of her characteristic use of pointed humor to silence a critic. Finally, the Reverend Olympia Brown recalls her attendance in 1866 at the founding meeting of the American Equal Rights Association, an organization formed by woman suffrage and abolitionist reformers to campaign for universal suffrage during the early years of Reconstruction; now Stanton is upon the stage, and Brown contrasts her later, maternal persona with the earlier version of a fifty-year-old Stanton—without the white curls and, perhaps, just being "herself." Brown found Stanton's early rhetoric as impressive as that of later years, but the younger Stanton lacked "the strong and undaunted manner in which she faced her audience and told them great truths"[†] that she acquired with age.[43]

By contrast, the selections in "Marriage and Maternity" both require considerably more contextualization than preceding chapters and present Stanton at the height of her powers on the stage, where she successfully wielded her sunny disposition, trademark white curls, plump features, maternal demeanor, and personal anecdotes to charm her audience. Stanton, Augusta Larned remarked astutely in 1873, "generally amuses and entertains most when you agree with her the least."[44] Stanton scholars have long been aware of the suspect nature of many of these diverting reminiscences, aired in lectures, journal publications, and finally in *Eighty Years and More*. But as Larned wryly detects, Stanton reckoned that humor, baby stories, and her personal experiences as a wife and mother softened the radical edges of her reformist demands. "What matters ultimately to Stanton," observes Ann D. Gordon, "is not, apparently, whether she recalls events accurately, . . . but whether she conveys to people the complicated tensions . . . that accompanied the advent of women's rights." Illustrated via others' memories in this and several chapters in *Stanton in Her Own Time*, these anecdotes skillfully portray, under the guise of laughter and everyday "home life," Stanton's mature sense as a reformer of the cultural origins of women's subordination. Enfranchisement alone, she came to believe, could not resolve such tensions; and she brought to the fore her exceptional gifts in rhetoric, logic, humor, and self-presentation to work on the minds of her audience— a performance Gordon characterizes aptly as a "well mastered . . . style of contributing to political dialogue while speaking as a woman."[45]

Margaret Stanton Lawrence, who attended one of Stanton's lectures in Chicago, penned one such admiring description of her mother's well-honed manner of delivery. Before her audience, Stanton skewered clergymen for their repression of women's voices and public roles by relating what is most likely a fictitious story of her post-Troy Seminary years. In this tale Stanton described herself as the leader of her church's girls' club; the teenaged girls raised money to fund a young man's tuition at Auburn Theological Seminary and to equip him in ministerial attire upon graduation. In her recounting, at his first sermon she and her fellow clubwomen learned a useful lesson in institutional religion:

> After dilating on how faithfully that club of girls had worked to educate the young man, in her round, rich voice, she asked that vast assembly, "And what do you think, my friends, he took for his text? That passage of the Scriptures which says, '*I suffer not a woman to speak in the churches.*'"
>
> Pausing a moment to let her hearers catch the full significance of the thing, Mrs. Stanton remarked in a slow, distinct tone, "We never educated another!" Her hearers burst into shouts of laughter and applause. Some man called out, "I should hope not."[46]

Such reactions, particularly from male audience members, illustrate typical responses to a strategy many scholars acknowledge: Stanton leveraged humor and her maternal persona to inoculate her radical commentary on controversial subjects, from marital rape and divorce to fertility limitation and religion. Not only did she succeed in doing so (to laughter and applause, as indicated above), but she also became, in the words of two of her biographers, a "celebrity" and a "rock sta[r]." "'You would laugh to see how everywhere the girls flock around me for a kiss, a curl, an autograph,' she wrote her daughter" Maggie in December 1872.[47]

The white curls, beribboned dresses, and ample frame apparently enhanced her rhetoric, as seems evident also from Olympia Brown's earlier memories of a younger Stanton at the founding meeting of the American Equal Rights Association. Moreover, this anecdote illuminates our understanding of another oratorical gift, Stanton's "round, rich" speaking voice, a characterization that harmonizes with other accounts. The San Francisco reporter attending Stanton's "Marriage and Maternity" lecture similarly delineated her "clear musical"[†] voice, while a 1994 *New York World* report adds another dimension to this declamatory power. Although Stanton did not speak "loudly," the reporter claimed she amply and easily projected her "deep, round musical voice" throughout the vast auditorium, with its two thousand attendees. Helen Potter, a professional impersonator, likewise highlights Stanton's "subdued force" in speaking.[48]

But the skillful authorial hand is also apparent in Stanton's lectures on the lyceum circuit. That her use of personal anecdote, jokes, and careful word choice rendered her subject matter less threatening and even pleasing is evidenced by the popularity of her lectures on "Our Girls," "Our Boys," and "Marriage and Maternity"—and by responses from reporters and audience members. In addition to characterizations of Stanton's self-presentation and deportment during this phase of her lecturing career, this chapter includes a male reporter's description and approximate transcript of a Stanton address to women on marriage and children, one of her most popular lyceum lectures. It bears the hallmarks of what Lori D. Ginzberg calls "classic Stanton": "[f]unny, ironic, condescending, rambling, and overblown."[49] As Lisa S. and J. Michael Hogan explain, successful postwar lyceum lecturers typically offered high-entertainment fare or stirring social reform talks grounded in uncontroversial moral or Christian idealism. Stanton deviated from both categories and, notably, held off the scandal and subsequent mainstream public alienation that hampered her late writings and addresses on religion, an achievement garnered in part by her rejection of "direct, explicit statements of her feminist views, even on the issue that most defined her public image: woman suffrage."[50] One example of that strategy can be seen in Stanton's identification in this lecture of the educational stages daughters require. While the first stage, self-development, is essentially the entire subject of the lecture, for this audience Stanton ranks mothering before citizenship in her hierarchy of tutelage. The central inequity, however, cannot be contained by breezy anecdotes: "woman is a living subject to man's desires,"[†] she declared, illustrating that religion, fashion, marital law and custom, and medical practices ensure that state of abject servitude.

The fact that Stanton could give such talks (as well as another on "Free Love" the same evening) with impunity speaks volumes to her skillful self-presentation and narrative style. Commenting on both aspects of Stanton's oratory, the Wisconsin writer and woman suffrage reformer Hattie Tyng Griswold explained that Stanton "compelled audiences. In those early days it was almost disgraceful to hear her, but the people came," she recollected in 1902. "When there, they remained, and they refrained largely from jeering."[51] The doctrine of "free love," "the repudiation of any relation between a man and a woman that violated the personal freedom of either," was derived from Charles Fourier's socialist theories, popularized in the 1840s through communal experiments that attempted (ultimately without success) to harmonize capital and labor. In the 1850s, sexual reformers, water-cure physicians, spiritualists, and free love anarchists, such as Thomas Low and Mary Gove Nichols, Marx Edgeworth Lazarus, and Stephen Pearl Andrews, surfaced previously suppressed aspects of Fourier's writings, namely his theory of the sexually liberated "passional attraction," in lectures and published tracts. Therein, these reformers attacked indissoluble marriage, promoted fertility control, and advocated more elevated sexual and spiritual unions. Although their individual positions on monogamy, diet, and sexual purity differed, free lovers shared Stanton's contention that a loveless marriage reduced its partners to an economic relationship akin to slavery and prostitution, and they all supported woman's rights.[52]

In an 1870 speech addressed to a private group of men and women, Stanton championed the virtue of "true free lovers" such as Mary Wollstonecraft and insisted that the freedom to improve upon mistakenly chosen conjugal partners and the liberty to discard constricting marital relationships would allow individuals to "advance to higher planes of development." Anticipating a judgmental reception of these words she exclaimed, "Why, that is nothing short of unlimited freedom of divorce, freedom to institute at the option of the parties new amatory relationships, love put above marriage, and in a word the obnoxious doctrine of Free Love. Well, yes, that is what I mean." Contrasting progressive and virtuous free lovers with "abject slaves" whose marriage is "seemingly so fair" in this speech, Stanton specifically condemned a couple who were "prominent advocates of women's rights." Ellen Carol DuBois proposes that in this speech Stanton likely refers to Henry Browne Blackwell and Lucy Stone, the latter a prominent leader of ASWA.[53]

The 1855 marriage of Stone and Blackwell was widely regarded as a prototype for enlightened wedlock; Stone retained her maiden name, and at the time of the ceremony the two authored and published a formal protest against the legal and civil restrictions marriage imposed upon wives. Stanton's attack is certainly consistent with the routine and ongoing rancor between NWSA and AWSA leaders, including Stone, about Stanton and Anthony's racist language and opposition to the Fourteenth and Fifteenth Amendments and Stanton's critique of marriage, advocacy of divorce, and remarks about free love. But she may also have alluded to rumors within reformist circles at this time in regard to Blackwell's dalliance with the married Abby Hutchinson Patton, a fellow activist and former member of the famed abolitionist Hutchinson Family Singers.[54] According to his sisters, in October of 1869, Blackwell was "refusing utterly to terminate" the connection, to Stone's "discomfort & distress"; and in April 1870 Stone feared he would "renew or take up the old snare."[55] Blackwell eventually disentangled himself from Patton; but these contexts provide a more nuanced understanding of Stone's commentary on Stanton—especially in regard to free love—in several chapters in *Stanton in Her Own Time.* As Isabella Beecher Hooker maintained in her 1870 letter to Susan Howard, during the 1850s Stone had enthusiastically approved Stanton's assertion of women's right to divorce and to refuse sexual intercourse within marriage;[†] further, she then considered both topics appropriate and even essential subjects for a national suffrage convention.[56]

Stanton's affinity for free love doctrine and her ability to espouse aspects of it without public condemnation and indeed with approval are on display in her popular lyceum lectures on marriage and maternity,[†] in which she advocated wives' right to limit family size and control the terms of their sexual interactions, particularly (and as her response to an audience member indicates) in regard to marital rape. Stanton's counsel—the necessity of educating men to respect women's self-sovereignty—is both typically elitist and informed by activist conventions that shared an uneasy alliance with components of free love doctrine. Abolitionist and woman suffrage reformers such as Stanton, Angelina Grimké Weld, and Lucy Stone omitted the word "obey" in their marriage vows to signal their power to refuse sexual intercourse.[57] As Linda Gordon explains, this right of refusal instantiated a "potentially explosive, conceptual change: the reacceptance of female sexuality" in a historical moment when male sexuality commanded religious, legal, medical, and cultural authority. As such it "was a key substantive demand in the mid-nineteenth century when both law and practice made sexual submission to her husband a woman's duty."[58] Significantly, Stanton's public recommendation for women to refuse the compliance demanded by biblical, legal, and cultural edict was reported without rancor by a male journalist and met by likely white, middle-class women with applause and laughter.

This reception is fascinating given public anxiety about her subject matter, a concern also evident in other chapters in which reformers are troubled by Stanton's nonchalant association of free love with woman's rights. As historian Adam Tuchinsky suggests, in his *New York Tribune,* Horace Greeley, with whom Stanton increasingly sparred in regard to divorce, also offered free love advocates, woman's rights supporters, and religious conservatives a welcoming environment for open discussions about marriage. These debates proved "so discomfiting to voices across the political spectrum," Tuchinsky observes, because "everyone agreed that the family institution bore some relationship to the emerging bourgeois order, but there was little consensus about what exactly that relationship was." Other social experiments, among them the Mormon polygamist community Stanton visited in 1871, likewise contributed to this uneasiness. Together, they prompted questions that would frame dissent within the woman suffrage ranks and inform commentary on Stanton. What is family? How does it engage in and contribute to public and private ethics, rights, and responsibilities? What is its role in an increasingly complex and industrializing world?[59]

These questions grew polarizing after the Civil War. "Criticisms of marriage and discussions of divorce and sexuality increasingly became subject to repression and censorship," suggests Joanne E. Passet. "Civic and moral leaders, convinced that the institution of marriage ensured social order, feared it was in jeopardy." Chief among the social purity reformers was Anthony Comstock, who harnessed the power of the federal government to criminalize women's reproductive health issues. In 1872 the New York City Young Men's Christian Association (YMCA) charged Comstock with the leadership of its New York Committee for the Suppression of Vice; the next year Comstock championed the passage of the Comstock Law, a federal obscenity statute that spawned numerous state laws, all prohibiting the circulation of pornography and other "obscene" information about contraception and abortion.[60]

Creating further dissension among woman's rights reformers, Victoria Claflin Woodhull and Stanton waded into public debates that Comstock considered obscene; the ways in which he reacted to both women also speak to the public's reception of their words and personae.[61] A series of sex scandals in the late 1860s, the trials of unwed mother Hester Vaughan for infanticide[62] and of Daniel McFarland for the murder of his ex-wife's intended,[63] culminated in the early 1870s with Laura D. Fair's murder trial[64] and the notorious Beecher-Tilton exposé. The Beecher-Tilton affair would prove particularly damaging for woman's suffrage activists, and it would destroy the career of Theodore Tilton, then a successful lecturer and editor.[65] Although knowledge about Henry Ward Beecher's extramarital affair with his parishioner, Elizabeth Tilton, circulated within Brooklyn and reformist sets by 1870, in an attempt to publicize the double standard in these cases, Woodhull exposed the Beecher-Tilton affair in 1872 in her *Woodhull & Claflin's Weekly*. Comstock quickly charged Woodhull with obscenity, and she was repeatedly jailed as she awaited trial. To protest the unfair legal and media treatment of all these women, Stanton called mass meetings, gave interviews, and published articles; she incorporated information about them in her lyceum lectures on marriage and maternity in the 1870s (without harassment from Comstock), but the publicity surrounding the three trials and Woodhull's arrests inevitably forced other suffrage reformers to state their own positions on free love. In the public imagination both branches of the woman's movement were tainted with the specter of free love: Beecher was elected president of AWSA in 1869; and Stanton, Woodhull, and both Tiltons were active in NWSA. Theodore briefly assumed its leadership in 1870 when it was (transiently) denominated the Union Woman's Suffrage Society.[66]

Stanton's San Francisco lyceum lecture on marriage and children† also documents the extent to which Stanton's reception impacted multiple audiences from diverse professional fields. Like Stanton—and often quoting her—"regular" (orthodox) and "irregular" (homeopathic) physicians cited ubiquitously the racist example of the Native American "squaw," who works as usual just prior to a simple delivery. To quote one later example from John H. Dye's *Painless Childbirth* (1884),

> When she realizes that the hour of delivery is at hand, she enters her cabin or betakes herself to some stream or spring, gives birth, washes the young "injun" in the cold water, straps it on her back, and before she has been scarcely missed, has returned a full-fledged mother, and resumes her labors.[67]

Whether she intentionally modeled herself on this idealized and racialized birth or not, it is worth noting that Stanton made similar claims for her own seven childbirths to her lyceum audiences† and in other public and private settings, and in doing so her reception impacted protofeminist medical reformers as well as woman's suffrage activists. "Taken together with the . . . increasing number of manuals on sexuality and contraception available," observes Lois W. Banner, "her lectures contributed to an effort on the part of American women to take some control over their sexual and reproductive lives."[68]

Comparing the claims in popular advice manuals by male obstetricians and female physicians on the subject of "painless" birth, Richard W. and Dorothy C. Wertz argue that while both believed the deleterious effects of "civilization" accounted for "unnecessary" pain in childbirth, they recommended strikingly different social behaviors to address the problem: "male authors . . . impl[ied] that women had pain because they were not truly feminine, because civilization had rendered them too 'sexually aggressive, intellectually ambitious, and defective in proper womanly submission and selflessness.'"[69] Many female physicians (and, arguably, some male water-cure and homeopathic physicians)—in the manner of Stanton's exposition—espoused a program of self-care that would lead to physical, psychological, intellectual, and professional independence. Not surprisingly, then, Stanton's lecture,[†] delivered lyceum season after season in the 1870s, "became the favorite text" for these early female self-help authors, and "[m]any women sought a painless birth as a sign of their own release from feminine roles that made them weak and dependent."[70]

The extent to which Stanton successfully packaged herself and her radical ideas for a lyceum or reform audience can be better understood in the context of the 1871 western lecture tour she undertook with Anthony. Both women spoke about the tragic case of Hester Vaughan. Anthony, however, did not always fare as well in those years as did Stanton. Her extemporaneous speeches, earnest and stoic demeanor, and single status occasionally threatened her audience, even—as was the case in 1871—when Stanton and Anthony spoke on the same, inflammatory topic. Poignantly, Anthony described the frustration of "sitting a lay figure and listening to the brilliant scintillations as they emanate from her never-exhausted magazine. There is no alternative," she confessed; "whoever goes into a parlor or before an audience with that woman does it at the cost of a fearful overshadowing, a price which I have paid for the last ten years."[71] As subsequent chapters will demonstrate, however, Stanton's enthusiastic reception would change with time; by the end of their lives, the roles would reverse.

The selections in the "Schism" chapter, including the commentary of William Lloyd Garrison,[†] Lucy Stone,[†] J. Elizabeth [Hitchcock] Jones,[†] Theodore Tilton,[†] the attendants of the 1869 American Equal Rights Convention (AERA),[†] Henry Browne Blackwell,[†] Isabella Beecher Hooker,[†] and Eleanor Kirk,[†] reflect the events surrounding what William S. McFeely movingly describes as "one of the saddest divorces in American history. Since Seneca Falls, if not earlier," he explains, "the antislavery movement and the women's rights movement had been seen . . . as one. . . . Now a breach was in the making, and it has never fully healed."[72] This rupture, composed of painful stages during which woman's suffrage leaders began to compete with abolitionists who advocated enfranchisement and civil rights for black men, also spurred a schism within the woman suffrage movement. Concerned that there was insufficient political will in Reconstruction America to enfranchise both African American men and all women, male and some female abolitionists asserted that it was "the negro's hour." In response Stanton and Anthony exchanged their former calls for universal suffrage with "educated suffrage" and repeatedly employed scurrilous epithets for the immigrant and black men who would precede (white) women to the ballot box. This chapter demonstrates the multiple ways that other reformers viewed these tactics. As in the chapter "Marriage and Maternity," Stanton's pronouncements on divorce and free love as well as on late 1860s and early 1870s sex scandals also inflected their perspectives. This breach, the events that preceded it, and the subsequent competition between NWSA and AWSA inevitably contributed to the trajectory of Stanton's legacy as well as her shifting allegiance from enfranchisement and organizational work to cultural concerns.

As the foregoing implies, no singular event produced this schism; nonetheless, the tragic divide centered upon a pivotal question. Can worthy ends sanctify compromised means? As selections in this chapter narrate, a precipitating event, two ballots (for African American male and women's enfranchisement, respectively) placed before Kansas voters in 1867 provoked this question for ostensibly unified AERA reformers, who were last glimpsed in Olympia Brown's observations at their founding meeting. Notoriously, during the Kansas campaign Stanton and Anthony allied with George Francis Train, whose racist commentary had for years appalled abolitionist and woman suffrage reformers; their outrage increased in the 1870s when Train championed both Mormon polygamists and the imprisoned Victoria Woodhull.[73] William Lloyd Garrison, revolted by the alliance and defensive at this time about his own public disputes with Wendell Phillips, disagreements that were proving damaging to his reputation, expressed the indignation that Lucy Stone and Stephen Symonds Foster echo: he found the partnership unprincipled, further collaboration with the Democratic party vile, and Train himself bestial and ludicrous. "He may be of use in drawing an audience," he wrote, "but so would a kangaroo, a gorilla, or a hippopotamus."† In another selection, however, Isabella Beecher Hooker considered Harry Blackwell and other Kansas Republicans' engagement with Train similarly compromised.† It is possible, then, that righteous indignation as well as defensiveness may have contributed to Garrison's† and Stone's† caustic reception of Stanton and Anthony.

The Fourteenth (ratified in July 1868) and Fifteenth (sent to the states for ratification in February 1869) Amendments to the Constitution, which pledged to secure the citizenship and enfranchisement of African American men, also created strains within AERA as for the first time the word "male" would be attached to "citizen" in that hallowed document. The "call" for AERA's annual meeting (12–14 May 1869) reflected this tension; in a contradictory manner, it proclaimed that the Fourteenth and Fifteenth amendments have "now virtually established on this continent an aristocracy of sex" and that "woman's enfranchisement is now a practical" or viable "question in England and the United States."[74] The discussion,† conflated in this chapter, ensued over several convention sessions and, in an increasingly heated fashion, also addressed the association of free love with woman's suffrage and condemned Stanton. At times the acrimonious outbursts grew so loud that individual voices could not be heard. After the convention, Stanton and Anthony formed NWSA; officially replying in kind, in October 1869 Stone and others formed AWSA.

During the convention itself, one reads important assessments of Stanton from Frederick Douglass,† Stephen Symonds Foster,† Lucy Stone,† and Mary Livermore.† Livermore and Stone revealed the anxiety that Stanton's pronouncements on divorce, free love, and Hester Vaughan's trial had produced, as do Stone's bitter remarks in 1879 on Stanton's association with Train, Woodhull, Laura D. Fair, and Mormons.† As mentioned above, Stone's rancor may derive from personal as well as political fears about the success of the woman suffrage movement. But the extent to which her concerns were astute may perhaps be judged by Anthony and Stanton's reception in *Puck* magazine's "Cartoons and Comments" piece and its accompanying centerfold cartoon (see fig. 6) the following year. Discounting women's claims that their enfranchisement would "purify politics," the editorial (likely penned by *Puck* editor Henry C. Bunner) retorted, "These ranting women . . . have not even been able to purify their own organization from the fatal association of free-lovers and spiritualists."† Famed satiric cartoonist Joseph Keppler's illustration sports mannish woman suffrage advocates who have left the care of their home and children to their husbands, grown whiskers and dressed as men, and elected an effete male candidate entitled "THE LADIES PET."[†] Not dissimilarly, the *National Republican* contrasted the "dignity" of AWSA's 1880 annual convention with NWSA, whose members it characterized as "long-haired brethren and the pantalooned sisters."[75] Perhaps in anticipation of this kind of depiction of woman suffrage, in her defense of the Kansas campaign Eleanor Kirk pointedly expounded upon Stanton's roles as exemplary wife and mother.[†]

Final skirmishing between Stanton,[†] Livermore,[†] and others reveal additional rifts within AERA, some breaking along gender and others along race lines—exposing white reformers' complex and ambiguous moral high ground, even for those who avoided the racist and elitist rhetoric of Stanton, Paulina Wright Davis,[†] and, to a lesser degree, Anthony.[†] British-born Henry Browne Blackwell, for example, who was led into antislavery and then woman's suffrage reform by Stone, was also prone to the racist arguments in which white activists sometimes engaged, an example of which is his pamphlet "What the South Can Do," an appeal to enfranchise white women in order to maintain white supremacy by increasing the numbers of white voters. According to the transcript, Blackwell's suggestion that the test oath should be abolished in the South met with hisses from the audience[†]—while, strangely, Stanton's calls for educated suffrage requirement, as "she did not believe in allowing ignorant negroes and foreigners to make laws for her to obey," received applause.[†76]

The poet, novelist, and political activist Frances Ellen Watkins Harper's commentary at this AERA meeting also engages with Stanton's statements, especially in comparison with Frederick Douglass's arguments, lending a nuanced impression of the ways that a black woman might respond differently from black men to Stanton's slurs, her rejection of the Fifteenth Amendment, and her calls at this convention and elsewhere for educated suffrage. Harper occupied a unique position in this meeting, where the discussion of "woman's" and "African American" rights was largely coded "white" and "male," respectively, by white suffrage reformers. Harper forthrightly introduced questions about racism in the workplace for African American women, even as she insisted that she would not "put a single straw" in the way of black men's enfranchisement. "But the white women all go for sex," she argued, "letting race occupy a minor position. She liked the idea of working women, but she would like to know if [the resolution] was broad enough to take colored women."† Despite Anthony and others insisting, "Yes, yes," however, Harper appears to remain skeptical, since at this point she offered eyewitness testimony of white female laborers' racism in Boston.[77]† Whether Stanton, Anthony, and others understood the full range of her rebuke is unclear from the AERA meeting's transcript, but her remarks do provide an important context for the occasionally contradictory ways in which reformers responded to Stanton's denigrating language at this critical moment and the ways such responses shaped her later activism.

Douglass himself generously treated and then deflected Stanton's racist and elitist epithets with humor. He strongly resisted, however, the idea "that there is the same urgency in giving the ballot to woman as to the negro. With us, the matter is a question of life and death." Douglass's full elaboration of the nature of this urgency is indeed dire: his examples included lynching, child murder, and school segregation, and they elicited "great applause" from the AERA members in attendance. Moreover, when asked by an unidentified attendee whether his concerns also applied to black women, Douglass conceded that truth. "Yes, yes, yes," he agreed; "it is true of the black woman, but not because she is a woman, but because she is black. (Applause.) . . . Woman! why, she has 10,000 modes of grappling with her difficulties."†

Despite the obvious painful tensions that characterized this and other discussions during the AERA convention, it is noteworthy that Foster, Douglass, Stanton, and Livermore all interjected humor; the audience's laughter suggests the extent to which (on the surface, at least) reformers at this point were agreeing to disagree with Stanton despite strong emotions—an atmosphere that would change quickly and dramatically but that, remarkably, would continue to characterize the Stanton-Douglass friendship. Although some scholars suggest that Stanton had first met Frederick Douglass around 1841, he himself recalls the date as 1840.†[78] He served as one of the vice presidents of the AERA, as did she. They shared intellectual and reformist interests, including a fierce streak of anticlericalism and an anti-Garrisonian willingness to dirty their hands with pragmatic politics. By June 1869, Douglass and Stanton dined together at Theodore Tilton's home, where they put aside their disagreement over the Fifteenth Amendment.[79] Stanton supported his controversial marriage to his white secretary, Helen Pitts, in 1884, a union that strained relations within his family and among his political friends and advocates in the black and white communities. But their fifty-year relationship endured periods of great stress, as at this fraught postwar moment.

Theodore Tilton (as Stanton's friend, unsurprisingly) and Isabella Beecher Hooker rendered a more positive reaction to the multifaceted controversies within this chapter of *Stanton in Her Own Time*. Because of her culturally powerful siblings (including Harriet Beecher Stowe, Henry Ward Beecher, and Catherine Beecher), leaders of both NWSA and AWSA were eager to ally with Hooker; each group courted her in 1869 and 1870 (see fig. 4). After conducting her own personal "investigation" by interviewing members of both NWSA and AWSA, Hooker ultimately joined forces with Stanton and Anthony, despite reservations. Alarmed at the radical content of Stanton's articles in *Revolution* and encouraged by husband John Hooker to approach Stanton and Anthony, Isabella Hooker proposed that she and her half-sister Harriet Beecher Stowe assume its editorial duties, requesting, however, pay for their labor and a domesticated new title for the paper. Stanton and Anthony were willing to pay the sisters—and Anthony hoped initially that Stowe might write a "woman's" *Uncle Tom's Cabin* in its pages—but refused to revise *Revolution*'s moniker.

Simultaneously, however, Stowe was facing tremendous public backlash in response to her September 1869 *Atlantic Monthly* piece, "The True Story of Lady Byron's Life," a posthumous defense of the embattled Lady Byron and an exposé of Lord Byron's relationship with his half-sister, an alliance that had produced a child. As she did with other sex scandals in the late 1860s and early 1870s, Stanton interjected herself into this controversy by publicly vindicating Stowe and Henry Ward Beecher, who had become implicated in November 1869 with the notorious McFarland murder. Press and clergy railed at Beecher for ostensibly supporting adultery, divorce, and bigamy when he officiated at the marriage of Abby McFarland and Albert Richardson. In response to the controversy, Stanton delivered a speech on the inequities of divorce laws for women and of men's coercive sexual ownership of their wives' bodies and children. Stowe felt further tarnished by Stanton's defense of her and Beecher as well as of Abby McFarland and retreated from any association with the inflammatory *Revolution*; Hooker, however, as her letter to Susan Howard suggests, offered occasional pieces in its pages and remained an NWSA ally and leader.[†80]

Despite their differing perspectives on Elizabeth Cady Stanton, Hooker,

Blackwell, and Tilton shared a perplexing need to reflect upon the extent of her "Americanness." Although perhaps only punning on the name of his newly formed association, in a December 1869 letter to Isabella Hooker—inviting her to join AWSA—Blackwell wrote, "By your tastes, principles, & social position, you belong to our phase of this Movement—you can help keep it *American* in spirit."[†] Blackwell, whose British family suffered no lack of self-esteem, emphasized the Beecher family's reputable societal position—as well as that of AWSA. By extension, however, he seemed to imply that Stanton, or NWSA, was not "American." While this potential allegation may actually reference only their organizations' differing nomenclature, as in "National" versus "American," when placed beside Hooker's comments in an 1870 letter to Howard, the apparent aspersion seems clearer. Hooker, who throughout the epistle attempted to defend Stanton for her association with Train and statements on divorce and free love, compared Stanton to "foreigners" denied the ballot. "They are here," she asserted, "& disfranchisement will not annihilate them—but fraternizing will educate & gradually make them an integral part of the body politic."[†] Hooker's sense of her own superiority was as inflated as Stanton's, and after joining NAWSA she believed it her duty to render respectable Stanton's priorities. In fact, she went so far as to suggest that Stanton not attend the 1871 NAWSA convention; and the evangelical tone Hooker displays throughout the letter reiterates her sense that she has been called to "raise up" and "educate" both Stanton and Anthony.

With an entirely different perspective in doing so, Tilton nonetheless used a strategy similar to Hooker's. In his published vindication of Stanton's actions at this time, Tilton also endeavored to elevate her in the public eye, but instead of questioning her nativity, he literally draped her in the flag. Tilton's Stanton is as prototypically American as Martha Washington. "The costume that most becomes her (and in which her historic portrait ought to be garmented)," he urged, is a blue dress and red shawl. This "array, . . . topped with her magnificent white hair, makes her a patriotic embodiment of 'red, white, and blue.'"[†] Read together and viewed in the context of reformers' general understanding of Stanton's old and respected lineage (in this chapter, for example, Eleanor Kirk suggests that Stanton's every gesture on the platform "proclaims her 'to the manner born'" and that her "natural pride in the good blood she bears in her veins gives her a dignity and queenly presence"[†]), these debates about the true nature of

Stanton's "Americanness" may indicate the pervasive way in which some kinds of unsettling ideas provoke xenophobic reactions, even among politicians and reformers with seemingly common cause, in the nineteenth as well as in the twenty-first century.

As suggested initially, the selections in "The *Woman's Bible* Controversy" range widely in tone, and they portray the extent to which the *Woman's Bible*-era Stanton was regarded as a fearful stranger within her own suffrage association, even as she was revered by freethought communities. Likewise, they illustrate the relentlessly evolving focus of her activism. Highlighting her friendship with the nation's best-known agnostic and freethinker, Robert Ingersoll, and the anticlericalism Stanton increasingly emphasized in writings of later years, Marie H. Garrison wrote presciently in 1903,

> This latter stand of Mrs. Stanton changes materially her position in history. Had she in all things stood shoulder to shoulder with Susan B. Anthony, their names would go down without a break to posterity, but she did not do this; therefore I am tempted to prophesy that when our children's children look backward at the scroll of our country's history they will see written side and side the two names,
> Elizabeth Cady Stanton and Robert G. Ingersoll.[81]

Garrison's prophecy has only partially come to pass. Stanton's "latter stand" did indeed affect her position in history, just as her relationship with and similarities to the lawyer Robert Ingersoll elucidate her reformist trajectory. Both activist leaders turned their backs on productive, "conventional" career paths and shared a remarkable ability to enchant a live audience in service of radical aims. Ingersoll, a friend and admirer of Stanton, abandoned his successful political calling "to pursue his campaign . . . for the separation of church and state," Susan Jacoby explains; "as contemporary newspaper accounts make clear, [he] was a master at reaching people who did not necessarily agree with him or who might have been downright hostile." Further, Ingersoll also viewed enfranchisement as only the first step toward women's achievement of full personal independence.[82] Thus, while in old age the reach of her personal touch ebbed, Stanton nonetheless mirrored the "Great Agnostic's" vibrant and radical appeal: late commentators such as Laura Curtis Bullard,† Adelaide Johnson,† and John Swinton† suggest that for eclectic progressives her dynamic powers had not diminished. Such was the case for the Kentucky freethought writer and woman suffrage reformer Josephine Kirby Henry, who also served on *The Woman's Bible* revising committee; Henry claimed that Stanton's inspiration always remained with her. "I know of no one who has exerted so great an influence on my life," she vowed in 1902. Moreover, Stanton's example lent courage. "Often as I have entered" the state capitol to petition for Kentucky women's property rights and enfranchisement, she recollected, and "when I saw the members of the General Assembly crowding into the legislative hall, my heart sank within me. . . . Suddenly some influence seemed to say to me: 'Fear not, be a faithful sentinel on the watch tower of liberty: remember Elizabeth Cady Stanton.' With this thought my fears fled."[83]

In regard to Henry's empowered sense of the impact of Stanton as a freethought leader, Kathi Kern suggests that while she is routinely considered a secularist ready to dismiss all theology, in fact, early and late Stanton thoroughly studied theological questions, understanding their importance to American women. Her goal, explains Kern, was "to refashion Christianity into a creed that was true to its radical potential," a position influenced by her interest in positivism.[84] In addition, however, from the earlier time of her residence in Boston in the 1840s and attendance at Theodore Parker's liberal sermons and Margaret Fuller's Conversations, Stanton was also influenced by Transcendentalist conceptions of deity as impersonal and of Jesus as a wise prophet whose truth-bearing commentary should be distinguished from sectarian doctrines.[85] These Transcendentalist notions would undergo socialist and nearly anarchist turns by the end of the century. "Had Jesus lived in Russia in the nineteenth century," Stanton argues in *Bible and Church Degrade Woman*, published by Horace L. Green at the century's turn,

> he would have been exiled as a Nihilist for his protests against tyranny and his sympathy with the suffering masses. He would have been driven from Germany as a socialist, from France as a Communist, and imprisoned as a blasphemer in England and America, had he taught in London and New York the radical ideas he proclaimed in Palestine.[86]

This comment should also be understood in the context of her enthusiasm for exiled radical and "nihilist" Sergei M. Kravchinskii, reported by Adelaide Johnson.[†] For Stanton these figures represented a model of individual conscience, educated in self-development through science, with their right to unique personal and political self-determination. Her faith resided in that growth and its promise of social progress.[87]

In light of Kern's assertion that Stanton wished to reform religion, just as she sought to reform other cultural aspects of American society, Horace L. Green's reaction to NAWSA's disavowal of its former leader perhaps suggests the extent to which this impetus stimulated freethinkers.[88] Green depicted Stanton as a savior and martyr—comparing her to Jesus of Nazareth, John Brown, Theodore Parker, and Giordano Bruno. In this view he likewise characterized the leadership of NAWSA as akin to those who crucified such martyrs, literally or metaphorically[†]—a perspective that Anthony ally Jean Brooks Greenleaf, despite her sympathy for Stanton, disputed.[†] But for Green, Stanton's persecution "prove[s] the truth of the new Gospel of Evolution,—that progress is the eternal law of the universe and can not be prevented or stayed by persecution."[†] Stung and uncharacteristically chastened by the words and actions of NAWSA leaders, Stanton was grateful to Green, and his journal continued to offer a stage and a receptive audience for her ideas (see fig. 10).

The 30 November 1902 *Blue Grass Blade*, published under the banner "Edited by a Heathen in the Interest of Good Morals," amply demonstrates this welcome receptivity of Stanton's skepticism; it further indicates that freethought communities respected her fierce advocacy of free love, women's reproductive health, and liberal divorce. Amid three articles dedicated to glowing assessments of Stanton in the paper's "Notes and Comments" section, the Iowa woman suffrage reformer and freethought author Harriet M. Closz elevated Stanton—along with the skeptical midwestern farmwife, writer, and free love anarchist author Kate Austin and the freethought pamphleteer, sexologist, marriage reformer, and free speech advocate Ida C. Craddock—to a new "Humanitarian Trinity."[89] All three women died within weeks of each other, and grief within their interlocking communities was profound; the mourning anarchist Emma Goldman called Craddock "one of the bravest champions of women's emancipation"; and of Austin she wrote, "Kate to me was not the Anarchist, the rebel, the thinker, the writer, . . . she was a mother, a friend. . . . She was all to me."[90] Understanding the differences in the three women's forms of activism, Closz nonetheless emphasized the connecting threads between them. "Though they traveled different paths the prophetic mind can discern in the not far distant future, the point where the three paths merge into one," she predicted, "and beyond a little way the goal of the emancipation of mothers." Twenty-first-century assaults on women's sexual and reproductive rights may suggest that Closz proved overly optimistic about timely access to this unified route, through which childbearing women's "past and present inequalities" might be eradicated; nonetheless, her commentary underscores the heady optimism that informed turn-of-the-century progressive thinking by Stanton and the ways in which she was envisioned, among the vanguard of leaders in revolutionary and empowering change for women.[91]

The other selections in this chapter, including NAWSA secretary Rachel Avery's report,[†] the commentary from attendees of the NAWSA convention in January 1896,[†] and Jean Brooks Greenleaf's reply to Green,[†] represent the wide array of woman suffrage perspectives on Stanton after the publication of *The Woman's Bible*. Taken together, however, they offer a snapshot of the organization's leadership on the cusp of change, locating a significant tension at the time between a "narrow" and a "broad" platform that also signaled the new direction of the suffrage movement as a whole. The anguished words of Anthony[†] at this meeting registered profound distress about her inability to protect her old friend. "Anthony was caught in the changing of the guard," argues Kathi Kern. "Her own belief about the necessary direction of the movement legitimated the new leadership she had hand chosen, their political conservatism, and their emphasis on pragmatic strategy at the expense of ideological boldness." Stanton was not the only victim. Her decisions also pushed her loyal followers and defenders to the margins of the movement and out of leadership positions, including Lillie Devereux Blake and Clara Bewick Colby, both mentioned in this chapter.[92] From that perspective, Colby's determination to humanize and honor Stanton[†] in her commentary in the chapter "Death and Legacy of Elizabeth Cady Stanton" reveals multiple lines of motivation.

The selections in "Not 'A Person of One Idea': The Aging Radical" from woman suffrage reformer, journalist, and novelist Laura Curtis Bullard; sculptor and woman's rights advocate Adelaide Johnson; and labor activist, journalist, socialist, and newspaper publisher John Swinton reflect the voices of Stanton supporters in the years preceding and following the publication of *The Woman's Bible*. Johnson's selection—spread out over two weeks as Stanton sat for a sculpture—is particularly revealing in that her report makes it clear that Stanton is trotting out standard anecdotes from her lyceum days and the reminiscences that would later appear in her autobiography. Johnson's reaction, then, offers an instantaneous assessment of Stanton's powerful storytelling abilities. Significantly, one such anecdote, regarding her weeklong visit with Rosalind Frances Stanley Howard, Countess of Carlisle,[†] invokes Stanton's influence upon an expansive transatlantic woman's rights community in England and France in the 1880s and 1890s, even as her power gradually diminished at home within NWSA and NAWSA.

Bullard also alludes to her transatlantic impact, as well as the sharply differing ways that the American public viewed Stanton, who remained "an object of affection to one class of her countrywomen, of aversion to another, and of curiosity to all."[†] In this view, the aging suffrage leader remained a vivid aspect of the national public gaze then, even when she offended. In seemingly pointed fashion Bullard also introduced this piece by recounting eager questions posed to her about Stanton by George Sand, whose queries likely imply that Stanton's public statements on divorce, women's reproductive health, and free love continued to resonate for transcontinental artists and reformers. The French novelist, playwright, autobiographer, and political writer George Sand, a pseudonym for Aurore Dudevant, explored protofeminist and socialist concerns in her own writings. Much admired by other female authors such as Elizabeth Barrett Browning and George Eliot, she led an unconventional sexual and professional life: legally separating from her husband, cross-dressing, and taking a number of well-known lovers, among them the poet Alfred de Musset and composer Frédéric Chopin. As Bullard—and perhaps Sand—was well aware, Stanton, in addition to wearing and promoting the Bloomer costume in her early reform years, publicly detailed the benefits women would garner in wearing male attire.[93]

Importantly, and in addition to reiterating Stanton's substantial transatlantic reputation, another late commentator on Stanton, Caroline Severance, even more overtly envisioned Stanton as companionate with Sand and with George Eliot. This perception and her admiring commentary lend complexity to characterizations of the two suffrage organizations as "conservative" (AWSA) and "radical" (NWSA); they similarly enable a more nuanced analysis of Stanton's reception by members of both organizations in several chapters of *Stanton in Her Own Time*. Severance is perhaps best known as the "mother of clubs," or the founder of the woman's club movement, although her interests were as varied as Stanton's. "Eliz. Cady Stanton was a woman of large nature physically and mentally," she wrote in an undated typescript memorializing Stanton posthumously, "one to whom we can well apply the tribute of Geo. Elliot [*sic*] to Geo. Sand: 'A large-brained-woman and great hearted man.'"[94] Like Bullard, Severance found common ground in the three women: for her, they were leaders of women and controversial agents who transcended gender boundaries. She honored each role.

Caroline Severance's remarks complicate our understanding of Stanton's reception within the woman suffrage movement in the late nineteenth and early twentieth centuries. Severance was not a younger generation "niece" but instead almost exactly Anthony's contemporary. Although allied with the women and men of AWSA (and before it the New England Women's Club, of which she was a founder) and distressed in the late 1860s by Stanton's advocacy of divorce and alliance with George Francis Train ("We are all in sackcloth and ashes over the strange, insane move of S.B. Anthony and Mrs. Stanton . . . hand in hand with George Francis Train!!!" she wrote then), Severance held close friendships with NWSA members and shared kindred interests with Stanton. She passionately embraced the water-cure movement, became an early leader of the Free Religious Association, and took up with dress reform and socialism. Perhaps more importantly, early in her career she became disillusioned with the feuding between woman suffrage factions, and, like Stanton, she turned increasingly to social problems outside the narrower quest for enfranchisement. By the time that Stanton was working on *The Woman's Bible*, the two "seemed to come to an understanding," suggests Severance's recent biographer, Virginia Elwood-Akers, "and they corresponded with each other until Elizabeth's death."[95]

Thus, amid the mixed but largely negative NAWSA reaction to Stanton in the last two decades of her life, radical woman's rights reformers, socialists, and nonconformist artists continued to praise and even (as John Swinton's commentary suggests especially) celebrate Stanton in the manner of her "rock star" lyceum years. The married and aging Swinton, who worked at the *New York Sun* during Henry Brewster Stanton's last two years there, likely responded so viscerally to Stanton because of her positions on women's rights, but also because of her turn to socialist and labor concerns in the 1890s. Since her exposure to the Transcendentalist Brook

Farm community experiment in 1845, Stanton had expressed an interest in associational living; but her late and more thoroughgoing enthusiasm was due in part to the influence of her daughter, Harriot Stanton Blatch, a well-known suffrage and labor leader in her own right, whom Swinton apparently mentions. (Stanton's eldest daughter, Margaret Stanton Lawrence, was not a public figure.)

In his letter to Stanton, Swinton described a bizarre dream, and in it he promoted a highly spirited form of admiration that also suggests how uniquely Stanton inhabited the unconscious mind of one old reformer. Envisioning Stanton standing on a rock in the middle of an enormous desert, Swinton imagined her assuming nearly messianic proportion, as she "discours[ed] upon righteousness and the judgment to come." Further, she was either associated or conflated with her daughter's more progressive labor opinions in his mind and, remarkably, with a "dancing girl in short skirts," spinning to "the Spanish bolero." Even the rock shivered![†] At the time of his death, almost exactly a year before Stanton's, Swinton was honored in *Harper's Weekly* as a "stalwart, bitter champion of the laborer"; his life "was one continuous battle for the rights of the lowly and oppressed."[96] Swinton's veneration was undoubtedly welcome to the vain, aging reformer—who, as Adelaide Johnson bemusedly narrated on several occasions during her sitting for the sculptor, demanded that she reduce her robust throat and chin.[†] "I loved flattery," Stanton confesses in her autobiography.[97]

Worshipful in her own manner, in this chapter's selections Adelaide Johnson recorded conversations with Stanton as she sat for her sculpture over a course of fourteen days;[†] notably, one such sitting offers a revelatory glimpse into Stanton's evolving thoughts on motherhood and woman's rights. According to one of these diary entries, Stanton wove personal anecdotes into her commentary on the "Matriarchate," a tactic she had also commonly employed in her lyceum lectures to enliven and illustrate political or philosophical analyses.[98] In other diary entries, Johnson recollected Stanton's rather bombastic tall tales about the care of her own and other people's infants as "very interesting."[†] She likewise found "ever inspiring" similar anecdotes during this sitting, memorable among them Stanton's jocular championing of the "gift of motherhood"[†] in an acerbic encounter with Arthur Cleveland Coxe, Episcopal bishop of western New York. Employing a standard argument, that women's reproductive organs unfitted them for governance and rational thought, Coxe "prated of 'womans [*sic*] disabilities,'" she wrote. According to the tale, Stanton disabled *him* with scathing humor.† The fact that the childless, artistic, and intellectual Johnson, an author and woman's rights activist in her own right, found such accounts as fascinating as did lyceum attendees of the 1870s, an audience that historian David Mead characterizes as "few intellectuals and a large body of plain citizens," indicates that Stanton's standard delivery included protofeminist content—in addition to the spoonful of sugar required by the lyceum circuit.[99] Importantly, however, this strategic combination of "sugar and spice" also reflects the evolution of Stanton's intellectual, personal, and political concerns. Her late analyses of the Matriarchate forged a connecting link between earlier and lyceum-era interests in the physiological education of women about reproductive health and her later attempts to reform institutional religion and to analyze the solitary nature of the human condition.

Delighting in this alleged early period and predicting its return, Stanton propounded with Johnson upon topics also found in her public remarks that same year, "The Matriarchate, or Mother-Age," an address Stanton composed for the National Council of Women in February 1891.[100] The three discussion topics Johnson mentions during this sitting—medieval witch trials, the maternal sources of power, and women's roles as soldiers and nurses—all figured in this address. In "The Matriarchate, or Mother-Age," Stanton cited early anthropologists Lewis Henry Morgan, Karl Pearson, and others to assert that in preclassical times women assumed positions of religious, political, and domestic authority; created matrilineal lines of inheritance; and established associational communities. The extent to which society could reestablish women's equal status, such scholars held, would also demonstrate its increase in civilization and democracy.

In "The Matriarchate," Stanton located women's civilizing force, physical and mental strength, and wise governance within maternity. "Thus," she observed, "instead of being a 'disability,' as unthinking writers are pleased to call it, maternity has been the all inspiring motive or force . . . towards a stable home. . . . Clearly the birth of civilization must be sought in the attempt of woman at self-preservation during the period of pregnancy and lactation." In a related manner, Stanton argued that "physical and mental vigor" produced "freedom," an expansive personal and political liberty that women enjoyed only during the Matriarchate, and she characterized the transitional decades between this pre-Christian Matriarchate and the "father-age" as a struggle for supremacy between the sexes. In this view, women, who had previously waged battle with strength but only to defend their own, retreated to nursing roles as men initiated territorial wars that would establish hierarchical aristocracies. By the Middle Ages, woman's sole remnant of Matriarchate power lay in her authority as tribal priestess. "From this last refuge," proposed Stanton, "she was driven by the introduction of the Christian religion, with its narrow Pauline doctrine, which made woman mentally and physically the inferior of man, and lawfully in subjection to him." From her perspective, in this period the former tribal priestess and übermother, deemed a witch by Christian priests, burned at the stake.[101]

Stanton found such scholarship an exciting example of women's historical liberation from the authority vested in the nineteenth century's modular family; she believed it also unearthed an important precedent for her long-standing view that childbearing and rearing were empowering modes of caregiving and self-reliance, rather than disabilities (as was the more typical contemporary understanding of both). Morgan, she argued, had proven the illegitimacy of other nineteenth-century historians, who "cling to the idea of 'the family unit,' because on that is based the absolute power of the father over the property, children, and the civil and political rights of wives."[102]

Johnson's excited glosses on Stanton's words underscore the curious fact that the then-unmarried Johnson, whose interests did not include children at this time, expressed such grateful appreciation for these "words of wisdom and goodness."† Considered together with lyceum attendees' reactions to Stanton's lectures in the 1870s, Johnson's diary may indicate that in the last quarter of the nineteenth century, women of various stations maintained a vivid interest in the importance of physical health as a precursor to domestic, intellectual, civil, and political equality. Stanton sketched this prophetic future in the address's concluding lines, where she urged stirringly, "our turn will come again." Significantly, in this vision Stanton does not call for female supremacy over men. Instead she looks out for "the as yet untried experiment of complete equality, when the united thought of man and woman will inaugurate a just government," homes and civilization devoid of poverty, crime, and human ignorance.[103] And in light of Stanton's optimistic hope for human equality and progress, Johnson likely internalized this message, for in 1896, when she married British businessman Alexander Frederick Jenkins in her Washington, DC, studio, the groom took her surname. Rather bizarrely, her sculpted busts of Anthony and Stanton served as bridesmaids, or perhaps tribal priestesses. Taken as a whole, the selections in this chapter stand in striking contrast to her critics in NAWSA and illustrate that Stanton was granted an enthusiastic reception by freethought, woman suffrage, socialist, anarchist, and sex radicals. The world was moving, indeed!

The last chapter in *Stanton in Her Own Time* documents her last days on earth and reflects posthumously on her life and legacy. Importantly and perhaps predictably, all the selections are self-consciously concerned with history. The fact that Stanton's daughters, Margaret Stanton Lawrence and Harriot Stanton Blatch, produced differing accounts of their mother's death speaks to the ways in which end-of-life stories inform the legacies of great figures and of those who follow in their footsteps. Lawrence narrates the day immediately preceding Stanton's death as fairly routine. Although almost completely blind, Stanton, with the aid of her secretary, works on her letters to the Roosevelts at her desk while the children talk and laugh; because of Stanton's "extraordinary" "powers of concentration," she continues undeterred until they demand her presence. Visitors arrive, Stanton sparkles as "the life of the party," and the assembled celebrants enjoy dinner. The next day Stanton arises but feels unwell. The children call the doctor, to no avail: "She had always hoped she would not have an illness at the end of her days, she had never been really ill; wonderful health had been her portion. At three o'clock in the afternoon the machinery in the clock ran down, and she quietly slipped away!" Lawrence remembered.[104]

Although Stanton had grown frail in the last year of her life and as early as 1884 had complained privately to Anthony of shortness of breath and heart trouble, both daughters reinforced the vigorous image their mother had held up to the world in justification of her theories about the independent woman (see fig. 11).[105] Lawrence's Stanton continued advocacy even in sightless old age—highlighting an (authentic) portrait of the publications that surfaced after the death of the suffrage leader. It was not stretching the truth to emphasize how actively her mind engaged the world up to the very day of her death, an intellectual youth and vitality that was no surprise to those who knew Stanton. Indeed, Adelaide Johnson imagined her consciousness illuminating the ether, even after death. On October 26 she penned in her diary, "This day the great the splendid Elizabeth Cady Stanton has passed on [*sic*] Well!!!! What does she see now, how is it to her active consciousness over there[.]"[106] In Lawrence's narration, the day before her death Stanton produced activist commentary with the same critical force of concentration in the face of her brood's antics that she had displayed when they were toddlers and young children. As deftly as the great Swiss salonnière Germaine de Staël, Stanton entertained her guests the evening before her demise. She glided into oblivion quickly, with no sign of the illness she had always regarded as a crime against self-regulation and a shameful mark of weakness.

Harriot Stanton Blatch—who sketched her narrative of her mother's death in a letter to Stanton's freethought friend and colleague Helen Hamilton Gardener—promoted an alternative version of the death of the "mother" of the movement, one that emphasized her legacy as the great stateswoman and orator and perhaps subtly pointed to Blatch's position as her successor.[†107] "Her own life, career, and political commitments followed too closely on those of Elizabeth Stanton for [Blatch] to separate the two subjects," observes Ellen Carol DuBois in examining the daughter's attempts to resurrect her mother's place in history in the 1920s. In addition, Blatch likely experienced, in Henry D. Thoreau's moving words from another context, the mourning survivor's desire to undertake a "double living": to honor and "fulfil [*sic*] the promise of our friend's life also, in our own, to the world."[108]

In terms of an immediate legacy for her mother, however, the second-generation feminist leader surely understood that Gardener would perpetuate her poignant and thrilling report of the dying giant, supporting herself against all odds in an upright posture to deliver a final address to humanity and to the eternity she skeptically but ever hopefully regarded as one with the physical and scientific laws of the universe. Blatch's Stanton also went into that good night swiftly and without serious illness, but in this rendering one glimpses the hint of a physician's material aid.[†] Family members claimed that Stanton had instructed her doctor to ease her out of life if she lost the control of her prized mind—and for no autopsy of her body to be conducted in the event of death.[109]

If each daughter recounted her mother's final hours with an eye to history, she couldn't be faulted. Each was aware that Anthony had already

overshadowed Stanton in the popular and mainstream reformist imagination. Both daughters would continue to fight this historical trend, and
Blatch and Theodore Weld Stanton would edit their mother's letters, diary,
and autobiography in service of the same cause (see fig. 12).

But what of Anthony herself? Her own remarks reinforced both her
palpable and wrenching grief and her anguish at losing forever her intellectual "word artist"—continued testimony to the enduring emotional and
practical partnership these two woman's rights reformers had enjoyed for
over half a century. In a letter describing Stanton's small, private funeral
to Clara Bewick Colby, published in Colby's *Woman's Tribune* on 8 November 1902, Anthony, too, may have been unconsciously cementing that
historical legacy for the public. As she described for Colby and her readers, amidst a mountain of flowers, nearly the only other material object of
mourning and memory was the portrait of Anthony—front and center over
the coffin. Anthony may not have believed herself capable of commanding
verbal artistry, but she summoned a graphic word picture: Stanton and Anthony are forever conjoined.[110] In another letter, to journalist Ida Husted
Harper, Anthony poignantly illustrated the aching silence she faced, standing alone now in an indifferent universe. "Well, it is an awful hush," she
wrote, adding,

> It seems impossible—that the voice is hushed—that I have longed to hear for
> 50 years—longed to get her opinion of things—before I knew exactly where
> I stood— It is all at sea—but the Laws of Nature are still going on—with no
> shadow or turning— What a world it is—it goes right on & on—no matter who
> lives or who dies!![111]

Anthony slightly amended her description of the universe's unfeeling progress to reiterate bittersweetly that she had been deluged with newspaper
reporters who practically camped on her doorstep. Bereft, she was unable
to find adequate words to convey her desolation (see fig. 13).

The posthumous portraits that emerged after the death of Elizabeth
Cady Stanton tell us what she represented as a public figure at the cusp of
the twentieth century. May Wright Sewall's commentary is significant for
what it does and does not say to readers. Stanton's powerful wit and intel-
lect are visibly at play at the centennial celebration of the nation's birth.
What is also apparent, however, is the extent to which a second-generation

suffrage reformer was unfamiliar with her former leader. Moreover, Sewall witnessed with perplexity and consternation Stanton's seemingly paradoxical actions and inflammatory, if spicy, rhetoric. "I have from time to time met her," she confessed, bringing to our attention the paucity of actual conversations she had shared with Stanton. Nonetheless, Sewall emphasized that Stanton's delivery of the "New Declaration, filled me with a kind of awe; her eloquence and logic were irresistible."[†] Apparently, Stanton still possessed the power to hook a live audience.

Equally revealing, however, is Sewall's mixed reaction of confusion and amusement at Stanton's typically mischievous pleasure in her mode of rhetorical destruction—her imagined "torturing" of her opposition. To Sewall, Stanton's devious delight seemed at odds with "the main point" in writing a suffrage address. "This combination of . . . statesmanlike grasp of great principles . . . with . . . delight in the prospect of being able to interrupt the solemnity" of the meeting was curious. "Has not that combination," asked Sewall, "baffled and charmed all of us . . . ?"[†] But Sewall's bewildered reception of Stanton's intellectual aims and methods further explains her eclipse—such that the Nineteenth Amendment is known as the Susan B. Anthony Amendment.

The last two selections, from Helen Hamilton Gardener and Clara Bewick Colby, respectively, represent what was likely Stanton's most enthusiastic audience, immediately after her death in 1902 until midcentury.[112] Both women served on the revising committee for Stanton's *The Woman's Bible*; both were personal friends. Helen Hamilton Gardener (a legal pseudonym for Alice Chenoweth) was a fervent freethought and woman's rights activist, acolyte of Robert Ingersoll, and author of fiction and nonfiction books such as *Men, Women, and Gods, and Other Lectures* (1855). Colby, a groundbreaking woman's newspaper publisher and the first female valedictorian at the University of Wisconsin, published serially both Stanton's reminiscences and in-progress extracts from her biblical commentary in the *Woman's Tribune* before each was published in its entirety as *Eighty Years and More* and *The Woman's Bible* (see fig. 5).[113]

Notably, Gardener and Colby make a point that stops just short of Nancy F. Cott's explication of "Feminism" as the successor of the nineteenth-century "woman's movement": "as an *ism* (an ideology)," she suggests, early twentieth-century "Feminism (capitalized at first) . . . presupposed a set of principles not necessarily belonging to every woman—

nor limited to women."[114] Stanton "knew that her work was not for woman only," argued Gardener. "Every blow she struck for woman was really a blow for man, quite as truly."[†] In similar fashion, Colby quoted from Tennyson's *The Princess*—a poem on female education, women's rights, and the "doctrine of love and mutual understanding" between the sexes—and perhaps thinking of Stanton's concluding thoughts, above, in "The Matriarchate," glossed those lines in verse with her assertion that "men will realize that the word of Freedom was not spoken by her for women only but for them also."[†115] It must be admitted that neither woman understood Stanton's reforms to include the twentieth-century ideological assumption that men as well as women can or should be "Feminists." Instead, their assessments remind us that while Stanton was overwhelmingly concerned with the multiple causes of women's subordination, other passions included her need to "worship as a God" a "son of Adam" and her maternal desire to ensure the physical, intellectual, and personal growth of her five boys. Those conjoined interests shaped her reformist vision for the progressive development needed for men as well as for women.[116]

In what is likely a related impulse, Colby and Gardener resurrected the maternal image Stanton flaunted during her lyceum career, and each self-consciously framed her within a soon-to-be-emerging "Feminist" history, with roots in Margaret Fuller's earlier literary and philosophical theories.[117] Alluding to Fuller's adaptation in *Woman in the Nineteenth Century* of Ralph Waldo Emerson's idea that women and men must develop into self-sustaining "units" before true unions are possible, Gardener claimed that Stanton "led the contest in this and other countries for what is commonly called the rights of woman—that is, for woman's right to stand as a unit among other units of the race."[†] Gardener alluded to Fuller's "Feminist" legacy even more explicitly when she describes the impact Stanton's advocacy would instantiate. In future years, mothers of all races will "be reckoned as self-respecting, self-directing human units, with brains and bodies that are sacredly their own," she predicted, adding that marital partners benefit from this feminine achievement, since they will participate in a companionship among equals.[†118]

In this summary of her friend's transatlantic advocacy, Gardener emphasizes women's independent wholeness outside of relationships, and in that characterization she is likely summoning not Stanton's frequent allusions to motherhood but instead her insistence—seen in her San Francisco lyceum lecture—that women reverse the cultural trend that honors wives and mothers and devalues "womanhood." Pointing to unmarried, successful women such as Anthony and Harriet Hosmer, Stanton had demanded in those lyceum lectures, "Are there no children of the brain?"† Further, Gardener nods to Stanton's magisterial late address, "The Solitude of Self," which she delivered on 18 January 1892 before the House Judiciary Committee hearing to debate a constitutional woman suffrage amendment for federal elections. Stanton had deliberately explained to the committee that she refused to repeat the justifications she had used in the past before this body to appeal for women's enfranchisement. Instead, as the *Washington Post* recorded her introductory remarks, she would speak on the solemn and heroically isolated state of "Individuality."[119]

Colby also situates Stanton within a broader, transatlantic "feminist" history whose grand players include Abigail Adams, Margaret Fuller, Susan B. Anthony, Lucy Stone, and Matilda Joslyn Gage in America and Harriet Taylor Mill, Priscilla Bright McLaren, Ursula Mellor Bright, and Elizabeth Wolstenholme Elmy in England. The primary interests that engaged these representative figures also hint at Stanton's multiple, at times conflicting, and occasionally fleeting activist concerns: temperance, abolition, woman's enfranchisement, educated suffrage, universal suffrage, history writing as activism, the religious sources of women's subordination, the Matriarchate, married women's property rights, liberal divorce laws, and free love.[120] Abigail Adams's desire for government to seek the consent of the governed and Fuller's quest for "absolute equality for women"† similarly populate this historical movement; and as Colby characterized both women's contributions, she likely understood Adams as the precursor of the natural rights liberalism Stanton advocated early in her career but never entirely discarded and Fuller as the antecedent of Stanton's identification of the cultural forces that exacerbate gendered difference. In the end, however, Colby honors Stanton most concretely for "necessary gifts for leadership"—for her unique ability to champion the transatlantic movement that "blossomed" from the "seed thoughts" of Adams, Fuller, and other "reincarnation[s] of the Immortals who have stood for Liberty and fought its battles in ages past." Under her guidance, this emerging, organic woman's history culminated in "specific and organized demand[s]" born out of an understanding that equality is composed of "educational, industrial, professional, legal, and political rights."†

In this posthumous analysis of Stanton's multitudinous and evolving forms of activism, Colby took pains to enumerate the ambitious and individual petitions that in her view fueled a twentieth-century "Feminist" movement. Equally vital, however, were memories of less cerebral gestures of mentoring: the example of daily actions that fashion character and shape a life. From this perspective Colby admiringly recounted early impressions of Stanton confidently striding through a train in the manner of men and prompting her "suffrage daughter" to introduce Stanton at an early convention, rather than waiting for a male representative to do so. Acknowledging changing times and her own growth as a person and a reformer, Colby admits that such physical acts appear unremarkable in 1902. Importantly, however, for the Colby of thirty years hence such quietly evocative expressions of implicit self-regard taught a powerful "lesson of self-respect." Emphasizing the high stakes for her younger self, Colby characterized that split second on the platform as "in reality a crossing of the Rubicon for me."[†] Extending Colby's metaphor, as her eloquent mentor was wont to do, I imagine that Stanton would have delighted in the notion that this moment of feminine self-sovereignty was also a point of no return.

Stanton in Her Own Time includes selections from manuscripts, nineteenth- and early twentieth-century publications, and scholarly editions. In my transcription of manuscripts, I have reproduced the writer's final revisions but preserved spelling, capitalization, and punctuation infelicities that do not obscure intelligibility. When paragraph indentation is missing, I have supplied indentation if the preceding line is short. Page numbers and nonauthorial notations appended to manuscripts have not been transcribed. With regard to the published selections, only those errors in spelling, punctuation, and capitalization that might produce misreadings have been corrected or acknowledged. When possible, I have selected the first printing of these publications. In this introduction, a dagger indicates that the referenced text is printed in this volume. Contextual information appears in the (sometimes lengthy) headnote prefacing each chapter or selection, and bibliographical information and contextual notes appear at the end of chapters and selections. The bibliography at the end of the volume includes all works cited.

My deep gratitude goes to series editor Joel Myerson for inviting me to undertake this project and for offering practical advice throughout. At the University of Iowa Press, Catherine Cocks and Susan Hill Newton have been unfailingly ready with answers, and Rebecca Marsh provided stellar copyediting advice and commentary. For generous help with primary materials and for multiple readings and thought-provoking questions, I thank Sandra Harbert Petrulionis. Phyllis Cole brought crucial insight to an early draft of the introduction, and William Hare and Kay Baker dedicated valuable time to proofing. Jennifer Ruth Cowfer transcribed and proofed many selections and located first printings of source material, and Samantha Gilmore assisted with citations and bibliography. I am grateful to Coline Jenkins for her permission to include Stanton material herein.

For their assistance in securing archival material, I thank Kathy Jans-Duffy, Seneca Falls Historical Society; Sarah Hutcheon, Alissa Link, Caitlin Reeves, and Amanda E. Strauss, Schlesinger Library, Radcliffe Institute, Harvard University; Kathleen Arthur and Amy Mantrone, University of Chicago Library; Dean Rogers, Vassar College Libraries; Brooke Black, Huntington Library; Lee Grady and Lisa R. Marine, Wisconsin Historical Society; Dorran Boyle, Ella Strong Denison Library, Scripps College; and Elizabeth G. Burgess, Harriet Beecher Stowe Center.

I cannot express adequate appreciation for years of aid and encouragement from Kay Baker—and from Bob Baker, whose dedication to justice also inspired the thematic concerns of this book. Thanks, too, to Alexander, whose delightful antics never fail to remind me that life after deadlines beckons. Finally, I owe an incalculable debt to Will—who makes anything possible.

NOTES

1. *The Woman's Bible*, 10. A number of women listed in both volumes did not contribute, and several enumerated in volume 1 asked to be removed from future publications. In addition to Stanton, who was the "overriding influence" on the books, only seven of the ostensibly twenty-three-member committee for volume 1 were actually contributors; and of the twenty-member committee for volume 2, only eight contributed (Kern, *Mrs. Stanton's Bible*, 139).

2. Discussing the sources of Stanton's antipathy to institutional religion, Elisabeth Griffith rightly instances nineteenth-century biblical teachings that justified and upheld slavery, intemperance, and women's subordinate status. "Whatever advances women tried to make—in education or employment or political rights—were held to contradict the will and the word of God as revealed in the Scriptures and interpreted by ministers" (*In Her Own Right*, 210).

3. Kathi Kern astutely characterizes the practical failures of Stanton's strategy: "Little

did she expect that the Bible debate would actually cement the unlikely alliance of religiously liberal, but politically pragmatic, figures like [Carrie Chapman] Catt, [Rachel Foster] Avery, and Alice Stone Blackwell with more conservative religious women like Anna Howard Shaw and Laura Clay" (*Mrs. Stanton's Bible*, 206).

4. In May 1869 Stanton and Susan B. Anthony founded the National Woman Suffrage Association (NWSA); in 1870 its name briefly changed to the Union Woman's Suffrage Society. Increasingly alarmed at the pair's resistance to the Fourteenth and Fifteenth Amendments and the association of woman suffrage with Stanton's social concerns, a block of reformers composed primarily of Garrisonian abolitionists formed their own organization, the American Woman Suffrage Association (AWSA), in the fall of 1869. Associated with Boston and the Republican Party, this group, including most prominently Lucy Stone, William Lloyd Garrison, Wendell Phillips, Julia Ward Howe, and Thomas Wentworth Higginson, focused its efforts upon enfranchisement. Scholars have long debated whether the two organizations' competition helped or hindered the women's advance toward the national electorate, finally reached in 1920. In February 1890 NWSA merged with AWSA. Stanton served as the first president of the merged entity, the National American Woman Suffrage Association (NAWSA).

5. Quoted in Kern, *Mrs. Stanton's Bible*, 67. Stanton had long held, publicly spoken about, and published the anticlerical sentiment that inspired these comments in 1885, but she did not begin working on *The Woman's Bible* until 1887, after the publication of the third volume of *History of Woman Suffrage*, the writing of which had consumed much of her time during the first half of this decade. In a letter to Clara Bewick Colby in November 1888, Stanton notes that she wants to focus her publications on "the religious bondage of woman." Her greater public concentration on this "bondage" in the years leading to the 1895 publication of *The Woman's Bible* is therefore reflected in my post-1887 selections in the chapter dedicated to this controversy. (See Lutz, *Created Equal*, 295; Stanton, *The Selected Papers of Elizabeth Cady Stanton and Susan B. Anthony*, 5:141. Note that *The Selected Papers* will hereinafter be abbreviated as *SP*.)

6. Ellen Carol DuBois explains this historical narrative, in which the publication of *The Woman's Bible*, combined with Anthony's increasing popularity, ensured that the breadth of Stanton's reforms were forgotten in the years after her death and that Anthony was posthumously credited with women's enfranchisement in 1920. "Her children [Theodore Stanton and Harriot Stanton Blatch] issued a single volume of her letters, but otherwise no effort was made to collect her writings or remember her to later generations of women. She was not even the subject of a full-length biography until 1940" ("Part Three: 1874–1906," 191–192). For a description of Harriot Stanton Blatch's efforts, see DuBois, *Harriot Stanton Blatch and the Winning of Woman Suffrage*, 242–273. Tragically, however, Theodore Stanton and Blatch heavily edited, combined, and then destroyed their mother's papers, and they also revised her autobiography; for the resulting misinformation inflicted upon her primary manuscripts and the historical record, see Griffith, *In Her Own Right*, xv–xvii; Gordon, Afterword, 480–481, 483n9; Ginzberg, *Elizabeth Cady Stanton*, 13–14.

7. "Mrs. Stanton on the Wheel," 525.

8. *SP* 2:361.

9. In this introduction, daggers (†) following quoted passages from Stanton's contemporaries designate writings included as selections in this volume.

10. Stanton "would rank with Charles Sumner as an orator, holding all the while her written manuscript in her left hand, and speaking with such beauty of diction and elegance of style, that you scarcely observe that she is reading," suggested Charles King. "In this particular she is inimitable" ("Notes from Washington," 40).

11. Greenwood, "The National Women's Suffrage Convention at Washington."

12. Stanton and Anthony's woman's rights colleague, the reformer and freethought author Matilda Joslyn Gage (1826–1898), was an active member in NWSA and served on the revising committee of *The Woman's Bible*. She contributed to *Revolution*, was a significant historian of women's history, and, like Stanton, wrote on the Matriarchate. She edited and published the *National Citizen and Ballot Box*; her most important work is *Woman, Church, and State* (1892).

13. Lutz, *Created Equal*, 318; Griffith, *In Her Own Right*, 217; Ginzberg, *Elizabeth Cady Stanton*, 187; *SP* 6:448–449, 448–448n1.

14. Ginzberg, *Elizabeth Cady Stanton*, 13.

15. While commending scholars' awareness of Stanton's divisive stances on race, class, and imperialism, Ann D. Gordon also makes the important point that "the exploration of *what* they signify needs better tools and maps than are currently in use." Similarly, Jen McDaneld observes that although scholars widely discuss Stanton's racism, because her large corpus is primarily ephemeral (addresses, newspaper articles), the subject remains understudied ("Stanton and the Right to Vote: On Account of Race or Sex," 124; "White Suffragist Dis/Entitlement: The *Revolution* and the Rhetoric of Racism," 243).

16. In 1844 a fellow reformer described Stanton as a "strong heart in a diminutive cage," but between 1860 and 1870 she reported her weight at around 175 pounds; by 1888 she weighed a stunning 240 pounds (and, perhaps even more remarkably, could still dance the Virginia Reel with her son at that time). In December 1889 she traveled to Dansville Sanitorium to slim down, but after a six-week stay, she had lost only five pounds (Taylor, *British and American Abolitionists*, 225; *SP* 2:160, 361; Griffith, *In Her Own Right*, 196–197).

17. *SP* 5:358, 359.

18. Griffith, *In Her Own Right*, 143; see also Ginzberg, *Elizabeth Cady Stanton*, 9. For social reformer Clarina Howard Nichols's more conservative waging of maternal politics, see Blackwell and Oertel, *Frontier Feminist*.

19. Griffith, *In Her Own Right*, 195–196.

20. For her miscarriage in the spring of 1849 and possible miscarriage in 1847 or 1848, see Wellman, *The Road to Seneca Falls*, 169.

21. *SP* 5:xxvi–xxvii.

22. In contextualizing her varied, intellectual, and quotidian maternal interests, I do not mean to imply that Stanton always enjoyed or succeeded at that role. Her Seneca Falls years, in particular, document a frustrated and intense ambivalence about child-rearing and domesticity. Her eldest son, Neil, the only Stanton child who failed to attend college and whom neither parent had ever been able to discipline effectively, offers one example

of the complexities involved in her maternal experiences in child-rearing. In 1863 Henry Stanton lost his job at the New York Custom House and his reputation in some circles after Neil, who was clerking for his father, stole bonds for shipments. The discovery of this theft unleashed Treasury Department and congressional subcommittee investigations and prominent media attention. Moreover, Neil hardly lived up to his mother's protofeminist principles for marriage. After marrying Frederika F. Anthony in April 1884, the couple separated in September of that year; the terms of their divorce, which Frederika was granted in 1886, indicate that Neil had never visited his daughter Florence, born in January 1885; moreover, he had to be forced by the court to pay child support (Griffith, *In Her Own Right*, 114–115; Ginzberg, *Elizabeth Cady Stanton*, 113–114; *SP* 4:xxvii, 407n3).

23. Before slaves were emancipated in New York in 1827, when Stanton turned eleven, Daniel Cady owned several slaves, who after emancipation remained as servants in the Cady household. According to Lori D. Ginzberg, 40 percent of African Americans in Johnstown were enslaved when Stanton was five (Griffith, *In Her Own Right*, 3–4; *Elizabeth Cady Stanton*, 20–21).

24. Wellman, *The Road to Seneca Falls*, 32.

25. See Griffith, *In Her Own Right*, 65, and quoted, 43; Ginzberg, *Elizabeth Cady Stanton*, 87–88. During Elizabeth Cady Stanton's childbearing years, because of his political activities, Henry was rarely at home for any length of time. At the time of their tenth anniversary, he resided with the family in Seneca Falls for more than six months, "a period longer than any in the coming decade," notes Griffith (64). Other reformers characterized the marriage similarly. "A woman unsuitably married like Mrs Stanton may find herself fettered," Henry Browne Blackwell wrote Lucy Stone in August 1853 (Wheeler, *Loving Warriors*, 57).

26. Organizationally experienced Quaker reformers Jane and Richard Hunt, Lucretia and James Mott, Mott's sister Martha Coffin Wright, Mary Ann and Thomas McClintock, and their daughters Elizabeth and Mary Ann McClintock collaborated with Stanton to call an impromptu woman suffrage meeting in Seneca Falls on 19 and 20 July 1848. The women wrote a "Declaration of Sentiments" in the manner of the Declaration of Independence, including a list of grievances regarding women's lack of civic, religious, and political stature. Most notably and controversially, Stanton insisted that the list include women's enfranchisement. Anthony did not attend, but members of her family were in the audience.

27. See *SP* 2:299. According to Morgan Friedman's "The Inflation Calculator" (http://www.westegg.com/inflation/), in 2014 dollars that would be $36,897.01 for a little over two months. "Measuring Worth" (http://www.measuringworth.com/uscompare/relative value.php) places the value at $37,400 in 2014 dollars. Lisa Tetrault emphasizes the vast crowds in these lyceum lectures, up to "thousands," giving lecturers enormous access and fame ("The Incorporation of American Feminism," 1037, 1038, 1041).

28. Ginzberg, *Elizabeth Cady Stanton*, 86, 87, 168–169.

29. *SP* 3:xxiv.

30. Quoted in Ginzberg, *Elizabeth Cady Stanton*, 167. For the couple's relationship in 1868 and separate households, see Banner, *Elizabeth Cady Stanton*, 109–110, 111; Griffith, *In Her Own Right*, 120; Ginzberg, *Elizabeth Cady Stanton*, 142.

31. *SP* 5:473, 473n2.

32. *SP* 1:182. As Ginzberg, following Ann D. Gordon, explains, Stanton's likely fiction-alized story about their meeting in May 1851 at the time of an abolitionist meeting is "slip-pery" (*Elizabeth Cady Stanton*, 208n1).

33. "Notes about Women." Tilton is the likely author of this piece, which appeared first in his *Golden Age*. In September 1896 Anthony forwarded to Stanton a letter from a fan who mistakenly remembered the lecture and white curls of Stanton as belonging to An-thony. "It is too funny the way peoples memories do carry you & me one for the other & both as one," she mused (*SP* 6:95).

34. Stanton delivered her first reformist speech, on temperance, in Seneca Falls, where she was visiting her sister, Tryphena, and brother-in-law, Edward Bayard, but she under-took no formal organizational work at that time. With characteristic self-satisfaction, she claimed that her maiden address moved both her audience and herself to tears (*SP* 1:25).

35. In the last decades of the century, leaders of NWSA and AWSA fought to establish their own branch as the "origin" of the woman's rights movement. With the publication of the multivolume *History of Woman Suffrage*, a chronicle of the movement told from the perspective of NWSA, and Anthony's successful promotion and identification of herself with the Seneca Falls meeting, Seneca Falls assumed a prominent place in women's his-tory. For Stanton and Anthony's successful historicizing of the Seneca Falls meeting and the multiple points of "origination" that preceded and networked with it, see Gordon and Collier-Thomas, *African American Women and the Vote*; Isenberg, *Sex & Citizenship in Antebellum America*; Terborg-Penn, *African American Women in the Struggle for the Vote*; Ginzberg, *Untidy Origins*; and Tetrault, *The Myth of Seneca Falls*.

36. For Stanton's 1866 congressional run and 1880 vote, see Griffith, *In Her Own Right*, 125–126, 171; Ginzberg, *Elizabeth Cady Stanton*, 12–13; *SP* 1:597n1; *SP* 4:14.

37. Ginzberg, *Elizabeth Cady Stanton*, 190–191.

38. Margaret Stanton Lawrence, "Who Was Elizabeth Cady Stanton? My Mother," Part 1:3, Elizabeth Cady Stanton Papers, 4.5.

39. It is important to emphasize, however, that by 1851, Stanton was fortunate enough to have the live-in assistance of Amelia Willard, who stayed with the family for thirty years and supervised other indoor and outdoor servants (*SP* 1:190n3).

40. *SP* 1:379.

41. In an early version of this advice, Stanton schooled her September 1851 *Lily* readers in the best ways to keep their boys off the streets, a prescription including vigorous romps, needlework, and indoor games (Stanton [E.C.S.], "Letters to Mothers. No. 1. The Boys of Our Village," 66).

42. *SP* 3:550.

43. Two New York papers similarly perceive the later Stanton's oratorical command in their reports of her surprise 1894 address before a mass meeting of two thousand. There Stanton's mere appearance incites the crowd's tumultuous applause, acclamation she si-lences instantly with a motion of her hand. See *SP* 5:619.

44. Larned, "The Woman's Congress," 363.

45. Gordon, Afterword, 476, 472.

46. Lawrence, "Who Was Elizabeth Cady Stanton? My Mother," Part 1:9, Elizabeth Cady Stanton Papers, 4.5.

47. Quoted in Griffith, *In Her Own Right*, 163; Ginzberg, *Elizabeth Cady Stanton*, 148.

48. *SP* 5:619; Potter, *Helen Potter's Impersonations*, 94. Note, however, that friend Theodore Tilton disagrees, characterizing her voice as "hardly musical."†

49. Ginzberg, *Elizabeth Cady Stanton*, 70.

50. Hogan and Hogan, "Feminine Virtue and Practical Wisdom," 417–420, 426, 432.

51. Griswold, "Elizabeth Cady Stanton," 149. Stanton's successful delivery can be usefully contrasted with the reception of reformer Mary F. Davis's similar claims for women's rights within marriage and for divorce at the November 1856 annual woman's suffrage convention. When Stanton could not do so, Lucy Stone arranged for Davis to speak on these subjects there; and while convention attendees listened "with respectful consideration," the *New York Observer* "called her speech 'too disgusting to be put in print' and said she deserved to be 'tongue-tied to prevent her foul mouth from being opened in public again'" (Million, *Woman's Voice, Woman's Place*, 227–228).

52. Spurlock, "The Free Love Network in America, 1850 to 1860," 767. See also Blatt, *Free Love & Anarchism*; Guarneri, *The Utopian Alternative*; Silver-Isenstadt, *Shameless*; and Passet, *Sex Radicals and the Quest for Women's Equality*.

53. DuBois, "On Labor and Free Love," 267, 266, 264.

54. For the extramarital relationship, see Kerr, *Lucy Stone*, 136–152; McMillen, *Lucy Stone*, 179–181. Letters between 1869 and 1870 between Lucy and the Blackwell family indicate the family's concern about the relationship. Kerr adds, based on the evidence of "third party" information about it, that extrafamilial individuals were also aware (144).

55. Emily Blackwell to Elizabeth Blackwell, 11 October 1869, Blackwell Family Papers, MC 411, Box 11, Folder 164; Lucy Stone to Emily Blackwell, 15 April 1870, Blackwell Family Papers, MC 411, Box 11, Folder 151.

56. See, for example, Stanton's extensive published argument that married women had the right to divorce and to determine when and how many times they conceive in December 1855. In a January 1856 letter to Anthony, Stone characterized Stanton and her publication as "strong and noble," and she further proposed that if suffrage reformers could fund a new paper, Stanton should serve as its editor. Moreover, as Stone organized the November 1856 woman's rights convention, she asked Stanton to address these topics. "Stone said she wanted to 'push' the issue of 'a wife's right to her own body,'" observes Million (*SP* 1, 306–308, quoted in, 313; *Woman's Voice, Woman's Place*, 227).

57. Throughout this lecture, Stanton is undeniably tone-deaf to women with other cultural or religious expectations or to those who were not fortunate enough to have married a reformer. Moreover, Stanton, whose healthy enjoyment of sex was well known to her friends, was also fortunately oblivious to the safe space she occupied, by virtue of her class and race, to publicly espouse this view. For the grave dangers African American women faced in this regard, see Martha S. Jones, who describes the poet and abolitionist Frances Ellen Watkins Harper's similar but private conversations in the South for freed

African American women to discuss sexuality, their daughters' futures, "the welfare of the race," and women's role in carving out their own identity (quoted in *All Bound Up Together*, 136).

58. Gordon, *Woman's Body, Woman's Right*, 98, 103.

59. Tuchinsky, *Horace Greeley's* New-York Tribune, 111.

60. Passet, *Sex Radicals and the Quest for Women's Equality*, 93.

61. A spiritualist, free love and woman's rights advocate, editor, and Wall Street businesswoman, Victoria Claflin Woodhull (1838–1927) for a time allied with NWSA. Isabella Beecher Hooker, Stanton, and, to a more limited degree, Anthony continued to defend her even when her actions scandalized the nation, in large part because they believed she was the victim of a pervasive double standard in the way that men's and women's behavior was judged.

62. In late 1869, Stanton visited in prison and petitioned for the pardon of the British immigrant Hester Vaughan, a woman engaged as a servant in Philadelphia. Abandoned by her child's father, Vaughan gave birth alone and was charged and convicted of infanticide after she and her dead baby were discovered; she was awaiting execution. Vaughan was eventually pardoned and returned to England. In the pages of *Revolution*, Stanton appealed to women, urging them to add their voices in Vaughan's support and condemning gendered double standards: "What a holocaust of women and children we offer annually to the barbarous customs of our present type of civilization, to the unjust laws that make crimes for women that are not crimes for men!" (Stanton [E.C.S.], "Hester Vaughan"; see also Griffith, *In Her Own Right*, 159; Thomas, "Elizabeth Cady Stanton and the Notion of a Legal Class of Gender," 148–149).

63. Daniel McFarland's excessive drinking, spending habits and uneven employment, and occasional abandonment eroded his marriage with Abby Sage McFarland; she attempted both separation and gainful employment to support the couple's children. Journalist Albert Richardson made platonic efforts to help the struggling woman after they met in 1866; thereafter they fell in love. After separating from McFarland in March 1867, Abby fled to Boston, and in the summer of 1868 traveled to Indiana, a state with liberal divorce laws, where she established residence and was granted a divorce in October 1869. Before she returned to New York, however, McFarland, who had previously threatened and wounded Richardson in a failed murder attempt in 1867, hid in the offices at the *New York Tribune*. On 25 November 1869, when Richardson arrived to retrieve his mail, McFarland shot him. Notified by telegram, Abby returned to New York, where Henry Ward Beecher married Richardson and Abby Sage on 30 November. On 2 December 1869, Richardson died. Found innocent by reason of temporary insanity, Daniel McFarland gained sole custody of their eldest child (Cooper, *Lost Love*, 98, 113–114, 117–133, 235).

64. Fair's marital history and business acumen cast her in disfavor with the mainstream and largely male press, judge, and jury. Married four times (widowed twice and divorced twice), Fair amassed a fortune in astute silver mine investments. For seven years she and Alexander Parker Crittenden, twenty years her senior and her married lover, conducted a public affair in San Francisco and Virginia City, Nevada. Crittenden promised Fair that his wife, Clara, would never visit San Francisco and that he would take advantage of lib-

eral laws in Indiana to obtain a divorce, thereafter marrying Fair. Breaking his promise, on 3 November 1870, Crittenden met Clara and his children in Oakland to take the ferry to San Francisco, and Fair shot him. She pled not guilty by virtue of temporary insanity caused by dysmenorrhea and was convicted and sentenced to death by hanging. Stanton visited her in San Francisco while she awaited her second trial (the first verdict was overturned on legal technicalities). At her second trial she was acquitted (Haber, *The Trials of Laura Fair*, 1–10, 140–141, 174).

65. An influential abolitionist and woman's suffrage reformer, Tilton (1835–1907) was also a good friend of Stanton's. Henry Ward Beecher married Theodore and Elizabeth Tilton and mentored Theodore early in his journalist career; but in 1866, when Tilton's successful lecturing circuit kept him away from home for extended periods, the married Beecher began visiting Elizabeth. In 1870, Elizabeth confessed their affair to Theodore, and the couple agreed to maintain its secrecy. Sometime thereafter, however, the two individually confided in Stanton and Anthony; rumors also circulated in Brooklyn, home of both Beecher and the Tiltons. Tilton further revealed the story to Henry Bowen, who published Tilton's *Independent*, and to an old friend, Frank Moulton, who offered to mediate with Beecher quietly, a process in which Stanton and Anthony became involved in 1871. Bowen, who ultimately feared publicity and the security of the *Independent*, fired Tilton, after which Moulton and Beecher funded a new paper for him to run, the *Golden Age*. When Victoria Woodhull began hinting that she would bring the scandal to light, Beecher and Moulton asked Tilton to intercede, a process which culminated in Tilton's biography of Woodhull. After Woodhull exposed the affair in 1872, leaders of AWSA defended and Stanton excoriated Beecher publicly. Tilton brought a civil suit against Beecher in 1875; the six-month trial ended in a mistrial verdict. Beecher was exonerated by the court and Plymouth Church, but the Tiltons' lives were ruined. Tilton ultimately expatriated to Europe, where he died in Paris (Gunter, "Tilton, Theodore"; *SP* 3:97–98n2; Applegate, *The Most Famous Man in America*, 408–414, 442, 451).

66. See Griffith, *In Her Own Right*, 142; *SP* 2:331–332. As late as February 1885 public distrust of free love and those associated with it remained strong. The editors of the *Nation* blamed the decline of the woman suffrage movement's momentum on the Beecher-Tilton scandal: it had "'received a severe blow from the figure cut by many of its leading supporters in the Tilton-Beecher scandal and by the adhesion of Victoria Woodhull and some other women of her kind. From this it can hardly be said ever to have recovered" (quoted in Kerr, *Lucy Stone*, 177).

67. Quoted in Wertz and Wertz, *Lying-In*, 113. Thomas Nichols offers an early example in his "The Curse Removed," 168.

68. Banner, *Elizabeth Cady Stanton*, 125.

69. Wertz and Wertz, *Lying-In*, 114.

70. Ibid., 115.

71. Quoted in Harper, *The Life and Work of Susan B. Anthony*, 1:396.

72. McFeely, *Frederick Douglass*, 266.

73. The Boston-born Democrat George Francis Train (1829–1904) was a quixotic international celebrity and entrepreneur, author, electric and popular lecturer, presidential

aspirant, and promoter. While financing railroad land grants across America in the 1860s, he partnered with Mormon leader Brigham Young and thereafter became one of the Mormon community's few public defenders. During the Kansas campaign he appeared occasionally with Stanton and Anthony to support the woman's suffrage ballot; and during that time he pledged to finance a newspaper for them (*Revolution*), as well as a multistate lecture circuit to publicize it. Shortly after its first issue was published in January 1868, however, they lost his money. Train traveled to England, where he was jailed for a year because of his support of Irish rebels. He returned to the United States in 1869. In response to these events and Stanton's plans to create a woman suffrage association, the "Boston" reformers founded the New England Woman Suffrage Association in November 1868. When Anthony Comstock imprisoned Woodhull on obscenity charges in 1872, Train protested by publishing the most sexually explicit passages in the Bible in his paper, the *Train Ligue*, an action for which Comstock also imprisoned him. Train was ultimately released but pronounced insane by the authorities, a legal and financial disability that would thwart his business ventures for the remainder of his life (Barker, "Train, George Francis (1829–1904)"; Bitton, "George Francis Train and Brigham Young"; Frisken, *Victoria Woodhull's Sexual Revolution*, 102–103).

74. Stanton, Anthony, and Gage, *History of Woman Suffrage*, 2:378.

75. Quoted in *SP* 4:45n18.

76. Although the *History of Woman Suffrage* frequently provides historians' sole glimpse of such encounters, one must always keep in mind that Anthony, Gage, and Stanton produced that record.

77. Harper here demonstrates what Martha S. Jones asserts generally—that "black women did not privilege matters of race over those of gender. Rather, they were active at the intersection of these two salient social categories and fashioned their tactics and their aims to suit this circumstance" (*All Bound Up Together*, 10).

78. Wellman, *The Road to Seneca Falls*, 161.

79. *Revolution*, "What the Press Says." Years later, visiting with her in Europe in the summer of 1887 as she worked on her *Woman's Bible*, he wrote to Amy Post, declaring that Stanton was "more radical than ever—She is a noble woman—and has no snobbery about her" (quoted in McFeely, *Frederick Douglass*, 333.

80. White, *The Beecher Sisters*, 149–153; Applegate, *The Most Famous Man in America*, 388–389; Campbell, *Tempest-Tossed*, 109.

81. Garrison, "Michelet's Motto for Elizabeth Cady Stanton," 23–24.

82. Jacoby, *The Great Agnostic*, 11–12, 118.

83. Henry, "Tribute to Elizabeth Cady Stanton."

84. Kern, "Free Woman Is a Divine Being," 94–95.

85. For the impact of Fuller on Stanton's developing reformist vision, Seneca Falls address, discussions of marriage and young women, and her late address "The Solitude of Self," as well as the influence other Transcendentalists and Unitarians such as Ralph Waldo Emerson, Theodore Parker, and William Henry Channing had upon her, see Cole, "Stanton, Fuller, and the Grammar of Romanticism."

86. Quoted in Kern, "Free Woman Is a Divine Being," 96.

87. For a good example of Stanton's willingness to reverse an anecdote's meaning in order to support disparate points, even within one talk, see her honorific discussion of Russian nihilists (as in her remarks upon them to Johnson or to a freethought audience), followed by her threatening reference to women's potential union with "Nihilists, Socialists, Communists, and Anarchists" in her "Closing Address" to the more conservative audience attending the International Council of Women in 1888, and Lori D. Ginzberg's differing view of the second comment (Stanton, "Closing Address," 432, 436; Ginzberg, *Elizabeth Cady Stanton*, 160–161).

88. This essay is unsigned, but it is likely Green's work. Stanton was enthusiastically embraced by freethinkers; but as Lori D. Ginzberg argues, although these skeptics strongly supported woman's rights, "they regarded their female counterparts with a combination of good fellowship and condescension that suggests at best an ambiguous welcome to women-as-equals into their ranks" ("'The Hearts of Your Readers Will Shudder,'" 215).

89. Closz, "Stanton, Austin, Craddock, the Humanitarian Trinity." Like Stanton, Austin was the mother of a large family—in her case, of five children. All three women shared related interests regarding religion's role in women's subordination, the importance of teaching women about their reproductive health, and free love, although Austin (1864–1902) and Craddock (1857–1902) promoted fertility limitation and free speech more aggressively; Comstock imprisoned Craddock repeatedly for her pamphlets on sexology and women's reproductive health. In fact, facing a possible five-year prison term and having suffered extreme mistreatment during previous imprisonments, Craddock took her life and wrote a public letter justifying the decision. Freethinking liberals tried "their best to turn 'The Craddock Tragedy' into a cause célèbre." On the day Stanton died "a memorial service in Chicago gathered 1200 attendees at Handell Hall to honor Craddock and to blast away at Comstock" (Miller, "Kate Austin," 189, 198; Schmidt, *Heaven's Bride*, xii, 219, 220–221).

90. Quoted in Schmidt, *Heaven's Bride*, x; Miller, "Kate Austin," 200.

91. Closz, "Stanton, Austin, Craddock, the Humanitarian Trinity."

92. Kern, *Mrs. Stanton's Bible*, 193, 200.

93. See, for example, Stanton's 22 July 1869 *Revolution* article, "Woman's Dress" (*SP* 2:252–254).

94. Speech on Elizabeth Cady Stanton, n.d., Caroline M. Seymour Severance Papers, mssSeverance, Box 5, Folder 36. Severance errs in this attribution, but both Sand and Eliot were commonly associated with this tribute, penned by Elizabeth Barrett Browning in honor of George Sand in her sonnet "To George Sand: A Desire" (1844).

95. Elwood-Akers, *Caroline Severance*, 84, 28, 82–83, 115–116, 165–166, 174.

96. Quoted in Winter, "Swinton, John."

97. Stanton, *Eighty Years and More*, 39.

98. As Cynthia Eller notes, the mistaken scholarly understanding of the Matriarchate, a "matriarchal prehistory," assumed "cultural dogma" among anthropologists, intellectuals, socialists, and feminists from the early 1860s through the end of the nineteenth century, culminating in Friedrich Engels's *The Origin of the Family, Private Property and the State*, and ensured that the "myth of matriarchal prehistory" became "a socialist origin

story. Soon after, first-wave feminists began to see the myth's potential to dislodge the idea that patriarchy was universal and inevitable"; promoters of the Matriarchate include Stanton, Matilda Joslyn Gage, and Charlotte Perkins Gilman (*The Myth of Matriarchal Prehistory*, 31, 32).

99. Mead adds that these audience members were composed of "farmers, mechanics, and shopkeepers to whom 'culture' meant useful knowledge and practical, provocative ideas" (quoted in Hogan and Hogan, "Feminine Virtue and Practical Wisdom," 420).

100. Anthony delivered parts of the speech for Stanton, who was then in England; and Clara Bewick Colby published it in the *National Bulletin* that same month as well as in the published transactions of the National Council of Women (*SP* 5:359nn1-2; Stanton, "The Matriarchate," 275).

101. Stanton, "The Matriarchate," 268, 273, 272, 273-274.

102. Ibid., 266.

103. Ibid., 274.

104. Lawrence, "Who Was Elizabeth Cady Stanton? My Mother," Part 3:27-28, Elizabeth Cady Stanton Papers, 4.7.

105. Stanton sternly warned Anthony to say that she had merely caught a cold (Griffith, *In Her Own Right*, 184).

106. Adelaide Johnson, Excelsior Journal 1902, Adelaide Johnson Papers, MSS27821, Box 2.

107. Author, woman suffrage activist, editor, and civil servant Helen Hamilton Gardener (1853-1925) was born Alice Chenoweth to Katherine A. Peel and Reverend Alfred Griffith Chenoweth in Virginia. Gardener early established her independence, moving on her own as a teen to Cincinnati for high school. After attending Normal School in Ohio, she initially worked as a teacher and principal before later editing the freethought *Arena* and publishing woman's rights tracts and novels. She retained her legal pseudonym through two marriages. After Stanton's death, Gardener became an important political federal liaison for NAWSA, maintaining an influential working relationship with President Woodrow Wilson, who named her to the U.S. Civil Service Commission in 1920, "at that time the highest federal position ever awarded to a woman" (Miller, "Gardener, Helen Hamilton").

108. Dubois, *Harriot Stanton Blatch*, 260; Thoreau, *Writings*, 114.

109. Griffith, *In Her Own Right*, 218.

110. See *SP* 6:457-458.

111. *SP* 6:455.

112. Woman suffrage reformer and newspaper editor Clara Bewick Colby (1846-1916) was born in England to Thomas Bewick and Clara Willingham, who came to the U.S. in 1854, where they established themselves as Wisconsin farmers. Colby's initiation in woman's rights and the focus of her activism remained newspaper editing until five years before her death, and her *Woman's Tribune* (1883-1909) is the second in its duration only to the Stone-Blackwell *Woman's Journal* (Jerry, "Colby, Clara Dorothy Bewick").

113. Kern, *Mrs. Stanton's Bible*, 141; Griffith, *In Her Own Right*, 185.

114. As Cott explains, while the "woman movement" or "woman suffrage" reads un-

grammatically today, that nomenclature was embraced in the nineteenth century as representative of all women. The word "feminism" only came into use regularly in the 1910s and was not synonymous with enfranchisement. Instead, it more greatly resembled the catholic set of reforms Stanton advocated. "Feminism" also distinguished itself from the "woman movement" in that it was "broader in intent, proclaiming revolution in all the relations of the sexes, and narrower in the range of its willing adherents" (*The Grounding of Modern Feminism*, 3).

115. Mantell, "*The Princess*: Tennyson's Eminently Shakespearian Poem," 52.

116. If her talks for women on marriage and maternity trumpeted education as a means of enabling girls to develop the self-reverence, healthy bodies, and rigorous minds more commonly instilled in boys at that time, in "Our Boys" Stanton urged a similarly androgynous tutelage for sons. In particular she critiqued the harsh disciplinary methods then deemed appropriate to inculcate masculine "chivalry"; encouraged practical, hands-on experiential games and tasks that would encourage analytical thinking about the way the world works; and promoted skills commonly taught young women, controlled self-deportment, and conversational skills (Hogan and Hogan, "Feminine Virtue and Practical Wisdom," quoted on 423).

117. Phyllis Cole has recovered the significant but differing ways in which Stanton and members of both AWSA and NWSA honored and channeled Fuller as a political, philosophical, and spiritual leader and symbol. As she explains, Fuller was important to several of the members of the *Woman's Bible* revising committee ("The Nineteenth-Century Women's Rights Movement and the Canonization of Margaret Fuller").

118. Gardener is likely thinking of an 1884 article in the *North American Review*, in which Stanton wrote, "'We must first have units,' says Emerson, 'before we can have unions.' We must have harmoniously developed men and women before we can have happy marriages." Stanton repurposed passages from that article, including the preceding quotation, in an essay she published just two weeks before her death as part of a series of debates on marriage and divorce in the *New York American*. In both cases, Stanton loosely quoted from Margaret Fuller's statement, first articulated in "The Great Lawsuit" (1843) and then in *Woman in the Nineteenth Century* (1845): "We must have units before we can have union, says one of the ripe thinkers of the times." Fuller referred to Ralph Waldo Emerson's conception of the self-reliant "unit" in "The American Scholar" and evolved unions in "Love" from his *Essays: First Series* (1841), as well as to numerous conversations between Fuller, Emerson, and a circle of friends that shaped his thinking in the 1840s. Gardener's second reference evokes Fuller's analysis of the ascending levels of marital partnerships (Stanton, "The Need of Liberal Divorce Laws," 236; *SP* 6:442–443; Fuller, *Woman in the Nineteenth Century*, 301, 282–290).

119. Quoted in *SP* 5: 424. For the speech itself, see *SP* 5:423–436.

120. For Harriet Taylor Mill, Priscilla Bright McLaren, Ursula Mellor Bright, and Elizabeth Wolstenholme Elmy's championing of and interest in married women's property rights, liberal divorce laws, and free love, as well as Stanton's influence upon the more radical branch of the woman's rights movement in England, the Women's Franchise League, see Holton, "'To Educate Women into Rebellion.'"

Figure 1. Elizabeth Cady at the age of nineteen or twenty, from the archives of the Seneca Falls Historical Society. Courtesy of Coline Jenkins.

Figure 2. Elizabeth Cady Stanton and her daughter Harriot, the future second-generation feminist leader, c. 1856, from the archives of the Seneca Falls Historical Society. Courtesy of Coline Jenkins.

Figure 3. Elizabeth Cady Stanton and Susan B. Anthony, c. 1870. Susan B. Anthony Collection, Ella Strong Denison Library, Scripps College. Courtesy of Coline Jenkins.

Figure 4. Isabella Beecher Hooker, c. 1873. Courtesy of the Harriet Beecher Stowe Center, Hartford, CT.

Figure 5. Clara Bewick Colby. Courtesy of the Wisconsin Historical Society, WHS-26612.

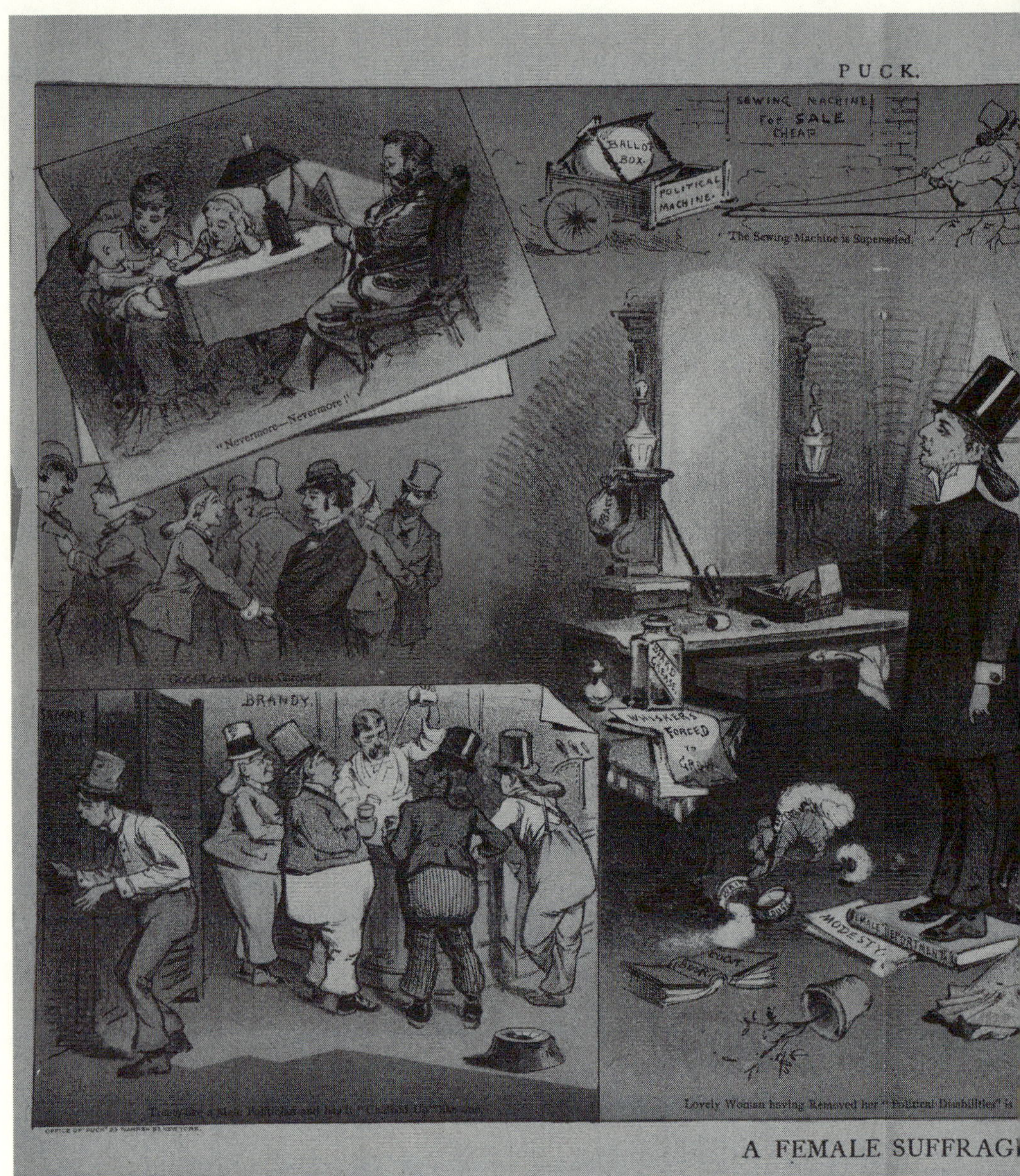

Figure 6. "A Female Suffrage Fancy," Joseph Keppler's centerfold cartoon in *Puck* magazine (1880). Courtesy of the University of Chicago Library.

Wife out Electioneering.

Bringing Miss Papers from the Polls.

A Handsome Fool gets the Office.

to Vote.

ANCY.

Figure 7. Henry Brewster Stanton in 1885, at age eighty. Elizabeth Cady Stanton Papers, 4.7, Archives and Special Collections, Vassar College Libraries. Courtesy of Coline Jenkins.

Figure 8. Elizabeth Cady Stanton, with Harriot Eaton Stanton Blatch and granddaughter Nora, c. 1892. Elizabeth Cady Stanton Papers, 4.7, Archives and Special Collections, Vassar College Libraries. Courtesy of Coline Jenkins.

Figure 9. Elizabeth Cady Stanton, c. 1895, with youngest son, Robert Livingston Stanton, and eldest daughter, Margaret Livingston Stanton Lawrence, with whom she lived in the last years of her life. Elizabeth Cady Stanton Papers, 4.7, Archives and Special Collections, Vassar College Libraries. Courtesy of Coline Jenkins.

Figure 10. Elizabeth Cady Stanton at her desk. Elizabeth Cady Stanton Papers, 4.7, Archives and Special Collections, Vassar College Libraries. Courtesy of Coline Jenkins.

Figure 11. Elizabeth Cady Stanton, two weeks before her death. Elizabeth Cady Stanton Papers, 4.7, Archives and Special Collections, Vassar College Libraries. Courtesy of Coline Jenkins.

Figure 12. The empty desk of the deceased Elizabeth Cady Stanton. Elizabeth Cady Stanton Papers, 4.7, Archives and Special Collections, Vassar College Libraries. Courtesy of Coline Jenkins.

Figure 13. Photograph of Susan B. Anthony in 1905, from the archives of the Seneca Falls Historical Society.

Figure 14. At far left, sculptor Adelaide Johnson shakes hands with Philadelphia National Woman's Party activist Dora Lewis, while Chicago social reformer Jane Addams looks on. The women pose before Johnson's group sculpture of Elizabeth Cady Stanton, Susan B. Anthony, and Lucretia Coffin Mott, *The Woman Movement*, on 15 February 1921, when it was placed in the Capitol Rotunda. National Woman's Party Records, Group I, Container I:160, Manuscript Division, Library of Congress, Washington, DC.

Chronology

1805	27 JUNE. Birth of Henry Brewster Stanton
1815	12 NOVEMBER. Birth of Elizabeth Cady to Margaret Livingston and Daniel Cady in Johnstown, New York
1820	15 FEBRUARY. Birth of Susan B. Anthony
1840	1 MAY. Marries Henry Brewster Stanton JUNE. During her honeymoon attends World Anti-Slavery Convention in London and meets Lucretia Mott
1841	FALL. Delivers first public speech on temperance in Seneca Falls, New York
1842	2 MARCH. Gives birth to Daniel Cady "Neil" Stanton (d. 1891)
1844	15 MARCH. Gives birth to Henry Brewster "Kit" Stanton, Jr. (d. 1903)
1845	18 SEPTEMBER. Gives birth to Gerrit Smith "Gat" Stanton (d. 1927)
1847	JUNE. Daniel Cady places the deed for home in Seneca Falls, New York, in her name FALL. With children, moves to Seneca Falls home
1848	APRIL. After passage of the New York Married Women's Property Act, legally owns home in Seneca Falls 19–20 JULY. Woman's Rights Convention at Seneca Falls: debut in organizational reform
1850	23–24 OCTOBER. Pregnant, contributes letter for the first national woman's rights convention in Worcester, Massachusetts
1851	9 FEBRUARY. Gives birth to Theodore Weld Stanton (d. 1925)

1852 — 20 OCTOBER. Gives birth to Margaret Livingston "Maggie" Stanton (d. 1930)

1856 — 20 JANUARY. Gives birth to Harriot Eaton "Hattie" Stanton (d. 1940)

1859 — 13 MARCH. Gives birth to Robert Livingston "Bob" Stanton (d. 1920)
31 OCTOBER. Death of Daniel Cady, whose will provides greater financial stability

1860 — MARCH. In first delivered speech in six years advocates woman's suffrage before the judiciary committee of the New York Assembly

1861 — Civil War begins, and woman suffrage reformers cease activism to support the war effort

1865 — Civil War ends
DECEMBER. Thirteenth Amendment ratified, ending chattel slavery

1866 — 10 MAY. Eleventh National Woman Suffrage Convention held, the first since the beginning of the Civil War
With other reformers votes to rename organization the American Equal Rights Association (AERA)
13 JUNE. Congress passes Fourteenth Amendment, granting citizenship to all persons born or naturalized in the U.S. but introduces the word "male" in its description of the electorate; sent to the states for ratification

1867 — Begins lecturing on woman's rights and the Bible
SEPTEMBER. Embarks with Susan B. Anthony on Kansas amendment campaign to extend suffrage to women
NOVEMBER. Begins lecture tour with Anthony and George Francis Train

1868 — Buys land and builds house in Tenafly, New Jersey
JANUARY. With Susan B. Anthony as publisher, edits *Revolution* with Parker Pillsbury
28 JULY. Fourteenth Amendment ratified
18–19 NOVEMBER. Founding meeting of the New England Woman Suffrage Association (NEWSA)

1869   26 FEBRUARY. Congress passes Fifteenth Amendment, establishing that citizens' enfranchisement cannot be restricted by race, color, or previous condition of servitude; sent to the states for ratification
12–14 MAY. Criticized at AERA meeting because of her stance on the Fifteenth Amendment and her racist and elitist commentary
15 MAY. With Anthony, organizes the National Woman Suffrage Association (NWSA) at reception at Woman's Bureau, *Revolution* offices
FALL. Lucy Stone and other members of NEWSA form the American Woman Suffrage Association (AWSA)
NOVEMBER. Embarks upon lucrative lyceum career, lecturing nationally eight months of the year for the next decade

1870   30 MARCH. Fifteenth Amendment ratified
17 MAY. Primary speaker at mass protest meeting following the acquittal of Daniel McFarland
26 MAY. With SBA announces resignation in final *Revolution* issue published by the pair

1871   29 JUNE. Lectures in Salt Lake City to 500 at Mormon Tabernacle
30 JUNE. Speaks in Salt Lake to large group of Mormon women
13 JULY. In San Francisco visits Laura D. Fair in jail, followed by a lecture for women only on "Marriage and Maternity"
15 SEPTEMBER. Death of Margaret Livingston Cady

1872   5 NOVEMBER. Susan B. Anthony tests NWSA's "New Departure" strategy, claiming the Fourteenth Amendment makes her, as a "citizen," part of the electorate and with fifteen others is arrested for illegal voting

1873   Anthony Comstock champions the passage of a federal obscenity statute that spawned numerous state laws, all prohibiting the circulation of pornography and other "obscene" information about contraception and abortion
19 JUNE. Does not attend the trial where Anthony is convicted—at the judge's behest—of illegal voting

1875   MARCH. Congress passes Civil Rights Act forbidding racial discrimination in hotels, public transportation, and places of entertainment and in the composition of juries

Supreme Court rules in *Minor v. Happersett* that the Fourteenth and Fifteenth Amendments offer no federal guarantee of women's right to vote

1876   4 JULY. Coauthors *Declaration of Rights of the Women of the United States*, which Anthony presents at the Philadelphia Centennial Exposition
AUGUST. With Anthony begins early work on *History of Woman Suffrage*

1877   End of Reconstruction
NWSA shifts gears to lobby for a Sixteenth Amendment ensuring women's right to vote, a strategy to which AWSA leaders are opposed, considering it a violation of the balance between federal and state authority

1878   JANUARY. Before the Senate Committee on Privileges and Elections delivers "National Protection for National Citizens" in support of Senate Resolution 12, the first federal proposal placed before the Senate that would prohibit states from restricting women from the electorate

1880   SPRING. Terminates lyceum lecture career
MAY. Harriot and Theodore sail for Europe, where he takes a job in Berlin as a foreign correspondent
FALL. In Tenafly, with Susan B. Anthony and Matilda Joslyn Gage, undertakes the serious work needed to complete *History of Woman Suffrage*
2 NOVEMBER. With Anthony attempts to vote in Tenafly

1881   MAY. *History of Woman Suffrage, Vol. 1, 1848–1861*

1882   MAY. *History of Woman Suffrage, Vol. 2, 1861–1876*
Sails to Europe with Harriot

1883   FEBRUARY. Delivers woman's rights addresses in England and connects with transcontinental suffrage activists
Anthony sets sail for England to join this transcontinental networking
16 NOVEMBER. Instrumental in the founding of the International Council of Women at a reception in Liverpool
17 NOVEMBER. With Anthony sails from Liverpool to the U.S.

1884   Theodore Stanton publishes *The Woman Question in Europe*

1885   NOVEMBER. Is the subject of the entire November issue of the
New Era magazine, edited by Elizabeth Boynton Harbert
12 NOVEMBER. Is the subject of NWSA-sponsored, nationwide
seventieth birthday celebrations

1886   MIDYEAR. *History of Woman Suffrage, Vol. 3, 1876–1885*
26 OCTOBER. Sails with Harriot Stanton Blatch and granddaughter Nora to their home in Basingstoke, England

1887   14 JANUARY. Henry Brewster Stanton dies of pneumonia
25 JANUARY. First vote on the Sixteenth Amendment is taken
up and defeated in the Senate
SPRING. Travels from Basingstoke to Paris to stay with Theodore
Stanton and his family
MAY. Sells Tenafly home
JUNE. Visited in Paris by Helen Pitts and Frederick Douglass,
who find her conducting preliminary work on *The Woman's
Bible*
OCTOBER. Returns to Basingstoke, England

1888   FEBRUARY. When conservative wing of British suffrage activists
balk at the prospect of attending the 1889 International Coun-
cil of Women, collaborates with more radical woman suffrage
reformers to organize a British delegation
MARCH. Returns to U.S.
Delivers multiple addresses at the International Council of
Women in Washington, DC
FALL. Lives with Margaret Livingston Stanton and her husband,
Frank, in Omaha, Nebraska

1889   Instrumental in enabling British suffragists Ursula Bright and
Elizabeth Wolstenholme Elmy to found and shape the radical
nature of England's Women's Franchise League, a group that
promoted middle-class and working women's right to citizenship
based on their paid and unpaid (maternal and domestic) labor
Begins publishing her "Reminiscences" in Clara Bewick
Colby's *Woman's Tribune*
APRIL. Is escorted by Neil Stanton from Omaha to Long Island,
where she spends the summer with Gat

NOVEMBER. Spends a month with Elizabeth Smith Miller in
Geneva, New York
DECEMBER. At Dansville, New York, sanatorium to lose weight

1890   FEBRUARY. Merger of NWSA and AWSA
Elected president of NAWSA
With Harriot Stanton Blatch, sails to England, where she re-
mains actively engaged with the Women's Franchise League
APRIL. Death of Frank Lawrence; after a few months Margaret
Stanton Lawrence returns to New York
OCTOBER. Encourages British suffragist Alice Clark to chal-
lenge the moderate branch of woman suffrage activists in
England
9 OCTOBER. With Harriot addresses the Bristol Women's Liberal
Association

1891   18 JANUARY. Death of Daniel Cady "Neil" Stanton in Logan,
Iowa
22 FEBRUARY. Anthony reads from her "The Matriarchate,
or Mother-Age" address to the National Council of Women
26 FEBRUARY. Anthony reads her presidential address, "The
Degradation of Disfranchisement," at the NAWSA annual
meeting
JULY. Spends the week at Castle Howard with Rosalind Frances
Stanley Howard, Countess of Carlisle and an executive committee member of the Women's Liberal Federation
31 AUGUST. Returns to New York City, where she takes up apartment housekeeping with Margaret Lawrence and Bob Stanton
until her death
SEPTEMBER. Spends three weeks in Rochester with Anthony and
sits for Adelaide Johnson, who is sculpting busts to be displayed
at the World's Columbian Exposition

1892   Resigns as president of NAWSA
18 JANUARY. Delivers "The Solitude of Self" before the House
Judiciary Committee and then later at the NAWSA convention—
her last appearance before both bodies

1893   Supreme Court strikes down the Civil Rights Act of 1875
MAY. World's Columbian Exposition in Chicago, where
Stanton's and Anthony's busts are on display

1894	7 MAY. Makes a surprise address at a mass meeting of two thousand, arranged by New York City suffragists
1895	12 NOVEMBER. Eightieth Birthday Celebration at the New York City Metropolitan Opera House, sponsored by the National Council of Women LATE NOVEMBER. *The Woman's Bible, Part I*
1896	28 JANUARY. Disavowed by NAWSA delegates
1898	*Eighty Years and More* *The Woman's Bible, Part II*
1902	26 OCTOBER. Death of Elizabeth Cady Stanton
1906	13 MARCH. Death of Susan B. Anthony
1919	4 JUNE. Senate passes the Nineteenth Amendment and sends it to the states for ratification
1920	18 AUGUST. Nineteenth Amendment ratified by three-quarters of state legislatures, Tennessee acting as the thirty-sixth state to do so 26 AUGUST. The ratification of the Nineteenth Amendment is certified by the secretary of state
1922	*Elizabeth Cady Stanton as Revealed in Her Letters, Diary, and Reminiscences*

"She Always Played to Win"

The Young Elizabeth Cady (1831–1922)

In their 1922 memoir of their mother, Harriot Eaton Stanton Blatch (1856–1940) and Theodore Weld Stanton (1851–1925) characterized what was for them the unique significance of Elizabeth Cady Stanton's early and late delight in dancing, music, and competitive games; that innate joy in artistry, physical activity, and spirited rivalry, they maintained, sharpened her activism. This insightful assessment was likely informed by their own rich experiences with suffrage and labor agitation in England, France, and America. Importantly, however, because both children married abroad after traveling to Europe, they were themselves instrumental in connecting their mother to the transcontinental woman's rights reformers through whom she would extend the reach of her influence in the 1880s and 1890s. In 1880 Theodore and Harriot journeyed together to Germany, where he was to take a position in Berlin as a correspondent for the *New York Tribune*. The next year he married Marguerite Berry in Paris; shortly thereafter, Harriot met the British businessman Henry Blatch, whom she married in 1882. Theodore and Harriot would ultimately settle in Paris and Basingstoke, England, respectively, and as a result England and France became new hubs for their mother's leadership.

Theodore Stanton edited *The Woman Question in Europe* (1884), "the first English-language study of the women's rights movement in Europe," and in his later career as a journalist he continued to write about the transcontinental woman's movement. In another first, feminist author, editor, and socialist activist Harriot Stanton Blatch became "America's first second-generation feminist leader," in England and then in America, where she returned after her husband's death. Her achievements were emphatically shaped, claims Ellen Carol DuBois, by Elizabeth Cady Stanton's "deliberate feminist mothering."[1] After her husband's death in 1915, Blatch regained her American citizenship and dedicated herself to woman's suffrage, authorship (*Mobilizing Woman-Power*, 1918, and *A Woman's Point of View*, 1920), the Socialist Party, and world peace.[2]

Thirza Lee (later Tilton) (1801–1877), an art teacher at Emma Willard's Troy Female Seminary, produced an evocatively concentrated portrait of the teenaged Elizabeth Cady during her student years there—one that contributes to biographical treatments of the youthful woman's rights leader as well as to analyses of the calculated rhetorical ways in which the older Stanton portrayed that time in lectures and in her autobiography.[3] The fifteen-year-old Cady entered the seminary sometime between the winter of 1830 and January 1831, when Lee was establishing herself as a newly accredited teacher.[4] Her selection, revealing the significance of religious teachings in Lee's own life,[5] is both brief and telling: the concerned teacher penned merely a few lines in Cady's commonplace book, a notebook that also displays extracts from other teachers, students, and friends written before and after Stanton's marriage. Nonetheless, with this concise and pious admonishment Lee amplifies a period that Stanton later identified as crucial to her development as a religious skeptic and cultural critic.

In *Eighty Years and More*, Stanton recalled that during her time at Willard's Female Seminary, the great evangelical revivalist Charles Grandison Finney spent six weeks in Troy, where in emotional mass meetings he forcefully dramatized the dire wages of sin. As she described that time, Troy students attended every session, daily, over the six weeks' duration, and fatefully, Elizabeth Cady was "one of the first [of Finney's] victims." The adult Stanton depicts the popular evangelist as a dangerous "epidemic," to which her "vivid imagination" was particularly susceptible; during one of these sessions, she remembered, Finney conjured a terrifying vision of hell, brimming over with "the burning depths of liquid fire" and fearfully punctuated by "the shouts of the devils echoing through the vaulted arches." Pointing excitedly to the ceiling, Finney exhorted prospective converts to witness, as he could, the encroaching demonic cavalcade. Over the course of weeks, claimed Stanton, Finney worked Cady into such an unstable state of mind that she could actually envision the fiends. Moreover, "the picture glowed before my eyes," she wrote, "and remained with me for months afterward. . . . Mental anguish prostrated my health. Dethronement of my reason was apprehended by friends." So overcome was young Cady that she retreated to Johnstown to recover. Fearing for her mental and physical welfare, so the story goes, in June her father, sister, and brother-in-law embarked upon a six-week scenic trip to Niagara Falls. Over the course of that vacation, readings in and conversations about rationalist philosophy restored her physical and mental health. "I found my way out of the darkness into the clear sunlight of Truth," Stanton recollected. "My religious superstitions gave place to rational ideas based on scientific facts, and . . . I grew more and more happy, day by day."[6] In this telling, her usable past illustrates the woeful effects of religion upon young women, even upon those as strong-minded as Elizabeth Cady. As Kathi Kern suggests, however, although this "failed conversion . . . played a shaping role in her politics[,] . . . the trouble is, in some sense, it may not be true." In point of fact, during Stanton's seminary years Finney only appeared twice; his first, quite brief visit to the area occurred in July 1831, a month *after* her restorative Niagara Falls vacation.[7]

We may never fully identify the authentic life events that shaped this narrative, but her art teacher's commentary may provide a slender thread of evidence that illuminates its themes and import to her later anticlerical positions and critiques of the cultural sources of women's subordination. In the pages of Cady's commonplace book, Thirza Lee responded directly to the actions and behaviors of a younger and less scripted version of the woman's rights advocate; and her extract and commentary produce another angle from which to view her religious experience at Troy Female Seminary. Lee signed and then dated her entry as "March—1831," approximately six weeks before Stanton located Finney and his six-week revival in Troy.

In an apparent attempt to instruct or chastise Elizabeth Cady, Lee quoted from John Angell James's *The Christian Father's Present to His Children*; its chapter "On Female Accomplishments, Virtues, and Pursuits" addresses pedagogical objectives for women. Although men's education fits them out for a public vocation, advises James, "the profession of ladies, to which the bent of *their* instruction should be turned, is that of daughters, wives, mothers, and mistresses of families." Young women may therefore pursue musical arts, painting, and foreign languages, as long as these amusements remain private rather than public occupations. Underscoring the frivolous aspects of the preceding talents, however, James counsels that a "female of few accomplishments, but many virtues" will make the best wife and mother; to that end, "mental improvement should be associated with *a correct knowledge of household affairs*," else husband and children "are both very likely to wander *from* home for comfort." James concludes this patronizing discourse with Lee's commonplace extract: "True Religion is the deep basis of excellence; Sound Morality its lofty superstructure; Good Sense, General Knowledge, Correct Feeling, the necessary furniture of the fabric; and unaffected Modesty and Fashionable Accomplishments, its elegant decorations."

James's appalling metaphorical portrait of the "correctly" educated woman (as a dwelling) only restates his previous assertions that her "appropriate" roles play out solely within its walls. In this cloistered analogy for the peerless woman, James makes "True Religion" the central feature of her "excellence"—grounding the foundation of the domicile for men's exclusive use. Ethics understandably merit the status of structuring framework for her character, but he relegates common sense and intellectual accomplishments to the "furniture" within this womanly "fabric" or edifice; modesty and the arts serve as superfluous but "elegant decorations."[8] One is tempted to imagine that forty years hence Stanton's words in her popular "Marriage and Maternity" lectures directly attack James's recommendations; in maturity she would demand that society educate girls to respect their "womanhood" over and above such "incident[al]" roles as wife and mother. "Our daughters are nouns—not adjectives," she would proclaim in the 1870s.[†]

Lee's gloss on James's counsel suggests that Elizabeth Cady, in the eyes of at least one beginning teacher, already displayed an intransigent vein of skepticism or was perhaps greatly in need of a crash course in religious and "womanly" (i.e., domestic) education. "I fear that you, my E.," Lee gravely cautioned, "are raising the superstructure without having lain [*sic*] the true foundation—If so," she added, alluding to Matthew 6:33, "I would only say in the words of the blessed Jesus, Seek first the kingdom of God and his righteousness." Although Lee's commonplace entry hardly constitutes a six-week indoctrination in the manner of Reverend Charles Grandison Finney, it may illustrate the kinds of interactions Stanton experienced with at least one of her teachers at Troy Female Seminary. They and other aspects of her experience there likely contributed to the Finney story spun for later audiences, as well as to her fierce advocacy for women's expanded cultural, educational, professional, and political roles.

Taking the failed Finney conversion narrative off the table, however, still leaves another question unanswered. What might have provoked Lee's rebuke? In *Eighty Years and More*, Stanton reprinted a speech she delivered at the Troy Female Seminary in June 1892 for the dedication of its Gurley Memorial Building. In this address, she related a prank she ostensibly played on a "Miss Theresa Lee," whom she does not identify as a teacher but who was tasked with ringing a bell to announce bedtime and morning prayer to students. Stanton claimed she surreptitiously kicked the bell down the stairs after everyone was in bed; when students and teachers poured into the hall in consternation, she and her roommate seized the opportunity to run in and out of students' rooms, disrupting bed linens and transferring clothing from one room to another—all without being detected.[9] Stanton, who relied heavily on Anthony for names and dates, may well refer to Thirza Lee here. Intriguingly, in her 1892 dedication speech she turned J. A. James's (and thereby, Lee's) advice for the education of young women on its head. Explaining that she and her roommate were never suspected as the perpetrators of this prank, she declared complacently, "Our standing for scholarship was good, hence we were supposed to reflect all the moralities."[10]

From Elizabeth Cady Stanton, Autograph and Commonplace Book, Thirza Lee, 1831[11]

"True Religion is the deep basis of excellence—Sound Morality its lofty superstructure—Good Sense, General Knowledge, Correct Feeling, the necessary furniture of the fabric—and unaffected Modesty and Fashionable Accomplishments, its elegant decorations"[12]. . [*sic*] I fear that you, my E., are raising the superstructure without having lain the true foundation— If so, I would only say in the words of the blessed Jesus, Seek first the kingdom of God and his righteousness.[13]

Thirza Lee

Troy Female Seminary March–1831

From Foreword, Harriot Stanton Blatch and Theodore Weld Stanton, 1922[14]

In recreations Mrs. Stanton had decided favorites. In the early days dancing was her chief delight. She was light as a feather on her feet, and always told with zest how she countered her father's pronunciamento that "she had been sent to Troy Seminary for the cultivation of her head, not her heels," with assertion that "he was mistaken as to the aim, for it was use of toes, not heels, which dancing was to inculcate." The playing of games she enjoyed throughout her life. She played as if her very life depended upon the outcome. She always played to win, and was sorely disappointed when she did not succeed. She was never known to give a game surreptitiously to a weak player. When she played chess she would even-up the contest by throwing out some of her pieces at the start, she would be generous in accepting the heaviest handicap, but when the game was once started, there was never anything for her or her opponent but a fight to the finish. She neither gave nor accepted quarter. She was as intense, as uncompromising, in a game as in a suffrage contest, and defeat was as painful to her in the one situation as the other.

NOTES

1. DuBois, *Harriot Stanton Blatch*, 45, 8, 12.

2. Perry, "Blatch, Harrieot Stanton."

3. The annual registers for the years 1830–1833 for New York State list a "Thirza Lee" as a teacher at the Troy Female Seminary during the years Stanton attended. She attended as a pupil in 1829, and after her graduation "she continued nearly ten years as teacher of Drawing and Painting" (Williams, *The New-York Annual Register for the Year of Our Lord 1830*, 189; Williams, *The New-York Annual Register for the Year of Our Lord 1831*, 170; Williams, *The New-York Annual Register for the Year of Our Lord 1832*, 200; Williams, *The New-York Annual Register for the Year of Our Lord 1833*, 216; Fairbanks, *Emma Willard and Her Pupils*, 199).

4. Citing a letter from the archivist of the Emma Willard School, Elisabeth Griffith suggests that Cady matriculated at midterm in January 1831, but several reliable sources— including Stanton's autobiography; Ann D. Gordon; *Emma Willard and Her Pupils*, a nineteenth-century history of the school; and other biographers—point to 1830 (*In Her Own Right*, 17, 238n8; Stanton, *Eighty Years and More*, 35; *SP* 1:xxiv; Fairbanks, *Emma Willard and Her Pupils*, 148; Lutz, *Created Equal*, 10; Banner, *Elizabeth Cady Stanton*, 12; Ginzberg, *Elizabeth Cady Stanton*, 22).

5. Fairbanks, *Emma Willard and Her Pupils*, 199.

6. Stanton, *Eighty Years and More*, quoted on 41, 43–44.

7. Kern, *Mrs. Stanton's Bible*, 42; see also 42–44 for further corrective information about Finney's appearances in Troy and other possible sources for her failed conversion story.

8. James, *The Christian Father's Present*, 2:57, 58, 65, 73, 74, 83.

9. Tilton (who because of his friendship with Stanton may have heard the tale from the horse's mouth) tells an alternate version of this story, in which Cady posed as a ghost to enact this prank, without her roommate and Lee (*Eminent Women of the Age*, 341).

10. Stanton, *Eighty Years and More*, 443.

11. Elizabeth Cady Stanton Autograph and Commonplace Book, Thirza Lee, MS P.84.848, March 1831, Boston Public Library/Rare Books, courtesy of the Trustees of the Boston Public Library/Rare Books, Boston, MA.

12. James, *The Christian Father's Present*, 2:83.

13. Matthew 6:33: "But seek ye first the kingdom of God, and his righteousness, and all these things shall be added unto you."

14. Harriot Stanton Blatch and Theodore Weld Stanton, foreword to Stanton and Blatch, *Elizabeth Cady Stanton as Revealed in Her Letters, Diary, and Reminiscences,* 1:xvii.

Seneca Falls and Early Reform Days
(1880–1911)

This chapter shows Stanton slowly acquiring the knowledge and confidence to participate in multiple reform movements. We see her speaking from the ranks of the audience, rather than from the stage, as she initiates her trademark weapon of scathing humor. In other reminiscences, Stanton offers guidance to young wives and mothers while meeting her own parental challenges, develops friendships among reform leaders such as Frederick Douglass, takes fledgling steps in convention organization in Seneca Falls in 1848 under the supporting wings of seasoned associates, and leads the newly formed American Equal Rights Association (AERA) as first vice president.

Among the contributors to this chapter is a fellow AERA vice president, Frederick Douglass (1818–1895), the former slave, abolitionist, and civil rights leader, masterful orator, author, journalist, and U.S. marshal and minister to Haiti. Despite his somewhat overblown praise for his old friend and occasional antagonist, the tone of this selection, written on the occasion of Stanton's seventieth birthday, rings sincere. Douglass recalled what was likely their first or early meeting, which he dates as 1840; and in this account Stanton's preaching of the "new gospel of woman's rights" amplified his own sensibilities about human dignity. Douglass—exalted in his own right for the power to move others—honors Stanton as a teacher and praises her fine skills in logical persuasion.

Mary Sherman Bascom Bull (1835–1881), about whom little is known, vividly if skeptically depicts the range and scope of Stanton's early activism in Seneca Falls. In *Eighty Years and More*, Stanton remembered "Mary Bascom," who was thirteen in 1848, as "a good talker on the topics of the day" and claimed her as one of three female intimates who "added much to [her] happiness" during her Seneca Falls days.[1] Bull's commentary on Stanton's articles in Amelia Bloomer's temperance journal, the *Lily*, illuminates Stanton's early interest in dress reform, when she and other woman suffrage advocates donned what would come to be known as the "Bloomer." They themselves first called the costume "Turkish" pants and "shorts" (as one of the objectives of the short skirts layered over trousers was to free women from heavy, trailing gowns). Introduced to the outfit by her second cousin Elizabeth Smith

Miller, whose father, Gerrit Smith, was also committed to dress reform, Stanton was enthusiastic about the shorts, but others found them threatening.[2] In 1852, describing her "remarks on the church" at a temperance convention over which Stanton presided as president (and notably, at a time before she had adopted her maternal self-presentation), a journalist argued defensively, "Mrs. Stanton's bearing at this Convention was dogmatic and egotistic in the extreme. And she is described by an eye witness, as resembling a man in her dress, having on boots like a man, pants like a man, dickey like a man, vest like a man."[3]

A more favorable account of Stanton's early reform work comes from the occasional essayist, poet, and editor Mrs. C. K. [Lucretia Russell Gray] Smith (1817–1911). Infant Lucretia was born in Reading, Vermont. In 1846 she and her husband founded and edited the Monmouth, Illinois, *Atlas*, a paper that became a daily in 1904. After her death her children collected and published selections from her writings, *A Souvenir Collection of Poetry and Prose from the Writings of Mrs. C. K. Smith* (1908). Although relatives described Smith at the end of her life as traditionally devout, she wrote and contributed to the *Free Thought Magazine* at the time of Stanton's death and attended a Junius—or "Friends of Human Progress"—meeting in earlier years.[4] Smith's memory of Stanton speaking from the audience in 1857 confirms Theodore Stanton and Harriot Stanton Blatch's contention that Stanton channeled her childhood exuberance and teenaged prankster spirit into activist tactics early in her career. Importantly, it also anticipates Stanton's later commentaries on the relationship between maternity and women's rights—and the welcoming reception she received from women whose interest in physical health as a vehicle for personal independence exceeded their enthusiasm for political enfranchisement.

The selection from Anna Elizabeth Henion (1840–1923), a Seneca Falls piano teacher who mastered the challenging and rambunctious Stanton brood, shows Stanton moving powerfully from the audience to the platform; she also provides insight into Stanton's home life in the early 1860s. Henion is listed in census records and directories as a single woman and music teacher who lived with siblings and her parents between 1867 and 1881; by 1895 she shared and co-owned her own home with her unmarried sisters.[5] Internal evidence suggests that Henion describes a relatively brief period between 1861, when son Theodore Stanton was ten and his sister Margaret was nine, and the spring of 1862, when Elizabeth sold the Seneca Falls house to join Henry in Brooklyn. At this time, after seventeen years of childbearing, Stanton re-emerged on the national public stage to assume positions of leadership; but with the exception of a flash-forward to her later career, Henion primarily highlights Stanton's advocacy within her community and her parenting skills within the home. Not surprisingly, Henry Brewster is missing from this picture, and Elizabeth Cady seems somewhat distracted, as she perhaps balanced increasing public reform efforts with parental duties. In that regard, Henion likewise offers a corrective to the "tall tale" nature of some of her employer's lyceum anecdotes seen in other chapters, where Stanton's ostensibly vast and peerless maternal expertise reigns supreme.

Universalist minister, woman suffrage leader, and noted orator Olympia Brown (1835–1926) described the convening of the Eleventh National Woman's Rights Convention several years later, on 10 May 1866 at the Church of the Puritans. Brown had to overcome bitter prejudice against female applicants when she attempted to gain acceptance to a theology school, and she faced similar difficulties when applying for ordination. Brown was, however, the first American woman to be ordained with "full denominational approval" in 1863. She married John Henry Willis in 1873 but did not take his surname. Considering her principled and brave stands in gaining ordination and, later, retaining her maiden name (for which she faced great criticism), her disappointed assessment of Stanton's demeanor in 1866 is revealing.[6] Also significant is her greater frustration with Wendell Phillips's dismissive comments about women's rights, in advance of the "schism" that would occur at AERA's annual meeting three years later.

Excerpt from Letter to the Editor of the *New Era*, Frederick Douglass, 1885[7]

Five and forty years ago in Boston, before the snows of time had fallen upon the locks of either of us, and long before the cause of woman had taken its high place among the great reforms of the nineteenth century, Mrs. Elizabeth Cady Stanton, then just returned from her wedding tour in Europe, did me the honor to sit by my side and by that logic of which she is a master, successfully endeavored to convince me of the wisdom and truth of the then new gospel of woman's rights.

I was then only a few years out of slavery, filled with detestation of the power it gave one man over another, and smarting with the insults offered to my manhood, by popular prejudice at the North. I was perhaps, on these accounts, all the more ready to listen to, and learn from a teacher of such splendid ability and liberality of spirits. No man is perhaps more debtor for her work in the world than myself. While she by her eloquence and reasoning, gave me a higher conception of the dignity and grandeur of woman than before, she also by her contempt for popular prejudice, in taking pains to impart to me the great truths with which her mind was illuminated, gave me a higher estimate of my abilities and possibilities as a "man and brother."

From "Woman's Rights and Other 'Reforms' in Seneca Falls," Mary S. Bull, 1880[8]

To this place as I have tried to describe it, came Mrs. Stanton in 1846 or 47.[9] She was then in the early bloom of a most attractive womanhood, fascinating in manner, cultured by travel, society and books; warmhearted, impulsive, "a very woman," for a secret was not safe an hour in her possession. She soon exerted a wide-spread influence over the younger and more advanced portion of society. The older and more conservative might point to her disregard of Sunday, of ordinary religious duties; but they were answered by an appeal to her conduct as a wife and mother, to her admirable housekeeping and charming hospitality, as proofs of Christianity in life and conduct. Most preachers of morals and religion fail to live up to their precepts; Mrs. Stanton's practice was better than her preaching. Her private life, laid open to the world, would reflect far more honor upon her than any public effort she has ever made. Mrs. Stanton would turn from her desk, where lay a manuscript of a lecture upon the wrongs of woman in marriage, to give a young girl about to be married the most loving sympathy and the wisest and most judicious advice. I know of wives who will never cease to hold Mrs. Stanton in loving and grateful remembrance,—however they may look upon her public career,—for advice given at that most important time, so wise and good that they feel they owe much of the happiness of their lives to her counsel.

Mrs. Stanton was then as bold and defiant as now of popular feeling or prejudice when it conflicted with her sense of justice. At a time when the prejudice against color was far greater than now, she boldly walked down the main street of this town in the broad light of a June day arm in arm with

Frederick Douglass; and she entertained as honored guests both Frederick Douglass and Charles Lenox Remond,[10] when they came here to lecture in the old chapel.

Mrs. Stanton greatly missed in coming here the excitement of her Boston life, where a convention was always at hand and a new "ism" daily to be talked over. In Mrs. Stanton's own account of the Convention, she says she met in Auburn in the Summer of 1848 Lucretia Mott, for the first time since the World's Convention in London.[11] Talking over with Mrs. Mott the theories that occupied them as they walked the streets of London together, was like the smoke of battle and strains of martial music to the old war horse,— the call to arms. Mrs. Stanton has never, her life through, gone willingly in a beaten path; whatever she is, she is original. We had had all kinds of conventions, but we were unconscious of our chains, blind to our slavery as women, our wrongs unread upon the statute-books. But when the idea was broached between the two ladies of a woman's convention conducted by women, it had the great merit to Mrs. Stanton of being *new* if nothing more. What to complain of, what particular wrongs, Mrs. Stanton knew no more than any other of the unconscious victims about her; but she "sniffed the battle from afar," and rushing into the arena threw down the glove as the champion of "woman's rights." In Mrs. Stanton's history of the suffrage movement, she tells the story of the first convention with such gleams of her own humor that one can hardly help suspecting that she saw the ludicrous aspect of the whole affair.[12]

Four ladies, Lucretia Mott, Martha Wright, Mary Ann McClintock and Elizabeth Cady Stanton, sitting around the tea-table of Richard Hunt, a prominent Quaker living near Waterloo, on Saturday evening July 15th, 1848, resolved to call a convention to consider the "Rights of Woman," and before twilight had deepened into night the call was written and sent to the *Seneca County Courier.* The convention was called for the 19th and 20th of July, and the next day (Sunday the 16th) after the tea-party at Mr. Hunt's, these ladies met in the parlor of Thomas McClintock, at Waterloo, to write their declarations, draw up resolutions and consider subjects for speeches.[13] To use Mrs. Stanton's own words "they found they had a herculean task before them." They knew women had wrongs,—had they not called a convention to complain of them?—but just what they were, or how to present them, no one knew.[14] They consulted the reports of peace and anti-slavery societies; but "all were too tame and pacific for the inauguration of such a rebellion as the world never saw." "Finally," says Mrs. Stanton, "a lady present read in a loud clear voice the Declaration of 1776." It was at once resolved to use that historic document, substituting "all men" for King George. Poor ladies! to have to resort to the product of a man's brain before they could even proclaim their wrongs! "But," to go on with Mrs. Stanton, "our ancestors had eighteen wrongs to complain of, and knowing that women must under any circumstances have more wrongs than men could possibly have to complain of, a protracted search was made through the statute-books, church usages, customs of society, to find that exact number." "Several well disposed men assisted in the search;" and Mrs. Stanton quotes the remark of a youthful lord present, "Your grievances must be grievous indeed when you have to go to books to find them out."[15] Reading this in Mrs. Stanton's account the other day brought back to my memory the fact of that "youthful lord's" confiding to *me*, as a fellow-lover of mischief without much reverence for elders and betters, his "audacious talk" to the grievance hunting ladies.

The momentous day, the 19th of July, was clear and bright, with mercury at 90°; Mrs. Stanton says, "Crowds on foot, on horseback and in carriages flocked to the old chapel." I do not remember a *crowd*, but we all differ as to terms, and Mrs. Stanton may have meant that zeal made up for numbers. I am certain that every man, woman and child present signed the declaration, and I find, on consulting, sixty-five names of women, thirty of men.[16] As "the crowd" came to the doors of the chapel they were found to be locked; but Mrs. Stanton and her adherents soon came upon the scene, "armed with the declarations, resolutions and the statute-books of the State of New York." No one had a key or seemed to know where to procure one. The convention was to be of women exclusively, no men admitted; but alas! right here upon the start, an appeal to the obnoxious sex was necessary. It was soon found that the doors of the chapel were barred by bolts drawn upon the inside, and the only way to obtain admittance was for some one to get in through the windows and draw the bolts. But these windows were so high from the ground that no one but a man or tall climbing boy could scale them. After some consideration, "an embryo Professor of Yale," was "boosted" through one of the windows, and quickly opened the doors and admitted the "Convention."[17] We all went in,—I say we, for I, though only a girl of thirteen, attended every session. I was one of the "little pitchers" of the last generation, and my father, just home from the Convention of 1846 and the succeeding session of the legislature, was much interested in the proceedings, and was, I think, one of the first speakers.[18] For the end shadowed the beginning. The ladies were obliged to turn to the men for aid before they could even organize their convention.

The *first* trouble was a very curious one, and it came near destroying the harmony of the proceedings here, and in Rochester a few weeks later almost broke up the convention. The ladies refused to work under a *woman* as a presiding officer. Here the matter was compromised by the appointment of James Mott as chairman; but in Rochester, where a woman was chosen to preside, the other officers resigned and were about to leave the hall in disgust. The question was settled in some way, I have forgotten how; but it strikes me as very ludicrous that the first act of a convention called to demand the rights of woman should be to refuse one of the rights claimed for her.[19]

"James Mott, tall, dignified, in Quaker costume," in the chair, his wife, Lucretia Mott, stated the object of the meeting. Elizabeth and Mary McClintock and Mrs. Stanton "each read a well written speech." The declaration was read and re-read by paragraphs and debated upon. The suffrage resolution was the only one not unanimously adopted. I remember Frederick Douglass'[s] speaking strongly in favor of that resolution.[20] Those were the days of Frederick Douglass'[s] fiery denunciation of all wrongs, social and moral. Time and the accomplishment of the great purpose of his life have greatly softened him, and he no longer pours forth those streams of fiery eloquence, so bitter, so sarcastic, that old Sojourner Truth was hardly to be blamed for the question suddenly asked by her in the midst of one of his speeches, "Frederick, is God dead?"[21] Mrs. Stanton also contended for that resolution.

Of course the impressions of such a child as I was are of little importance, none I might say, except as corroborating the history of the time as told by others. I remember all that passed perfectly well (except of course the speeches), and the whole scene comes before me as vividly as if yesterday,— the old chapel with its dusty windows, the gallery on three sides, the wooden benches or pews, and the platform with the desk and communion-table, and the group gathered there; Mrs. Stanton, stout, short, with her merry eye and expression of great good humor; Lucretia Mott, whose presence then as now commanded respect wherever she might be; Mary Ann McClintock, a dignified Quaker matron with four daughters around her, two of whom took active part in the proceedings. These ladies, Elizabeth and Mary McClintock, were beautiful women, with dignified and self-possessed manners not often seen in women brought up as they were in a country town of that day. . . .

Of this first convention may be said with absolute truth, that however ridiculous the affair might seem, how like playing at something of importance, the women concerned in it were ladies and more than that were pure hearted good women, if mistaken. Reading over the different accounts of the convention, besides talking with many persons who remember the proceedings perfectly well, I find the contrast between that first effort and those that have followed it so great, that I think Mrs. Stanton must often have looked back upon those days in 1848 with regretful longing, when she has sat as presiding officer and heard the women who have since disgraced the platform of the woman's rights party, with brazen faces and tongues, pour forth their diatribes at society and its restrictions.

Mrs. Bloomer if present at the convention in 1848 was then only as an auditor, for she had not yet awakened and found herself famous.[22] This convention, Mrs. Stanton's reputation and genial hospitality, and the notorious Bloomer dress, for a long time made this village a sort of Mecca for the vagabond reformers of the day. Very often the chapel was lighted up of an evening and a champion of woman's rights addressed the people. While we were sometimes honored by the presence of true good women like Frances Gage, or women of undoubted genius like Elizabeth Oakes Smith, we often had some very funny kinds of persons stray this way. . . .[23]

But though we had in these intermediate years a succession of the "apostles of reform," it was the Bloomer dress and *The Lily* that gave us our wide spread notoriety.

This dress was as wrongly named as America. To neither of the ladies, Mrs. Bloomer or Mrs. Stanton, whose names are connected with that costume the world over, belongs the credit of originating it. The history of the costume afterwards so famous, and of the paper that made its fame, is something after this wise:— . . .

. . . The first number of *The Lily* appeared in January 1849, Amelia Bloomer and Anna C. Mattison, editors. I cannot recall Mrs. Mattison, who or what she was; but it matters the less as her connection with the paper ceased with the first issue, and Amelia Bloomer reigned alone.[24]

I have some numbers of *The Lily* before me as I write, one issued in 1849, when the paper was entirely loyal to the cause of temperance and before Mrs. Stanton had gained admission to its columns. It is a small, insignificant sheet worthy of the name given it, but showing some inherent vitality in existing at all with such a name. . . . About 1850 Mrs. Stanton's attention was called to *The Lily*, little known even in this place except to the members of the society whose organ it was. This society was organized upon a strictly conservative and religious basis. Mr. and Mrs. Bloomer were both members of the Episcopal Church, Mr. Bloomer one of the officers of the Church, and *The Lily* up to this time was conducted in a conservative manner, and was considered unimpugnable by most persons when Mrs. Stanton made her first sally upon the posts.[25] Mrs. Stanton however understood human nature and woman nature perfectly well. She was a leader in social affairs, her house a social center, distinguished persons were often her guests, and an invitation to her parties was not often declined by any one, from clergymen down. A visit to Mrs. Bloomer, a judicious invitation or two, and the citadel was won, and *The Lily* was henceforth the organ of the woman's rights party as represented by Mrs. Stanton. A number of the paper issued after this change had taken place is also before me, nearly double in size,—print, paper, all improved, and issued semi-monthly. It was, judging from the old files of *The Lily*, a far more spicy affair than the present organ of Mrs. Stanton and Miss Anthony, *The National Citizen*.[26] Mrs. Stanton, over her signature of E. C. S., was merciless in choosing her themes, sparing neither institution nor individuals. A large distillery was built by prominent business men near her house. As soon as it was in running order, a card of thanks from E. C. S. appeared in *The Lily*, addressed to Messrs. ——, for the magnificent bouquet just presented to her by that firm at a cost of ten thousand dollars. I cannot find that article, as that number of *The Lily* is missing from my files; but I well remember my father's characterizing it as being as keen a piece of irony as he ever saw written, and it had the desired effect of making a sensation.[27] Another time E. C. S. asserted in *The Lily* that among the numerous personifications of the devil he had never assumed female form.[28] Of course tradition was against her, and a young clergyman, a modest quiet man, who held all advanced doctrines in horror and would not for the world have appeared in *The Lily*, was indiscreet enough to whisper to a friend that Mrs. Stanton was wrong, instancing the temptation of St. Anthony. Poor man! The next number of *The Lily* contained E. C. S.'s apology and recantation, expressing also her obligations to a reverend gentleman well skilled in legendary lore.[29] But I am wandering from the Bloomer dress. I have tried to show, however, how it was that Mrs. Bloomer became Mrs. Stanton's coadjutor in her work of reform. Early in the year 1852, Mrs. E. S. Miller, the daughter of Gerrit Smith, came here to visit her cousin Mrs. Stanton. Mrs. Miller then lived in the country near her father's residence at Peterboro, going every day to visit her father in all weathers. She often found her long dresses much in her way on dusty country roads, and sometimes bethought herself of a costume she had seen Mrs. Fanny Kemble wear in mountain climbing in Massachusetts, years previous.[30] The Winter of 1852 was characterized by very open weather, and Mrs. Miller put her long-thought-of project into execution by cutting off one of her gowns just below the knee, and making Turkish trowsers of the material thus gained. This costume she wore with great comfort in her walks from her house to her father's, and in coming here she remembered our clay mud and the absence of sidewalks upon many of our streets,—Mrs. Stanton's own house being at the end of a long muddy lane, a very "slough of despond" in bad weather. Mrs. Miller brought the costume with her as a matter of convenience, little dreaming of the commotion she was about to excite. Doubly welcome was she to her cousin with this costume, for Mrs. Stanton had worn the gloss of novelty off from most of her themes and was sighing for a new sensation, a new reform. Here it was ready to her hand, and forgetting, or not heeding, all she had said of the advantages of the long flowing robes over the male costume in her first speeches, she rushed with renewed ardor into "dress reform." As soon as the necessary stitches could be taken, Mrs. Stanton made her first appearance in the new dress. Never shall I forget that first appearance! Mrs. Stanton is not slight or sylph-like in her proportions; she is, not to put too fine a point on it, the reverse. Imagine her then in a full black satin frock cut off at the knee, with Turkish trowsers of the same material, her wrap a double *broché* shawl, and on her head the hideous great bonnet then in fashion. I have seen scarecrows that did credit to farmers' boys' ingenuity, but never one better calculated to scare all birds, beasts and human beings than was Mrs. Stanton in the Bloomer dress. She was accompanied by Mrs. Miller in the same dress, and followed by a crowd of boys yelling, singing and laughing, while every door and window was lined with staring faces. The whole town was roused as never before.

In the next number of *The Lily*, was an article from E. C. S. upon "Dress

Reform," and a hint that the editor would soon assume the costume.[31] Of course Mrs. Bloomer had so identified herself with Mrs. Stanton that when the latter said *a* Mrs. Bloomer must say *b*. Hence one bright day in the latter part of May, *three months after* Mrs. Miller had brought the costume into town, Mrs. Bloomer walked out of her house "*à la* Bloomer." She had a far better figure for the dress than had Mrs. Stanton, and looked better in the Bloomers than any other person I have ever seen wear them. For one thing she discarded the bonnet then universally worn and assumed a round hat, something like the sun and sea-side hats now worn. Oh! the excitement of that Summer! Reporters from the city papers were seen in our streets, evidently expecting to find all the female population wearing the hideous toggery. . . . I think that it was also in 1853 (but my memory for dates is imperfect) that Mrs. Stanton, accompanied by her baby and nurse, went to Albany and in the short dress presented to the Legislature of our state the first petition for female suffrage.[32]

Mrs. Stanton did not long wear the Bloomer dress, in spite of her assertion that she had assumed it for life; she "dropped it like a hot potato," to use her own expression, after wearing it a year or two. I have seen persons delighted to get out of a scrape, and have heard such persons express satisfaction; but never have I seen any one so happy, so heartily glad to be rid of an incubus, as was Mrs. Stanton when she had the courage (and far more was required to lay aside the dress than had been necessary to assume it) to cast off the ugly toggery.[33] "I can go out without being stared at now," was her heartfelt exclamation of satisfaction to a friend in the street the first time she went out after assuming again, to use the words of a Bloomer and woman's rights advocate, "the garb of woman's slavery."

From "Elizabeth Cady Stanton—Letters from Susan B. Anthony, Lucy N. Coleman and Mrs. C. K. Smith," Lucretia Russell Gray Smith, 1903.[34]

We first met Mrs. Stanton some forty years ago and heard her, at that time, make a speech of five words that "brought down the house" and perfectly squelched her opponent. We were in attendance at the meeting of the "Friends of Human Progress," held near Waterloo, N.Y. When we entered the meeting George W. Taylor was presiding and Lucy N. Coleman was speaking on a resolution in favor of giving women equal rights with men.[35] When Mrs. Coleman was through, a man, who had the appearance of a farmer, arose near the platform and commenced an argument (?) against the resolution before the house. The particular point he made was that women had it much easier than men. He said that while men labored in the hay and harvest field in the hot sun, women only had light work to do in the house, in the shade, out of the sun's rays, and while men were chopping down the forests and clearing the land the women had to do only light needlework, rock the baby and get the meals. For a moment he was interrupted and compelled to cease speaking by the cheering in the gallery by people who had come, as they expressed it to "see the show and hear the fanatics." At that moment a most dignified appearing woman, with such a head as we had never seen on the shoulders of a woman—a head like that of Daniel Webster's[36]—arose in the audience and asked permission of the chairman to ask the gentleman who was speaking a question. The chairman gave the permission, and this intelligent appearing woman, whom we afterwards learned was Mrs. Stanton, put this question to the man occupying the floor: "DID YOU EVER BEAR CHILDREN?" This question, so deliberately and calmly put, was not replied to, but it had a tremendous effect. The opponent of women's rights dropped into his seat as if he had been knocked down by a club, and the applause was not only great on the floor, but it turned the tide in the galleries and the resolution was passed unanimously—not a dissenting voice, not even from the man speaker, who was perfectly squelched.

From "Elizabeth Cady Stanton. Some Reminiscences of Her Family Life, at Seneca Falls, N.Y., by an Old Acquaintance," A.E. [Anna Elizabeth] Henion[37]

Elizabeth Cady Stanton lived in Seneca Falls, N.Y. during the first sixteen years of her married life; but I remember her best during the early years of the Civil War.[38] She was then a handsome woman, with a most attractive face, winning smile, and cordial manner which instinctively won confidence. And I remember hearing how all sorts and conditions of persons went to her for advice; women with drunken husbands who therefore failed to support them; women with refractory children difficult to manage; men and women who were hard up, not knowing which way to turn; women who asked information about housekeeping; girls who asked advice about marriage. To each and all she gave wise counsel and ready sympathy. She always enjoyed young people, over whom she had a stimulating influence;

and at one time held weekly or fortnightly "conversationals", after the manner of the French salon, for her own and their benefit, at which time the art of talking (which some people contend is becoming a lost art) was sedulously cultivated, for there was no other entertainment!![39] On these evenings all the great questions of the day, together with literary matters in general, were discussed, and the persons who participated have never forgotten the pleasure and profit derived therein.

Mrs. Stanton was also a fine housekeeper, a gift usually denied, I believe, to the "strong minded". How often I have heard men and women who had no acquaintance with her deliver themselves of the following: "She had better stay at home and work in the kitchen, and attend to her housekeeping, and take care of her family, than to go around the country speechifying." Nevertheless, Mrs. Stanton was a notable housekeeper and excellent cook, and one of the best suppers I ever ate was at her house when every article on the table was made by herself as her maid was absent.

But it was as a teacher of music that I came nearest to her. Her two younger children, Theodore and Margaret, were my first pupils.[40] I distinctly recall when I went to her house to ask the privilege of instructing them. I really stood very much in awe of her, for I had always heard her spoken of as a very gifted woman of remarkable ability; and, beside [*sic*], didn't she go on a platform and make addresses like a man!! So I rang the bell with a beating heart, and when she came to the door, proffered my request in trembling tones. She smiled, kindly. "Why," said she, "I don't believe you could teach them. Mrs. L. has been teaching them for some time, and I have stopped their lessons for they haven't learned a single note." "O', Mrs. Stanton," I entreated, "if you would only let me try, I could teach them to read notes, I know." "Well," she assented, "you can come next week on such a morning and begin, and we will soon determine if there is any progress. I would be glad to have them learn as I am very fond of music." So I began with all the enthusiasm of youth. I was determined that notes should get in their brains if such a thing was possible. Theodore, I should say was ten years of age, and Maggie, as she was called, seven or eight; and they were very bright, attractive, children. The beginning of the study of music is drudgery at the best, but things went smoothly for a while. They could soon read notes, could play some simple studies, and a duet. Their mother was pleased with their progress, and I was congratulating myself that I had accomplished something worth while when one morning an incident occurred. I was giving Theodore his lesson as usual, but I noticed his attention wandered frequently to the window, through which he could see his brothers and playmates playing, apparently having no end of sport and enjoyment. He suddenly stopped playing. What is the matter, I inquired. I am not going to take any more music lesson, he replied. Why, Theodore, I said, what is the reason? 'Cause I want to go out and play, and I am going to, he added with decision. In vain I coaxed and entreated and promised it should be a short lesson. Theodore was firm. He was going out to play with the boys whose shouts reached his ears most enticingly. Mrs. Stanton happened to come into the room. I appealed to her. I will say here that one of her favorite theories about the bringing up of children was the uselessness of coercion. When differences arise between parents and children she would say impressively, sit down and talk over matters rationally with them; it will have far greater effect than arbitrary compulsion. In fact, she didn't believe in compelling children to do anything. She would not even rudely awaken them in the morning. "Let them sleep their sleep out, then they will get up cheerful and happy", etc. So when I appealed to her she stopped short; "Theodore, be a reasonable being," said she, and passed on. I was discouraged, for Theodore had not the slightest intention of being a reasonable being. He was going out to play, and that ended it; and he started to carry his purpose into effect when a bright thought struck me. "Theodore", said I, "if you will come back and take your lesson like a good boy and do just as I want you to, I will sing for you 'Grasshopper sitting on a sweet potato vine.'" This was a moving ditty then quite in vogue, and I believe even still warbled occasionally by college students.

There was only one verse:

> "Grasshopper, sitting on the sweet potato vine,
>> The sweet potato vine,
>> The sweet potato vine,
> Turki gobbler, came up behind
> And yanked him off the sweet potato vine."

This was repeated as many times as the singer could improvise stories between, and created a great deal of fun. As I said before, Theodore had started to go out of the room; but, as he heard my offer, stopped short. Will you sing ever so many verses? he asked. I assented. And tell lots of stories between? he asked. I agreed to this. Then, said Theodore, I'll take my lesson, which he proceeded to do in a most amicable manner. And his mother coming into the room shortly after, found everything peaceful and happy; teacher, pupil and music, all harmonious. But, alas, the voice of reason had not accomplished the change, but the most unblushing bribery. At the close of the lesson I carried out my part of the agreement, improvising ridiculous stories embodying experiences of the Stanton family between the verses, amid shouts of laughter from the children. After this I had plain sailing, promises to sing this fascinating song would effect the most painstaking performance of studies and even the odious scales on the part of Theodore . . .

Soon after this, the Stanton family moved from Seneca Falls to New York, much to the regret of their friends.

I think it must have been ten or twelve years later that one day it was announced in the village papers that Elizabeth Cady Stanton would speak in the public hall on a certain evening. Her theme was partly political and partly her favorite subject, Woman Suffrage. It was her first appearance in public in our village since her departure, and her friends turned out en masse. I remember the address was fine, and I was full of enthusiasm. I remember her characterization of the imbecile Buchanan and stolid Grant, and how, when she came to her favorite theme, Woman Suffrage, she brought forth her arguments with telling effect.[41] The audience applauded heartily, although many did not agree with her. At the close of the lecture, a great many remained, and went up and shook hands with and congratulated her. I wanted to speak to her, but felt shy, was afraid she would not remember me, etc. But I finally mustered courage, and gradually found my way to where she was standing. Suddenly she turned and saw me. There was a gleam of recognition in her eye. She held out her hands, "How do you do," she cried, "I am very glad to see you; does the grasshopper still sit on the sweet potato vine?!!"

From *Acquaintances, Old and New,*
Among Reformers, Olympia Brown, 1911[42]

During the war all work for woman's rights was suspended. Women employed themselves in scraping lint and making bandages, preparing needle books and pin cushions, holding fairs, raising money and otherwise working for the soldier. The first call after the war for reformatory effort was in the spring of 1866. I had been settled a short time over my little church at

Weymouth, Mass., when I received a letter from Susan B. Anthony inviting me to attend a Woman's Rights Convention in New York City. I had never been in New York City and unsophisticated as I was, it seemed like a great undertaking. I prepared myself for the event by getting an entire new outfit of clothing. . . .[43]

Thus equipped I set forth with a beating heart for the great city, filled with speculations as to the people that I should meet and the speeches that I should hear. . . . Early in the morning I arose and after breakfast repaired to the church more than an hour before the time for the meeting.

I saw a large placard on the side of the church announcing "WOMAN'S RIGHTS CONVENTION HERE TODAY." . . .

As I recall that meeting now it seems to me that it was very small and the audience quite out of proportion in number and character to the distinguished speakers on the platform. There I saw for the first time Henry Ward Beecher, Theodore Tilton, Parker Pillsbury, Susan B. Anthony, Mrs. Stanton and others.[44] Mrs. Stanton was the speaker of the occasion. As I remember her at that time, her hair was quite dark and drawn down over her ears according to the fashion of that day. She read her manuscript, and while it was exceedingly well read and the style of writing was in the same grand eloquence which always characterized her utterances, yet her whole appearance upon the platform was in striking contrast to the strong and undaunted manner in which she faced her audience and told them great truths in later years when her beautiful white curled hair added a charm to her radiant face.

But, however she appeared at that time or any other, whether she read or spoke, she was always the great statesman and the grand orator. . . .[45] In the afternoon Wendell Phillips gave a lecture addressed to women of which the burden was that women should first give up fashion and folly and become more serious and earnest, and he repeated several times, as a sort of refrain "Albany can do nothing for you." I think the few women who had the courage to venture out at that small meeting were not the ones who needed the lecture and the oft-repeated assurance that Albany could do nothing for us was rather disheartening.[46]

After the afternoon session a number of people repaired to the ante-room where they organized "The American Equal Rights Association," which was to work equally for women and negroes.

NOTES

1. One would think it more likely, however, particularly given Stanton's poor memory for facts and dates, that Mary's mother, Eliza Bascom, was intimate with Stanton at this time. Judith Wellman describes Eliza as "a retiring woman" who was uncomfortable with the idea of delivering public speeches but did engage in temperance, diet, and antislavery reform (*SP* 4:31n3; Stanton, *Eighty Years and More*, 153; Wellman, *The Road to Seneca Falls*, 121).

2. Elizabeth Smith Miller (1822–1911), daughter of abolitionist and philanthropist Gerrit Smith and Ann Carroll Fitzhugh, was a lifelong friend of Stanton. She supported abolition, woman's rights, and dress reform, contributing to the design of the Bloomer costume. Ultimately settling in Geneva, New York, she married banker Charles Dudley Miller and published a popular cooking and household manual, *In the Kitchen* (1875) (Gamber, "Miller, Elizabeth Smith"). Stanton's cousin, the abolitionist and dress reformer Gerrit Smith (1797–1874), philanthropically dedicated his wealth to (among other reforms) the free-state cause in "Bloody Kansas"; as one of the "Secret Six," he also funded the militant efforts of abolitionist John Brown (McKivigan, "Smith, Gerrit"). Gayle V. Fischer argues persuasively that the origins of the Bloomer in 1850s America are hard to pin down, but that various proponents were seeking a "freedom dress" that would liberate women from the seven plus layers of petticoats, with up to twelve layers of fabric encircling their waists, that produced "as much as twenty-five to thirty-five yards of cloth just in the skirts without the petticoats," in addition to corsets. Early woman's rights activists such as Stanton likely imitated the Turkish pantaloons style, but whether Elizabeth Smith Miller was influenced by American or European hydrotherapy spa pantaloons or (as Bull claims in her reminiscence) by British and European women such as Fanny Kemble and George Sand is less clear (Fischer, *Pantaloons and Power*, quoted on 20, 21, 79–94).

3. Quoted in Lutz, *Created Equal*, 78.

4. Slightly contradicting her relatives, the anonymous writer of her memorial suggests that Smith was a "sincere believer" in the afterlife and was "genuinely liberal" ("Death of Mrs. C. K. Smith," 624, 625, 626; Scott, *Newspapers and Periodicals of Illinois 1814–1879*, 246).

5. I thank Seneca Falls Historical Association Collections Manager Kathy Jans-Duffy for her extraordinary generosity in locating Henion's typescript for me, for researching in and providing me with copies of Seneca Falls directories in order to establish Henion's places of residence over a course of many years, and for identifying Henion's death date. In these records, Henion is identified alternately as "Anna," "Anna E.," or "Anna Elizabeth" in all but one 1867 directory, in which she appears, perhaps mistakenly, as "Ann" (Child, *Gazetteer and Business Directory of Seneca County, N.Y., for 1867–8*, 159; Evans and Crofoot, *Seneca Falls and Waterloo Village Directory, 1874–5*, 60; Child, *Reference Business Directory of Seneca County, N.Y. 1894–'95*, 304; *United States 1860 Census*, AmericanAncestors.org; *United States 1880 Census*, AmericanAncestors.org).

6. Kujawa, "Brown, Olympia."

7. Frederick Douglass, Letter to the Editor of the *New Era*, *New Era* 1, no. 11 (November 1885): 345–346.

8. Mary S. Bull, "Woman's Rights and Other 'Reforms' in Seneca Falls," *Good Company* 5, no. 10 (1880): 330–332, 333, 334–335, 336.

9. In the spring and summer of 1847 Stanton oversaw the remodeling of her Seneca Falls home. The entire family likely moved into the home by fall of that year (Lutz, *Created Equal*, 40; Griffith, *In Her Own Right*, 48–49; *SP* 1:63–64n3).

10. Garrisonian abolitionist and civil rights orator Charles Lenox Remond (1810–1873) was born to free parents in Massachusetts. He and Douglass lectured together in the 1840s, but his postbellum career was shortened by tuberculosis (Sewell, "Remond, Charles Lenox").

11. For the likely more accurate account of their first meeting again in Boston in 1841 after their introduction the year before, see Wellman, *The Road to Seneca Falls*, 161.

12. The report of the Seneca Falls meeting appeared in the first volume of *History of Woman Suffrage* (1881), but Matilda Joslyn Gage began publishing in her *National Citizen and Ballot Box* drafts of the initial chapters as early as 1878 in what Lisa Tetrault calls a "rudimentary form of peer review" (*The Myth*, 115). "What would eventually become the *History*'s first chapter, 'Preceding Causes,' debuted in the *National Citizen*'s September 1878 issue. The 'especial object of the publication of the Woman Suffrage History by its editors in a newspaper,' they explained, 'is that all dropped facts may be picked up, all mistakes corrected, and everything made right before it is put into book form.' Additional draft chapters appeared in serialization over the next four years—eight chapters in all— with the final one appearing in February 1881" (Tetrault, *The Myth*, 228n16). Bull mentions Gage's paper, so she may have thought she was participating in correcting Stanton's rhetoric. Ann D. Gordon notes that Stanton discussed early plans to write a history of the woman suffrage movement in 1848 and again in 1855, asking for Lucretia Mott's advice (*SP* 1:361, 361–372). Bull's quotations from Stanton in this selection seem to have been largely drawn from the *National Citizen and Ballot Box* of April and May 1879.

13. As Judith Wellman explains, on Sunday, 9 July, Stanton joined a tight-knit group of Quaker reformers, among them the antislavery, women, and Native American rights leader, peace advocate, and Friends minister Lucretia Coffin Mott (1793–1880); her merchant and reformist husband, James Mott (1788–1868); Lucretia's sister, the antislavery and woman's rights reformer Martha Coffin Wright (1806–1875); Mary Ann and Thomas McClintock, with their two oldest daughters, Elizabeth and Mary Ann McClintock, at the home of Jane and Richard Hunt in Waterloo, New York. Mott and her husband were traveling in the area in order to hold meetings with the Seneca at their Cattaraugus reservation, with free black communities in Ontario province, and with reformist administrators at the state prison in Auburn, the town where Martha Wright lived (Faulkner, *Lucretia Mott's Heresy*, 134–139). The conversation there, much of it, according to Stanton, driven by "the torrent of [her] long-accumulating discontent," led Richard Hunt to suggest that they take some concrete action. In order to capitalize on the serendipity of the well-known Lucretia and James Mott's presence and ability to attend, they published the announcement on July 11 in

the *Seneca County Courier* for the convention, to be held in two days at Seneca Falls's Wesleyan Chapel, July 19 and 20. On July 16, Stanton returned to Waterloo, and with the McClintocks drafted the Declaration of Sentiments, listing women's inequities in the manner of the Declaration of Independence and including a demand for woman's enfranchisement. Henry B. Stanton didn't attend the convention, having declared that his wife's suffrage resolution "will turn the proceedings into a farce" (Wellman, *The Road to Seneca Falls*, 188–189, 191–192, quoted on 193).

14. As Lisa Tetrault notes about Stanton's rhetoric, "The implication of naiveté is surely intentional and reinforces the utter newness of what they were doing" and thereby establishes Seneca Falls as an "origins" story for the movement. "Mott was a seasoned reformer and speaker (and the others were antislavery Quakers)" (*The Myth of Seneca Falls*, 122–123). Moreover, Stanton had already delivered her maiden speech to a temperance crowd of women in 1841 (*SP* 1:25).

15. Citing Stanton's commentary in the 17 September 1868 issue of *Revolution*, Judith Wellman identifies the "youthful lord" as Charles McClintock, the son of Mary Ann and Thomas McClintock (*The Road to Seneca Falls*, 277n28).

16. One hundred people—sixty-eight women and thirty-two men—signed the Declaration of Sentiments, but many other attendees, including Bull, did not sign. Judith Wellman indicates that the signers represented about one-third of the total number of people who attended any one session (*The Road to Seneca Falls*, 201–202).

17. Stanton's nephew, Daniel Cady Eaton (Wellman, *The Road to Seneca Falls*, 194).

18. In 1846 Bull's father, Anselm Bascom, a lawyer, legislator, abolitionist, and legal reformer, had been designated the Seneca Falls delegate to a New York constitutional convention called to debate women's property and political rights. There, "Bascom became a leader in the battle for married woman's property provisions and the fight for black suffrage"; as a delegate in 1847, he particularly championed African American male suffrage. On Thursday, July 20, the second day of the Seneca Falls convention, after chair James Mott opened the meeting, Elizabeth Cady Stanton read the Declaration of Sentiments; upon its conclusion, first Lucretia Mott and then Ansel Bascom initiated responses (Wellman, *The Road to Seneca Falls*, 148–149, 198, 201).

19. Quaker abolitionist Amy Kirby Post (1802–1889), who attended the conference at Seneca Falls and signed the Declaration of Sentiments there, organized the woman's rights convention in Rochester on 2 August 1848, where, despite protest by Stanton and others, Abigail Bush was elected as the presiding officer. Stanton later regretted this early timidity (Griffith, *In Her Own Right*, 59; *SP* 1:123–126).

20. Bull conflates the meetings, which proceeded over two days of morning and afternoon and evening sessions, and confuses the cast of characters. See Wellman, *The Road to Seneca Falls*, 194–204.

21. In her 1863 *Atlantic Monthly* essay "Sojourner Truth, the Libyan Sibyl," American reformer and novelist Harriet Beecher Stowe (1811–1896) reported this exchange between Douglass and the former slave, abolitionist, and woman's right advocate Sojourner Truth (c. 1799–1883). The abolitionist and woman's rights leader Wendell Phillips (1811–1884) was purported to have relayed the story to Stowe. As Nell Irvin Painter argues, Stowe's

representation of Truth's question made Truth "an electrifying presence and a symbol of Christian faith and forbearance, a talisman of nonviolent faith in God's ability to right the most heinous of wrongs. When Douglass had come to doubt, Stowe's Truth still believed in the power of God and the goodness of white people" (*Sojourner Truth: A Life, a Symbol*, 161). Painter discusses the "daunting" task of confirming the incident and Truth's more likely question (160–162, quoted on 161).

22. Temperance, woman's rights and dress reformer, and editor Amelia Jenks Bloomer (1818–1894), out of town, arrived for the second day (Wellman, *The Road to Seneca Falls*, 197). She served, at her husband's appointment, as the deputy postmaster of Seneca Falls (Griffith, *In Her Own Right*, 64).

23. Temperance, antislavery, and woman's rights reformer, author, and lecturer Frances Dana Barker Gage (1808–1884) also wrote for Bloomer's *Lily*. Author, woman's rights lecturer, and temperance reformer Elizabeth Oakes Smith (1806–1893) was most active as a reformer before the Civil War (Sigerman, "Gage, Frances Dana Barker"; Crawley, "Smith, Elizabeth Oakes").

24. Anna C. Mattison and Amelia Bloomer are listed as editors in the first and second issues, January (*Lily* 1, no. 1 [January 1849]: 4) and February 1849 (*Lily* 1, no. 2 [February 1849]: 12).

25. In addition to his service as Seneca Falls postmaster, Dexter Bloomer was the editor of the *Seneca County Courier*. According to Wellman, in early 1840s Seneca Falls at all levels of society, citizens embraced temperance reform, organized through the Independent Temperance Society, paving the way for other reform efforts there later in the decade (*The Road to Seneca Falls*, 82–87).

26. Stanton and Anthony's woman's rights colleague, the reformer and freethought author Matilda Joslyn Gage (1826–1898), edited and published the *National Citizen and Ballot Box*.

27. Stanton [E.C.S.], "My Bouquet," *Lily* 4, no. 6 (June 1852): 52.

28. Stanton [E.C.C.], "For the Lily. The Devil," *Lily* 3, no.1 (July 1851): 51.

29. Stanton [E.C.S.], "The Devil Again," *Lily* 3, no. 8 (August 1851): 63.

30. British actress and author Fanny Kemble (1809–1893) married the Philadelphia slave owner Pierce Butler; the fraught marriage informed her subsequent sentiments and writing on antislavery and woman's rights (Moore, "Kemble, Fanny").

31. Bull is mistaken in her timeline. Stanton began wearing the costume by the spring of 1851. The article to which she alludes is perhaps Stanton's March 1851 "Sobriny Jane," the name she gives Elizabeth Smith Miller in this article. Stanton claimed that "my cousin Sobriny" took up the "Turkish trowsers" in December 1850, that a "dozen" Seneca Falls women were going to do the same immediately, and that the *Lily* editor was contemplating the change of attire (Griffith, *In Her Own Right*, 71; Ginzberg, *Elizabeth Cady Stanton*, 80; Stanton [E.C.S.], "Sobriny Jane," 23).

32. Bull may be conflating several events. Four months pregnant and dressed in Bloomers, in April 1852, Stanton addressed a temperance convention for women; in her talk she advocated divorce in cases of male drunkenness. She left all four of her children at home (Stanton, Anthony, and Gage, eds., *History of Woman Suffrage*, 1:481–483; Griffith, *In Her*

Own Right, 76). Stanton delivered a speech to the woman's rights convention in February 1854; it was later printed, and copies were delivered to the legislature. Stanton addressed the legislature directly for the first time in 1860 (*SP* 1:240).

33. Scathing commentary from the press, from family members, and even from ostensibly protofeminist male Garrisonian allies pressured woman's suffrage workers back into their long skirts (Fischer, *Pantaloons and Power*, 98–109).

34. Lucretia Russell Gray Smith, "Elizabeth Cady Stanton—Letters from Susan B. Anthony, Lucy N. Coleman and Mrs. C. K. Smith," *Free Thought Magazine* 21, no.1 (January 1903): 49.

35. This gathering is likely the summer 1857 meeting of the Friends of Human Progress, or Junius meeting, in Waterloo, New York. In 1848 the Congregational Friends (later denominated the Progressive Friends and then the Friends of Human Progress) established their meeting on, in Lucretia Mott's words, "radical principles"—in part because both sexes and sympathetic non-Quakers were allowed to attend and participate. The Congregational Friends meeting was assisted pivotally in its organization by the Quaker couple Mary Ann and Thomas McClintock, who moved to Waterloo in 1837. Its central focus was "abolition, woman's rights, and peace." Stanton and eighteen other signers of the Seneca Falls Declaration of Sentiments commonly attended the Junius annual conferences (Wellman, *The Road to Seneca Falls*, 215). According to Ann D. Gordon, George W. Taylor founded a Progressive Friends meeting in Collins, New York, and he attended the Waterloo meeting in 1857 (*SP* 1:357n9). Abolitionist, educator, woman's rights lecturer, and freethinker Lucy Newhall Colman (1817–1906) survived two husbands and her only child; she altered the last name of her second husband, Luther Coleman (Densmore, "Colman, Lucy Newhall").

36. Politician and lawyer Daniel Webster (1782–1852) was well known for his oratorical power and charisma. Webster's head was the subject of admiration among his contemporaries, several of whom shared Smith's assessment of its resemblance to Stanton's. Webster's head "is of magnificent proportions," enthused William Lloyd Garrison, "the perfection of vast capaciousness; his glance is a mingling of the sunshine and the lightning of heaven; his features are full of intellectual greatness" (Baxter, "Webster, Daniel," quoted in Fisher, *The True Daniel Webster*, 39).

37. A. E. [Anna Elizabeth] Henion, "Elizabeth Cady Stanton. Some Reminiscences of Her Family Life, at Seneca Falls, N.Y., by an Old Acquaintance," typescript, n.d., Collection 37, Box 38, Folder 6, 1–8, 9, courtesy of the archives of the Seneca Falls Historical Society, Seneca Falls, N.Y.

38. Stanton took possession of her Seneca Falls home in 1847 and sold it in April 1862, moving to Brooklyn in May to join Henry Brewster Stanton, who had taken a position as deputy collector of the New York Custom House in 1861.

39. From 1839 to 1844 in Boston, Transcendentalist, journalist, and early American feminist philosopher Margaret Fuller gave "Conversations," primarily for women, to foster self-development; Stanton lived in Boston from 1842 to 1847 and attended what was most likely the fourth season, 1842–1843. Stanton's Conversation Club rotated their meetings

in members' homes; in imitation of Fuller's practices, attendees read and thought about a common subject, presented ten-minute essays for discussion, and ended (with a non-Transcendentalist flair) with dancing and more conversation. See Cole, "Stanton, Fuller, and the Grammar of Romanticism," 537–540; Stanton, *Eighty Years and More*, 152–153.

40. Based on Henion's locating this period of time as early Civil War years and her estimating Theodore Stanton to be ten years of age, Stanton likely employed Henion in 1861, ten years after Theodore's birth in 1851. In 1861 Stanton's three eldest boys, Neil, Kit, and Gat, were away in Geneva, New York, at Dr. Reed's school. Theodore, Maggie (age 9), Hattie (age 5), and Bob (age 2) were at home. In denominating Maggie and Theodore as Stanton's "younger" children, Henion may imply that they were the youngest of her children who are old enough to benefit from piano lessons.

41. Henion's descriptions of James Buchanan and Ulysses S. Grant appear verbatim in Stanton's well-known lecture, "The True Republic," an address also espousing women's development in all aspects of cultural life, including the political. Ann D. Gordon suggests that Stanton delivered this talk in her lecture series of 1870–1871 (*SP* 2:365n1; "The True Republic," 15:7).

42. Olympia Brown, *Acquaintances, Old and New, among Reformers* (Milwaukee: Tate, 1911), 32–33, 34–36.

43. Brown describes the convening of the Eleventh National Woman's Rights Convention on 10 May 1866 at the Church of the Puritans. Woman suffrage workers ceased their efforts for women's enfranchisement during the war; this meeting marked their renewed engagement in the campaign for universal suffrage for African American men and all women. At the two-day meeting, attendees voted to change their organization's name to the American Equal Rights Association (DuBois, *Feminism and Suffrage*, 62–65; *SP* 1:583–589).

44. Renowned preacher, electric lecturer, and author Henry Ward Beecher (1813–1887) was one of the most well known and beloved figures in America. The son of notable Calvinist preacher Lyman Beecher, his influential family included the novelist and social reformer Harriet Beecher Stowe and suffrage activist Isabella Beecher Hooker. He himself would serve as the first president of AWSA in 1869. "His volcanic preaching was so widely celebrated," observes Debby Applegate, "that tourists by the hundreds took the Sunday ferries, nicknamed 'Beecher Boats,'" to hear him preach. "His exuberant knack for controversy made him the darling of the popular press, and his every word was printed and reprinted in even the most remote corners of the country" (*The Most Famous Man in America*, 4). The radical abolitionist and woman suffrage advocate Parker Pillsbury (1809–1898), unlike leading abolitionists such as Wendell Phillips and William Lloyd Garrison, actively pursued universal suffrage after the Civil War. In part because of his alienation from other abolitionists, Pillsbury accepted Anthony's offer to serve as coeditor of *Revolution*, a position he held until 1870 and which increased the distance between him and former Garrisonian allies (Robertson, *Parker Pillsbury*, 143–156). Editor, author, abolitionist, and woman suffrage reformer Theodore Tilton (1835–1907) was a popular lecturer and a lifelong friend of Stanton's.

45. Stanton's words included her proposal "to bury the black man and the woman in the citizen, and our two organizations in the broader work of reconstruction" (*SP* 1:587).

46. "Albany" is a reference to the New York legislature and the promise of woman's enfranchisement in that state. See *SP* 1:588–589 and 589n2 for Phillips's extemporaneous morning speech and bitter reactions to it by abolitionist and woman suffrage reformers Frances Dana Gage (1808–1884) and Josephine S. Griffing (1814–1872). Abolitionist, renowned orator, and woman's rights advocate Wendell Phillips (1811–1884), despite his idealistic Garrisonian commitment to universal rights for men and women, blocked women's attempts to pursue this objective during the critical Reconstruction passage of the Fourteenth and Fifteenth Amendments to the Constitution. The AERA meeting was convened because Phillips had previously used his power to deny Anthony and Lucy Stone's request to merge the American Antislavery Society with the women's rights movement. During Reconstruction, as abolitionist leaders gained power with the Republicans, they tempered their 1850s-era idealism; in Parker Pillsbury's view Garrison and Phillips were "motivated by their newfound celebrity" and thinking of their own legacy (DuBois, *Feminism and Suffrage*, 63; Robertson, *Parker Pillsbury*, 154).

Marriage and Maternity

The Public "Mother of the Gracchi" (1869–1888)

The selections in this chapter document one of the more controversial and still highly relevant evolutions in Stanton's activism, as well as the reception typically accorded her shrewd maternal self-presentation. The latest of these commentaries, remarks from Grace Greenwood (Sarah Jane Clarke Lippincott) at the 1888 "Conference of the Pioneers" session at the International Council of Women, may even indicate that by her seventies, Stanton had grown careless about cloaking the reasons for its adoption. Periodical and travel writer, newspaper correspondent, and editor Grace Greenwood (1823–1904) identifies the canny rhetoric and mode of delivery that characterized Stanton's lyceum and lecturing appearances; and from her perspective, the woman's rights activist's radical intentions penetrate the benign mask. But Greenwood is an outlier in this assessment. In promoting herself as the mother of a movement, Stanton doled out controversy with a spoonful of sugar, and the crowds apparently swallowed it whole.

The 14 July 1871 *San Francisco Chronicle* reports on one of Stanton's "Marriage and Maternity" lectures, a variant of conversations with women she had engaged in both casually and formally since the time of her residence in Seneca Falls. Stanton's advice may sound simplistic, arrogant, and patronizing, but as Elisabeth Griffith notes, these talks on children and marriage, including "Our Girls" and "Our Boys," were her most popular 1870s lyceum lectures.[1] And the question-and-answer session suggests women were eager to hear the message she was delivering: that woman's "rights" extend beyond the ballot box; that they begin with reproductive health; and that they are restricted by legislative, judicial, medical, and religious edicts to which women should not consent. The speech as a whole reflects the influence of homeopathic and water-cure philosophy on Stanton; and as in the case of her interest in reproductive limitation, those reform networks demonstrate the varied nature of her woman's rights platform—and its appeal to women who may not have cared about enfranchisement.[2]

Although in her lecture Stanton rambles over a number of seemingly unrelated subjects—including Mormon polygamists, New York newspaper editor Horace Greeley and male cooks, single women, baths, clothing, Mrs. Winslow's Soothing Syrup, and divorce—in terms of her social program they are closely intertwined.³ She understood and situated them within the context of specific medical and cultural developments at midcentury, seismic shifts for women that were also responsive to conflicts between civil rights and federalism during and after Reconstruction.⁴ Between 1840 and 1860 information about women's reproductive health and the commercialization of fertility control and abortion increased dramatically; and women took advantage of this information and accessibility.⁵ Between 1870 and 1890, however, in a backlash fueled by the American Medical Association and social purity reformers, state and federal governments criminalized the circulation of information about and products related to contraception and abortion, beginning in 1873, with the Comstock Law. "The most general result," writes historian Janet Farrell Brodie, "was to drive abortion underground, making it far more difficult, expensive, and dangerous to obtain." Women endured this criminalization of basic health necessities until the 1960s with the liberalization of sixteen states' laws and then more conclusively in 1973 with the U.S. Supreme Court's *Roe v. Wade* ruling.⁶ This particular iteration of Stanton's lecture preceded Comstock and offers an important perspective on the way such a talk was received in the expanding western states and territories.

Stanton's 13 July 1871 lecture in San Francisco formed part of a western tour she and Anthony were undertaking; and as such this piece also offers a glimpse of regional media coverage of Stanton in the West, where women's enfranchisement gained earlier traction in the territories than it did in the East and where Stanton spoke privately with and publicly about women whose marital situations or sexual choices fueled her commentary: Laura D. Fair, whose murder trial for the point-blank shooting of her lover had become a national scandal, and polygamous Mormons. Stanton visited Fair in her San Francisco jail cell, and both women spoke out in her defense—Anthony, unfairly, receiving biting criticism from the press and Stanton garnering praise for doing so. This important distinction highlights the ways in which Stanton influenced her audiences via words, rhetorical techniques, personal mannerisms, self-presentation, and dress. For Stanton, Fair exemplified the ways in which women fall victim to illiberal divorce laws and judicial double standards. "Give Laura Fair the benefit of the doubts and legal subterfuges that Sickles, Cole, and McFarland enjoyed in Courts of their peers," Stanton thundered, "and I am content."⁷

Twenty-seven years later, Stanton recollected this "Marriage and Maternity" lecture as one in which all attendees wore women's clothing. "To our astonishment," she wrote,

> the next morning, a verbatim report of all that was said appeared in one of the leading papers. . . . As I always wrote and read carefully what I had to say on such delicate subjects, the language was well chosen and the presentation of facts and philosophy quite unobjectionable; hence, the information being as important for men as for women, I did not regret the publication.[8]

Stanton may indeed have been "utterly astonished" to see the report of her address in the *San Francisco Chronicle* on 14 July, but the jocular tone of the reporter's language and Stanton's practice of planting information she wished to be dispensed about herself—as well as the extremely circumspect language she employed when questioned closely about abortion and divorce for Roman Catholics—may suggest otherwise.[9] Nonetheless, the reporter's description of Stanton's "clear, musical voice" and "tastily" beribboned attire (reporters often rendered menacing woman's rights speakers' "harsh," "mannish" voices and "inappropriate" garb) imply the talk was nonthreatening to male ears; moreover, the applause, laughter, and earnest and enthusiastic commentary suggest how well it was received.

In fact, Stanton's personal anecdotes about and recommendations for "painless" childbirth brought one woman to her feet with a spontaneous entreaty to spread this message to "every lady in the land." Why? Stanton's compelling appeal and ability to establish familial, female bonding about a subject of momentous concern may provide the answer—because in nineteenth-century America, women were deeply fearful of dying in childbirth.[10] In describing Clara Bewick Colby's similarly "radical feminist vision" for her *Woman's Tribune*, Kristin Mapel Bloomberg maintains that in the sprawling western states and territories (where Stanton often lectured), women had grown isolated from their eastern family networks; as a result, they fiercely sought such vital connections. In the words of historian Glenda Riley, because of this isolation, frontier women regarded "the ability to bond with other women" as an actual "survival technique."[11] Importantly, Stanton's own expanding vision of activism would increasingly emphasize the essential connections between women's physical well-being and cultural and political independence, an insight that appealed to nineteenth-century women broadly and in greater proportion than did the demand for enfranchisement.

Historians have long understood that early American women confronted grave peril during their childbearing years. Ironically, however, as the regular obstetricians and gynecologists licensed by the American Medical Association after its inception in 1847 gradually replaced midwives, their "heroic" measures (among them, repeated and copious bloodletting; disastrous mistreatment with forceps; and ill-timed, contraction-inducing drugs) unwittingly increased the incidence of debilitating pain, injury, and death during and after childbirth. "'Meddlesome midwifery,'" explains Judith Walzer Leavitt, "the inappropriate interference by medical attendants in the form of forceps and drug abuse, can be implicated in some of women's worst postpartum problems" in nineteenth-century America.[12]

Water-cure and homeopathic, or "irregular," doctors of both sexes and regular male obstetricians all promoted painless childbirth, but their recommendations for achieving it were different. During and after childbirth, irregular physicians used warm-water baths to ease pain, and they decried heroic interventions during birth itself, favoring an approach that allowed nature to take its course. During pregnancy, they recommended an early form of prenatal care: healthy diet, exercise, water treatments, ample drinking water, douches (the last was also advocated in coded terms for family limitation), and corsetless dress reform. Finally, albeit inadvertently, because many physicians disputed new findings on the role of germs in infection, water-cure treatments likely decreased women's risks of contracting puerperal fever; even at midcentury, daily bathing was not a standard convention for Americans.[13]

The physical toll of regular physicians' ostensibly orthodox procedures, of fashionable dressing, and of the prevalence of venereal disease rendered many married women, as Stanton allowed in her San Francisco lecture, "weak." Another source of debility resulted from frequent childbirth, and for this problem, she urged women to consider its medical, marital, legal, and religious sources. The bottom line, as Stanton argued in her discussion of polygamous Mormon women's augmented fertility, is that "woman is a living subject to man's desires."

The phrase "birth control" did not yet exist; instead, reformers used coded terminology such as "regulators," "checks," and "the laws regulating and controlling the female system." Stanton's nomenclature for this idea includes women's "bodies and the laws which govern them," their "development as wives, as mothers," the "preservation of their own womanhood," "nature's laws," "the true laws of generation," "woman's perfect independence," and the necessity of "baths" before she asserts, "Woman must at all times be the sovereign of her own person." Such euphemisms derived from reformers' excessive reserve and from wary caution, even preceding the 1873 Comstock Law.[14]

Both concerns—and the possibility that Stanton had anticipated her remarks might be published—may account for her vague and circuitous responses, as well as her angry shift in tone when pushed to address abortion during the question-and-answer portion of the lecture. Significantly, her abrupt retort stands in sharp distinction to the tenor and content of the rest of her lecture and to previous defenses of and sympathy for women who sought abortions and for those prosecuted for infanticide. In an 1854 address and in her 1869 vindications of British immigrant Hester Vaughan,[15] for example, Stanton depicted such women as the victims of legislative and judicial systems designed and controlled by men.[16] Denied the right to consent to or craft judicial legislation and to be tried by or serve on a jury of their peers, Stanton insisted, women were forced to make unnecessarily dangerous decisions with grave consequences for themselves and their children—born or unborn.[17]

Prior to their California appearances, Stanton and Anthony addressed large crowds in Denver and in Salt Lake City, where they held meetings with Mormon audiences, an experience that Stanton draws upon in her commentary. In Salt Lake City, Stanton also spoke to women alone. Stanton admired Mormon women's support of their own enfranchisement, which Utah granted in 1870, but—as she suggested in her San Francisco lecture—the ballot for women of all sects is only "the first step toward her entire equality with man, [n]ot . . . an end, but solely . . . a means to an end."[18]

Stanton's position on Mormon women's faith is casually dismissive and reflective of her secularist bias. Nonetheless, when Stanton and Anthony welcomed newly enfranchised Mormon women to the platforms of NWSA meetings, they received fierce criticism from Republican-leaning AWSA leaders, who found plural marriage repugnant (as indicated, for example, by Lucy Stone's selection in "Schism"—"Excerpt from Letter to Harriet Jane Hanson Robinson"). Deeply rooted antipolygamist sentiment tracing back to the 1850s provoked this distaste. "Polygamy . . . exposed the underlying weakness of the American legal system, its vulnerability to degeneracy," explains Sarah Barringer Gordon. In this view, the democratic system's inherent liberties—particularly in the territorial West—might fearfully degrade the traditional concept of marriage. Fueled by this concern, mid-1850s Republicans condemned what they viewed as mirror evils: slavery and polygamy.[19] Twenty years later, in her 1890 presidential address before NAWSA, Stanton attacked the newly merged organization for its narrow platform; its membership, she pronounced, should include Mormon, Native American, and African American women. Similarly, at the annual meeting of the New York State Federation of Women's Clubs in 1899, Anthony shut down a proposed resolution to protest the congressional seating of the newly elected polygamist, Mormon Brigham H. Roberts. When women's groups and the media castigated Anthony vituperatively, Stanton defended her collaborator's stance in a published statement in the *New York Evening World*.[20]

From "'The Coming Girl.' Mrs. Elizabeth Cady Stanton's Portrait of the Perfect Female," *Chicago Tribune*, 1871[21]

Mrs. Stanton sailed out, in all the conscious majesty of veteran womanhood. The mother of the Gracchi could not have looked more imposing, or smiled with more benign dignity.[22] A faint odor was wafted from her garments as she swept through the chancel with her thirteen stone avoirdupois,[23] like the balmy breezes that blow off the shores of Araby the Blest.

From "Address and Poem," Grace Greenwood [Sarah Jane Clarke Lippincott], 1888[24]

Stately Mrs. Stanton has secured much immunity, by a comfortable look of motherliness and a sly benignancy in her smiling eyes, even though her arguments have been bayonet thrusts and her words hot shot.

From "Gossip from Gotham," *Daily Morning Chronicle*, 1869[25]

To tell the truth, Mrs. Stanton has not a very revolutionary appearance; neither is she meek mannered, but simply quietly elegant and evidently gifted with great gifts and firmly imbued with a vast deal of firmness. To my thinking, she has all the venerable appearance of a matron, whose good man is in comfortable circumstances, presiding over the ménage of an extensive country establishment. She is, however, a lady of great mental culture, a fluent speaker, and of course believes every word she utters.

"For Women Only. Mrs. Elizabeth Cady Stanton Discourses on Marriage and Maternity," *San Francisco Chronicle*, 1871[26]

"Mrs. Stanton's lecture on 'Marriage and Maternity' this afternoon, sir," was the salutation from the Chief Thunderer to the Head Local yesterday noon.

"But, sir, it is to women only."

"What have we to do with that, sir? Know you not that the CHRONICLE is a live paper? Are you not yet aware that we know no such word as 'impossible?'"

> "Go; make thyself like to the nymph of the sea.
> Be subject to no sight but mine—invisible
> To every eye-ball else. Go; take this shape
> And hither come in it. Hence, with diligence."[27]

We paused and wondered how this was to be accomplished, when suddenly a

BRILLIANT IDEA FLASHED

Athwart our brain, and quick we hied away to Uncle Smith's curiosity shop on Clay Street, and finding him in clever mood, we eagerly inquired if he knew a fellow named Prospero. He said he did: that he was knocking around town, and had but last week pawned with him his other clothes. Yielding to our urgent demand, he produced the garments, when, to our joy, behold the invisible cloak which Shakespeare wove, was there. Grasping it with eager clutch we effected a temporary loan, not on, but of it, and throwing it around our form we stalked into the street, unseen by any eye,

THROUGH THE PORTALS OF PLATT'S HALL,

Past the sharp-eyed and determined Susan B., who stood watch and ward within, to see that no masculine foot polluted the spot sacred for that [time] to the assemblage of wives and mothers of the city. Reaching a [s]eat where we could see and hear, we gently awaited the result. The hall speedily filled with women. We never saw so many women before all by themselves.[28] There were big women and little women; tall women and short women; lean women and fat women; women with spectacles and women with eye-glasses; women with bonnets and women with hats; ugly women and pretty women—all spread out in rows before the admiring glance of one solitary man. It seemed to be new to them also. There were

TITTERING AND GIGGLES.

An air of strangeness spread around. One young lady, with a drab silk dress, jaunty little black b[a]sque jacket, trimmed with crimson, and a hat and feather perfectly stunning, who sat just in front of us, remarked to her companion that it was the funniest place she was ever in in her life; that she could almost swear that there was a man near her. When she reads this account she will know she was right. At a few minutes past 3 o'clock Mrs. Stanton came upon the platform, accompanied by Mrs. Schenck[29] and Miss Anthony. She was tastily dressed in a blue silk dress, with blue grenadine overskirt, white gossamer scarf, and her hair bound with blue ribbon. She was introduced by Mrs. Schenck, and in her clear, musical voice began:

I have always advocated the ballot for woman as the first step toward

HER ENTIRE EQUALITY WITH MAN,

Not as an end, but solely as a means to an end. To-day woman is a living subject to man's desires. In passing through Salt Lake I found that the Mormons had made this idea the basis of a[l]l their religious teaching.[30] But how false is this idea of religion. No being ever moved on earth with higher and more reverent respect for woman than our Savi[o]u[r]. No oth[e]r teacher ever equaled Him in the teaching of purity in woman and respect in man. These women in Salt Lake believe that the greater the number of their children the greater their honors in Heaven; that their mission on earth is simply to

"MULTIPLY AND REPLENISH THE EARTH"—[31]

That and that alone; and to carry out this law every other law of nature or of God is violated. It is the prevalent opinion, based upon Mormon books and Mormon preaching, that these women are contented, satisfied and happy.[32] But my experience among them has taught me to the contrary conclusion. They are subject to all the jealousies and heart-sores of their monogomatic [sic] sisters. Yet they, for religion's sake, make their lives a perpetual self-sacrifice; they suffer here in hope of glory hereafter.[33] It is also a common belief that a woman among the Mormons is held sacred during the entire period of her ante-maternity.[34] It is no such thing. Women are there treated in that [matter] just as they are treated elsewhere—without regard to their nature and their rights. Girls of from 15 to 17, whose [girlhood] has not yet [ripened] are wives and

BEAR CHILDREN EVERY YEAR.

Everywhere it is so, and none the less so in Utah.[35]

We must educate our daughters in this order: First—To regard their own lives and bodies and the laws which govern them. Second—Their duty as parents. Third—Their duties as citizens. Fourth—To supply life with its luxuries and topperies. But now we reverse this order. Our daughters learn [music and worsted and]

SILLY ARTS AND ACCOMPLISHMENTS,

But not a thought or a word is given to their development as wives, as mothers, or as citizens. We who have reached and passed middle life cannot do much in this matter to remedy it as concerns ourselves; but we can for our children—so train and teach them that their coming lives will fill grand positions in their varied spheres. I would have mothers feel that their daughters have full and equal rights in all things with their brothers, and that they are entitled to be so considered in the world's opinion. It is a divine right of woman that she may do, and do rightly, whatever it is right that man may do. Horace Greeley has said that what we want is

SIXTY THOUSAND GOOD COOKS,

Instead of sixty thousand men voters.[36] Well, I know we do, and I propose that we educate the men to do it. [Applause and laughter.] Men are adapted to this work. They can stand any amount of heat. They don't mind any amount of smoke. A dozen of them will get together, and smoke a room so full that you can't see across it. They like smoke, and cooking will give them plenty of it. Men are the best cooks. Now, the best book on cooking ever written was written by a man. The quickest cooking I ever knew of was by a man on shipboard. He only had one spoon, which he would dip into everything, and, between [fl]avors, he would lick it. A woman wouldn't have done that—she would have dirtied a dozen towels and consumed vastly more time. But, in sober earnest, we must reverse the modern education of our daughters. Our girls must be taught first their own happiness: that their womanhood was the first consideration; wifehood and motherhood were mere

INCIDENTS OF THEIR LIVES.

The preservation of their own womanhood was the one prime object of their lives. As it is now, we look up to wives and mothers, and down upon womanhood. This is wrong. Our daughters are nouns—not adjectives.[37] I have a reverence for such women as Harriet Hosmer, for Susan B. Anthony, and for the host of women who have done great things in this world, even though they have not borne any children.[38] Are there no children except the children of the flesh? Are there no children of the brain? Ah! a higher civilization than this will realize that a grand thought, a grand idea is worthy of its homage and its admiration. We must educate our girls that they are independent; that in the society of the refined they may be happy; that they may live peaceful, glorious lives, and take high seats in Heaven

WITHOUT EVE[R] SEEING A MAN.

The idea that woman is weak inherently is a grand mistake. She is physically weak, because she neglects her baths—because she violates every law of her nature and her God—because she dresses in a way that would kill a man. I feel it to be my mission to arouse every woman to bring up her daughter without breaking her up in doing it. Our female idea of dress is all wrong. I have conversed with many physicians who tell me that it is almost impossible to find a

PERFECT FEMALE SKELETON.

[Here Mrs. Stanton illustrated the difference between the ribs as they should be and as they are made by dress, by interlacing her fingers.][39] It is a rare thing to find a woman perfectly well—but we can, if we choose, entirely revolutionize this. Even the Bible says that maternity is a curse—most women accept this doctrine as true; it is simply [horrible;] it is

A MONSTROUS LI[E].

The Bible has been translated by men and for men. *Will*, in the original, has been made *shall*, in the translation. God never meant [such] a monstrous [d]octrine to be promulgated as His will.[40] We must educate our daughters that motherhood is grand and that

GOD NEVER CURSED IT,

And the curse, if it be a curse, may be rolled off; as man has rolled away the curse of labor, as the curse has been rolled from the descendants of Ham.[41] My mission among women [is] to preach the new gospel. If you suffer, it is not because you are cursed of God, but because you violate his laws. What an [incubus] it would take from woman could she be educated to know that the pains of maternity are no curse upon her kind. We know that among Indians the squaws do not suffer in childbirth. They will step aside from the ranks, even on the march, and return in a short time [bearing] with them the new-born child. What an absurdity, then, to suppose that [our] enlightened Christian women are cursed. But one word of fact is worth a volume of philosophy: let me give you some of my own experience. I am the mother of seven children. My girlhood was spent mostly in the open air. I early imbibed the idea that

A GIRL WAS AS GOOD AS A BOY,

And I carried it out. I would walk five miles before breakfast, or ride ten on horseback. After I was married I wore m[y] clothing sensibly. The weight hung alone on my shoulders. I never compressed my body out of its natural shape. My first four children were born, and I suffered very little. I then made up my mind that it was totally unnecessary for me to suffer at all: so I dressed lightly, walked every day; lived as much as possible in the open air, ate no condiments or spices, kept quiet, listened to music, looked at pictures, read poetry.[42] The night before the birth of the child I walked three miles. The child was born without a particle of pain.[43] I bathed it and dressed it, and

IT WEIGHED 10 ½ POUNDS.[44]

That same day I dined with the family. Everybody said I would surely die, but I never had a relapse or a moment's inconvenience from it.[45] I know this is not being delicate and refined, but if you would be vigorous and healthy in spite of the d[is]eases of your ancestors, and your own disregard of nature's laws, try it. [Loud applause; one enthusiastic lady r[i]sing and requesting Mrs. Stanton to advise every lady in the land to do the same.]

Mrs. Stanton resumed: I can only advise them to dress right, take baths, and exercise freel[y]. Every mother in the land has it within her own [power] to be

SECOND ONLY TO GOD

In the making of her [offspring] just what it should be. T[his] is a serious responsibilit[y]; but it is one that God imposes upon every mother in the land. Children are born, not [made]. The mother's whole thoughts are centered upon her unborn child. It is, indeed, a holy period, and if her mind and body are in the proper condition, how great and grand will be the result. I have seen the original painting of which I see copies all over your land, which represents the ideal woman standing above the surrounding objects, while the man looks reverently up to her. This, to my mind, is the

TRUE IDEA OF WOMANHOOD.

We are to be the sovereigns of this world: but woman must understand her true position before she can take the first step toward this position. It is better now to learn and practice the true laws of generation, than to attempt to remodel the old and the bad; for with them we can make our children what they please, and insure the happiness of future generations.

It is a sad thing for a mother to have a dissolute son or an idiotic child. I know of one family where there are seven idiot children. Why? The father is a drunkard. I want to teach women that the begetting of a child by a drunken or a licentious father is a sin—is a crime; and I hold that the law which binds a woman to such a man

IS IN ITSELF A CRIME.

It is the woman's duty to break such obligations. I honor the woman who sunders such a tie. [Applause.] But what a selfish thing is that woman who is clothed and fed—who owes all that she has to some man who calls her wife, and yet has not a thought to bestow on those outside; who sneer at divorce, and who would ostracize the divorced woman from society. But to such I would say: Had you a daughter linked to a man whose soul and body were black with licentiousness and drunkenness, would you want her to be dragged down with him for life? This is the proper standpoint from which a woman should judge of this matter. In the matter of

MARRYING OUR DAUGHTERS

We pay a wonderful amount of attention to the clothes of the bride. She is furnished with a stock that would last her ten years, but how many mothers care for their souls or bodies? Young people who intend to marry should spend two or three years in open-air exercise in the study of physiology. If this were done we should have glorious results. Why, we don't pay as much attention to the raising of our children as we do our horses, cows and sheep. Oh! what a leap forward we might take into a higher life if we would make one combined effort. It is possible for parents to determine what their children shall be, and make them so before they are born. Oh, mothers! let us turn over a new leaf and make [a race of]

GODS, AND POETS AND STATESMEN.

Another idea. It is of more importance what k[ind] of a child we raise than how many. It is better to produce

ONE LION THAN TWELVE JACKASSES.

We have got jackasses enough; let us go into [the li]on business. Suppose our great statesmen, Clay, Webster, and others like them, had had only the society of refined and educated women, they would not have, as they did, looked upon women only in a physical light.[46] If men have dolls for wives, they [will seek the]

[SOCIETY OF INTELLECTUAL COURTEZANS].[47]

We must have a new type of womanhood. We need it more than gold. Courtezans ruled France and brought her to her ruin. Courtezans will rule this country unless woman rises to her true dignity. The old idea of the oak and the vine is pretty, but it is mere poetry; the emergencies of life prove its falsity—the lightning strikes them both alike.[48] And now I must say

A WORD ABOUT BABIES.

I never met six women in my life who really knew anything about babies. When babies cry, don't, for mercy's sake, give them that fearful curse of childhood,

MRS. WINSLOW'S SOOTHING SYRUP.[49]

Babies don't cry unless something is wrong, and if you bathe and feed it properly it will not cry. My first child was brought to me pinned up and crying. I immediately unpinned it; the nurse stood aghast, but the baby didn't tumble apart. You

DON'T PIN UP A KITTEN OR A PUPPY,

Why should you a baby? The clothes that you put on children are all wrong. They should be fed regularly and dressed loosely; once in two hours is often enough to feed any baby. Nursing them at night is all wrong. Often a child cries simply because it wants water, yet I have met mothers who didn't know that their children wanted water.

Mrs. Stanton continued in like strain, repeating the earnest advice about the use of soothing syrups, and the article of pins came in for another scorching. She then stated that it was her custom to answer such questions as might be asked, and she was now ready to hear any thing [*sic*] that might be offered.

A number of questions were asked. One lady inquired: "How can we follow your advice and

KEEP FROM HAVING CHILDREN?"

Mrs. Stanton announced that all truths run in parallel lines, and woman's perfect independence is the answer to that query. Woman must at all times be the sovereign of her own person. Another lady anxiously inquired: "What are we [to do when]

MEN DON'T AGREE WITH US

A[b]out th[i]s matter."

Mrs. Stanton replied that the men must be educated up to the higher civilization as well as the women.[50] That the same powerful force that governs the passions can be controlled and directed into the brain force, and made to result in great deeds. Women, with their dress, their dances, waltzes, bare arms, bare necks, are a[l]l stimulating men's passions, and [d]oing just the opposite of what they ought to do.

One lady asked a question which hinted at prevention by other than legitimate means, and Mrs. Stanton promptly replied that such views of the matter were

TOO DEGRADING AND DISGUSTING

To touch upon, and must be classed in the category of crime alongside of infanticide.[51]

A lady asked, with an evident air of sincerity, what a devout Roman Catholic should do in a case where she ought to obtain a divorce, which her Church forba[d]e?

Mrs. Stanton answered that she thought her whole lecture was an answer to that query.

It was then announced that Mrs. Stanton would lecture again this evening upon Woman Suffrage and Free Love: after which the crowd dispersed.

Drawing closely around us our invaluable cloak, we elbowed our way nimbly out, catching the remark made by a pouti[n]g and rosy matron that, "maybe she would think as Mrs. Stanton did when she got to be as old as her."

NOTES

1. Griffith, *In Her Own Right*, 164.

2. Stanton became particularly interested in homeopathy as she anticipated the birth of her first child, but she was also influenced by her brother-in-law Edward Bayard, a well-known homeopath first in Seneca Falls and then in New York City.

3. Stanton's educational conversations to women were anticipated in the late 1840s and 1850s by water-cure speakers, such as Paulina Kellogg Wright Davis (1813–1876), Thomas (1815–1901) and Mary Gove (1810–1884) Nichols, physician Harriot K. Hunt (1805–1875), and Jane Elizabeth Hitchcock Jones (1813–1896); Hunt and Davis were also active in woman's rights reform. Prominent water-cure physicians like Thomas and Mary Gove Nichols also published and lectured on women's social and cultural rights, although they were less interested in enfranchisement than was Stanton. Mary Gove Nichols "was among

the new voices of medical expertise that effectively competed with the church as arbiter of morality. The health reform movement was not merely medical; it was political. It offered an authoritative endorsement of women's strength" (Brodie, *Contraception and Abortion in 19th-Century America*, 126–130; Silver-Isenstadt, *Shameless*, 2).

4. Amanda Frisken argues that Victoria Woodhull's political activism and her advocacy of woman's unfettered sexuality and enfranchisement shed light on the limits of Reconstruction and "the intertwining of radical political movements in the 1870s. [Woodhull's] revolutionary program coincided with Radical Reconstruction; by 1876 both movements were in decline"; Ellen Carol DuBois rightly observes that Woodhull's socialism also contributed to this cultural backlash. Both observations similarly illuminate Stanton's growth as an activist as well as the resulting shift in her reception (Frisken, *Victoria Woodhull's Sexual Revolution*, 20; DuBois, "Woman Suffrage and the Left," 26–27).

5. Brodie, *Contraception and Abortion in 19th-Century America*, 254. Demographic analysis indicates that fertility rates between 1800 and 1900 dropped from slightly more than seven live children (this number excludes miscarriages and stillbirths) to 3.56 children for most native-born American white women, with 75 percent of that number accounted for by "active fertility control, including abortion and birth-control techniques." Immigrant and black women showed slightly higher fertility rates, however—with more than five children for black women and with German and Irish immigrants averaging more than seven live births by the century's end (Leavitt, *Brought to Bed*, 14, 19–20).

6. Brodie, *Contraception and Abortion in 19th-Century America*, 255.

7. Quoted in Haber, *The Trials of Laura Fair*, 135. Stanton referred to the equally notorious murder trials of Daniel Sickles (1859), George W. Cole (1867), and Daniel McFarland (1870), three cases that established the legal theory of "unwritten law." According to this precedent, the shocking discovery of a wife's seduction induced temporary insanity, during which time a husband might justifiably murder the male violator of the sanctuary of his home. Because the mainstream press and legal system considered Fair an "outspoken actress, successful businesswoman, and wily mistress who never hesitated to invade the public sphere," the "unwritten law" did not apply (Haber, *The Trials of Laura Fair*, 5–6, 3).

8. Stanton, *Eighty Years and More*, 290.

9. See, for example, Stanton's 2 November 1880 letter to her son Theodore, describing her attempt to vote; enormously satisfied with herself, she added that she wrote up a full accounting of her actions for various press outlets. Several of them gratified her request for self-promotion (*SP* 4:14–15).

10. Judith Walzer Leavitt argues that "death fears remained central to women's perceptions of their birth experiences" through the early twentieth century; statistics demonstrate that "maternity-related causes" of death by the early twentieth century were "65 times greater" than they were in the 1980s (*Brought to Bed*, 21, 23).

11. Bloomberg, "Cultural Critique and Consciousness Raising," 36–38, quoted on 37. Writing Anthony from Chicago in 1875, Stanton reinforces this sense about midwestern towns as well. "The people in the country towns are crazy to hear lectures," she wrote (*SP* 3:151).

12. Leavitt, *Brought to Bed*, 147. For more on the professionalization of gynecology and obstetrics as specializations in the nineteenth century, heroic measures and their often tragic results, physicians' misunderstanding of their own role in contagion and the spread of puerperal fever between patients, the formation of the American Medical Association, its increasing control of women's at-home birth experiences, and the AMA's role in criminalizing reproductive control, see Wertz and Wertz, *Lying-In*, 109–131; Leavitt, *Brought to Bed*, 142–170; Donegan, *"Hydropathic Highway to Health,"* 65–83.

13. Donegan, *"Hydropathic Highway to Health,"* 111–133, 96.

14. Janet Farrell Brodie considers the subject of this lecture to be birth control, although as Griffith observes, Stanton's personal decisions regarding family limitation are hard to pin down. Brodie adds that Stanton was also active with freethought groups and in 1876 was designated as an honorary vice president in their National Liberal League, one of the groups that fought the Comstock Laws (*Contraception and Abortion in Nineteenth-Century America*, 5, 6, quoted on 5). See also Lutz, *Created Equal*, 235–236; Griffith, *In Her Own Right*, 65–66; Hogan and Hogan, "Feminine Virtue and Practical Wisdom," 416. For an alternative interpretation of Stanton's position and terminology, see Davis, *The Political Thought of Elizabeth Cady Stanton*, 170–172.

15. Vaughan was charged with infanticide, convicted, and later pardoned. See Introduction, note 62.

16. For the section of her 1854 speech that addresses this concern, see *SP* 1:243–245.

17. Despite the general truth of Stanton's critique, the courts' treatment of women's reproductive health decisions was relatively evenhanded in regard to the adjudication of Comstock's lawsuits. Between 1873 and the 1910s, which saw the advent of Margaret Sanger's reformist efforts, contraceptives were "accepted" by a pragmatic judiciary. "Court decisions sanctioned sexual and commercial disobedience," argues Andrea Tone, "adumbrating an implied right to personal and entrepreneurial privacy that superseded the right of the federal government to interfere in the bedrooms and businesses of the nation" ("Black Market Birth Control," 438).

18. Anna Elizabeth Dickinson, the wildly popular orator and abolitionist, also visited Salt Lake City, an experience that inspired her late 1860s lyceum lecture "Whited Sepulchres." Like Stanton, Dickinson linked the necessity of a Mormon woman's exertion of an independent control of her body and mind to broader institutional restrictions on all American women's rights (Gallman, *America's Joan of Arc*, 70).

19. The Mormon electoral majority in the territory of Utah enabled Mormons to claim the protection of federalism to support their marriage practices, just as Southern states claimed Constitutional support for slavery before the Civil War (Gordon, "The Liberty of Self-Degradation," 819–826, quoted on 819–820).

20. Griffith, *In Her Own Right*, 199; *SP* 6:312–313, 314–315.

21. *Chicago Tribune*, 13 December 1871.

22. Second-century BCE brothers Tiberius and Gaius Gracchus (the Gracchi) were tribunes who introduced land reform and other populist legislations in ancient Rome. Members of the Populares, a group of politicians who appealed to the average citizen and

opposed the conservative Optimates in the Roman Senate, the brothers have been considered the founding fathers of socialism and populism.

23. The "stone," a British unit of weight, is the equivalent of fourteen pounds avoirdupois, so the reporter estimates Stanton to weigh about 182 pounds. Stanton's weight between 1860 and 1870 remained right around 175 pounds (*SP* 2:160, 361; Griffith, *In Her Own Right*, 196).

24. Grace Greenwood [Sarah Jane Clarke Lippincott], "Address and Poem," *Report of the International Council of Women* (Washington, DC: Rufus H. Darby, 1888), 353.

25. *Daily Morning Chronicle*, 27 May 1869.

26. "For Women Only. Mrs. Elizabeth Cady Stanton Discourses on Marriage and Maternity. Peculiar Ideas on Matrimony, Divorce and Babies. Important Questions and Sensible Answers. Full Report by Our Invisible Reporter," *San Francisco Chronicle*, 14 July 1871.

27. Albeit taking some liberties, the *Chronicle*'s anonymous journalist loosely quotes Prospero's directive to Ariel in Shakespeare's *Tempest*, act I, scene ii.

28. In her autobiography Stanton claimed that six hundred women filled Platt's Hall; in her diary for 13 July 1870, Anthony records that there were four hundred in attendance (*Eighty Years and More*, 290; *SP* 2:434).

29. Elizabeth T. Schenck, a widow, was an officer in NWSA for California. See *SP* 2:295n1.

30. Mormon Orson Spencer's influential 1853 pamphlet illuminates Stanton's contentions. According to B. Carmon Hardy, Spencer claimed that Old Testament patriarch Abraham's example replicates "the social and family patterns of heaven" ("Lords of Creation," 142). As Abraham was both righteous and childless, "God gave . . . Abraham . . . wives and concubines so that he could fulfill the first and greatest commandment, to 'effect the perpetuity and increase of God, in an endless succession of families.' . . . The 'law of Sarah' permitting one's husband to enter plural relationships, thus raised wifely submissiveness to divinely mandated principle" ("Lords of Creation," 142–143).

31. Julie Dunfey observes that "the security and status of [female Saints'] position, in the church and in society, were linked to their reproductive capacity and to their virtue. The great object of marriage relations . . . was the multiplying of the species" ("'Living the Principle,'" 531).

32. Joseph Smith formulated his "revelation" on polygamy in 1843, but when the Mormon community established itself in Utah and issued a public proclamation of this doctrine, plural marriages increased, and the general American public reacted antagonistically. Stanton may refer to the pamphlets and letters that Mormon women published to defend their faith; chief among their claims was their contention that plural marriages protected women and society from "infanticide, alcoholic and abusive husbands, desertion, divorce," prostitution, and sexually transmitted disease. Many examples appear beginning in 1872, when the biweekly *Woman's Exponent* was established, but earlier examples that speak to Stanton's talking points exist, such as Belinda Marden Pratt's "Defense of Polygamy by a Lady in Utah" (1854). Polygamy, argued Pratt, ensures that women are "honorable wives of virtuous men, and mothers of faithful, virtuous, healthy, and vigorous

children" (Hardy, "Lords of Creation," 138; Dunfey, "'Living the Principle,'" 527–531, quoted on 527, 531).

33. "Female Saints' diaries and letters," observes Julie Dunfey, "reveal the difficulty and sadness of 'living the principle.' As Martha Spence Heywood said, 'Tis rather trying to a woman's feelings not to be acknowledged by the man she has given herself to and desires with all her heart.' . . . Mormon women, however, hoped for the benefits of plural marriage in another world. As Lucinda Lee Dalton said: 'Only for the sake of its expected joys in eternity, could I endure its trials through time'" (Dunfey, "'Living the Principle,'" 534).

34. Julie Dunfey suggests that in their published letters and pamphlets Mormon women emphasized the dangers of sexual intercourse during pregnancy. Belinda Marden Pratt argued that women must abstain at this time because "her heart should be pure, her thoughts and affections chaste, her mind calm, her passions without excitement" ("'Living the Principle,'" quoted on 531).

35. Stanton's "Overland Letters" column in the *Revolution* issues of 13 and 20 July reflects similar themes. She found the women "refined" and "lovely" but (as she commonly did for organized religious sects of all kinds) condemned the Mormon belief that "woman is only sure of heaven by being tied to some man, and its highest seats by having a dozen children tied to her"; instancing the overflowing cemetery, Stanton criticized Mormon women's frequent childbirths from an early age ("Overland Letters").

36. Powerful newspaper editor of the *New York Tribune*, Horace Greeley (1811–1872) was not a strong supporter of woman suffrage at this time, and he and Stanton engaged in numerous skirmishes. The 7 October 1869 *Revolution* quotes Greeley to declare, "As to employment for women . . . this country is in present, pressing need of one hundred thousand scientific, skillful, thoroughly qualified cooks; but very few American born young women are seeking to adapt themselves to this urgent national need" ("Women's Right to Cook"). In the *Independent*, a weekly paper, on 24 September 1863 Greeley expresses an early version of this idea: "This day, there are thousands of refined, expensively educated women vainly seeking employment in our city; yet if every one of them was a skillful, able, scientific cook—a genuine 'artiste' in the preparation of food—she could find a good place in three days, and very soon command liberal wages" ("The Educational Problem").

37. Stanton also includes this metaphor in her popular "Our Girls" lyceum lecture, where she also declared, "It is a great truth to impress on the mind of every girl that she is an independent creative will power" (*SP* 3:491).

38. Harriet Goodhue Hosmer (1830–1908), the American sculptor, well known for flaunting convention, trained in Italy in the early 1850s with the British sculptor John Gibson (Groseclose, "Hosmer, Harriet Goodhue").

39. Irregular physicians and dress reformers asked women to replace constricting corsets and the heavy petticoats that placed pressure on the hips with loose, comfortable clothing. The middle- and upper-class practice of contracting young women's waists produced "compressed and permanently deformed lower ribcages." Moreover, corsets and heavy skirts further restricted women's movement, making them sedentary and ill-prepared for childbirth (Wertz and Wertz, *Lying-In*, 110).

40. Stanton refers to the King James Version, Genesis 3:16: "Unto the woman he said, I will greatly multiply thy sorrow and thy conception; in sorrow thou shalt bring forth children; and thy desire *shall be* to thy husband, and he shall rule over thee," a verse quoted in medical texts as justification for the inevitable suffering of pregnancy and childbirth in the nineteenth century. Stanton's point was not new among reformers. Water-cure physician Thomas Nichols argued that "the pains and perils of gestation and childbirth . . . have come to be considered as among the necessary evils of life, to be borne patiently, and with humble submission to the will of God, who has laid this terrible curse upon woman in consequence of the sin of Eve" ("The Curse Removed," 167).

41. Genesis 3:17–19 and Genesis 9:18–25.

42. For the prevalence of the belief in eugenics among late nineteenth-century feminists and the notion that the mother's ideas could imprint themselves on her unborn child, see Gordon, "Voluntary Motherhood," 263–264.

43. Books and tracts by the Nicholses and other physicians offered models of and strategies for "painless" births. In one such accounting, Mary Gove Nichols relates the experience of one of her recent patients, a first-time mother. "I said, after the birth, 'Were these efforts painful?' She hesitated, and then said, '*Slightly*'" (quoted in "Water-Cure in Childbirth—Again," 117).

44. Stanton bragged about the ease of her first six pregnancies and births; the last one was difficult, but she admitted it only to her closest friends. For the children's birth weights, her commentary to Lucretia Mott about her "savage" (easy) delivery, and her admission to Anthony and Elizabeth Smith Miller on the difficulties of her last pregnancy and birth, see *SP* 1:178, 316, 383, 387, 387n1, quoted on 212; Ginzberg, *Elizabeth Cady Stanton*, 95–97.

45. In an attempt to counteract the impact of their interventions during the birth itself, heroic physicians recommended an extended postpartum confinement, or "lying-in," for women—keeping them in a horizontal posture for ten days to six weeks (Donegan, *"Hydropathic Highway to Health,"* 77).

46. Statesman and lawyer Henry Clay (1777–1852) served in both the Senate and House (there as the Speaker) and as secretary of state. As was the case with similarly renowned politician and attorney Daniel Webster (1782–1852), he was a gifted orator. As congressmen, Clay, Webster, and John C. Calhoun were esteemed the powerful "Great Triumvirate." Contemporary published reports and rumors about extramarital sexual activities tarnished the reputations of Clay and Webster (Remini, *Daniel Webster*, 307–309; Remini, *Henry Clay*, 251–252).

47. Stanton here seems to extend her earlier reference to Clay and Webster to extramarital, companionate intellectual relationships. See Stanton's 11 August [1875?] letter to Elizabeth Smith Miller: "I do not believe in man having a wife for breeding purposes and an affinity [mistress] for spiritual and intellectual intercourse" (quoted in Griffith, *In Her Own Right*, 157).

48. Stanton refers to the nineteenth-century allegory of the masculine oak around whom the feminine and decorative vine wraps her gentle tendrils. Typically, the vine cannot support herself without the strong oak in literary depictions.

49. Mrs. Winslow's Soothing Syrup, first sold in 1832 for a host of infant ills and adult pains, was a morphine-based treatment; its success made the family of Stanton's colleague Laura Curtis Bullard independently wealthy.

50. Some free love and other associationists, such as John Humphrey Noyes's New York Oneida Community, placed responsibility on men for self-control. See Gordon, "Voluntary Motherhood," 256–258; Brodie, *Contraception and Abortion in 19th-Century America*, 65–67; Silver-Isenstadt, *Shameless*, 144–147.

51. Stanton skillfully shifts the terms of her interlocutor's question (which may allude to fertility limitation or abortion) to abortion in this exchange. For an alternate interpretation of Stanton's advice, see Davis, *The Political Thought of Elizabeth Cady Stanton*, 170–172.

Partnership of Elizabeth Cady Stanton and Susan B. Anthony (1885–1915)

Stanton and Anthony forged their enduring bond within political and personal spheres. This unique feature of their relationship was nowhere more apparent than when Anthony spent weeks at a time in Tenafly; at such times the two women shared domestic and reformist labors. Highlighting vital similarities between these endeavors, Stanton recalled, "We took turns on the domestic watchtowers, directing amusements, settling disputes, protecting the weak against the strong, and trying to secure equal rights to all in the home as well as in the nation." In like spirit, Anthony referred to the Stanton brood as "my children." Moreover, in an autobiography in which her husband appears but fleetingly, Stanton penned her fond dedication to Anthony: "I dedicate this volume to Susan B. Anthony, my steadfast friend for half a century."[1]

One child of this partnered mothering, Margaret Livingston Stanton Lawrence (1852–1930), Stanton's first daughter and fifth child, chronicled aspects of her mother's life on multiple occasions, but unlike her siblings Theodore Weld Stanton and Harriot Eaton Stanton Blatch, Margaret was, in her own words, "a lukewarm suffrage saint."† The Vassar graduate wrote of herself in 1885, "I have no remarkable genius in any direction but I have some practical talent in the ordinary affairs of life." Following the death of her husband, Frank Lawrence, in 1890, she returned to New York City and, after additional schooling, became a "'physical director' at Teacher's College." In 1892 she and her younger brother Bob moved into an apartment with their mother, where Lawrence nurtured her aging mother.[2] Lawrence's description of the two women's writing collaboration is noteworthy for her humorous but frank expression of frustration at the ways in which Stanton and Anthony's labors removed these fond children's mother from their lives. It also illuminates the reformers' ability to put aside differences, in service of their friendship and their common cause.

Despite her popularity on the stage, their fellow woman suffrage advocate, the phrenologist and author Helen Potter, leaves an elusive trail today, including birth and death dates. An innovator in the art of performing dramatic readings of addresses originally delivered by actors and other famous literary and historical figures, Potter used makeup, costume, and rhetorical technique to personify her subjects. Her participation in the woman's movement continued throughout her career; as late as 1912, still single, she appeared on the stage in New York City with militant British suffragette Emmeline Pankhurst (1858–1928) and Stanton's daughter Harriot Stanton Blatch.[3] As Theodore Tilton and other contemporaries also maintained, in this selection Potter insisted that one can scarcely "memorializ[e]" the pair separately. Her sprightly narration of events surrounding the country's 1876 centennial celebration of the American nation's birth in Philadelphia and the 1895 celebration of Stanton's eightieth birthday also displays pivotal moments when Stanton and Anthony resolved disagreements between themselves and with a united will addressed political infighting within NWSA and NAWSA.

Another commentator on the friendship, the physician, superb orator, and minister Anna Howard Shaw (1847–1919), became, under Anthony's leadership of NAWSA, one of her most fiercely loyal lieutenants and eventual president of the organization. In her autobiography Shaw shrewdly portrayed a "divine transfer of power," in which the dying Susan B. Anthony passed the presidential torch to the reluctant Shaw in order to "legitimize her own leadership" of NAWSA.[4] But this selection from *Anna Howard Shaw: The Story of a Pioneer* reads neutrally—as a humorous example of the familiar interactions between and of the strengths and weaknesses of Stanton and Anthony.

Suffragist and journalist Ida Husted Harper (1851–1931) took the place of Stanton and acted as Anthony's "word artist" during the last years of the aging suffrage activist's life. With Anthony's aid she wrote the fourth volume of *History of Woman Suffrage* (1902), and after Anthony's death she completed the fifth and sixth volumes of the monumental history (1922). She also wrote Anthony's biography, *The Life and Work of Susan B. Anthony* (1898), completing its final volume in 1908. Divorced from her former husband, the lawyer and union advocate Thomas Winans Harper, in 1890, at the turn of the century she lived in Anthony's home in Rochester, New York, to conduct their shared labors.[5] Importantly, the combined efforts of Anthony, Harper, and these publications—including the selection in this chapter—fused and subsumed Stanton's "pioneering" origins narrative at Seneca Falls into the Susan B. Anthony story. In this admiring reminiscence of Stanton's commanding legal mind, authorial power, and captivating oratorical presentation, Harper emphasizes that Anthony's role in propelling Stanton's "worldwide fame" is incalculable.

From "As a Mother," Margaret Stanton Lawrence, 1885[6]

Editor New Era:

Your letter was read aloud to us, in which you said that you intended to devote the November number of your *New Era* to my mother, in honor of her seventieth birthday; and that you desired to have a pen picture of our family life, and I, being the only child at home, was thereupon delegated to be the special artist for the work.

As my mother could not set forth in glowing colors her own domestic virtues, and as Miss Anthony, who is a part of our household, is now in the agonies of Vol. III. of *The History of Woman Suffrage*, buried under mountains of illegible manuscripts, I, with much hesitancy, undertake the task. . . .

But to return to my picture of mother and Susan. They are busy all day and far into the night on said Volume III. As our house faces the south the sunshine streams in all day. In the centre of a large room, 20 by 22, with an immense bay window, hard wood floor and open fire, beside a substantial office desk with innumerable drawers and doors, filled with documents, —there *vis-à-vis* sit our historians, surrounded with manuscripts and letters from Maine to Louisiana. In one drawer are engravings of some of the leading advocates, fifteen in number, all waiting to take their places in this last volume. *Entre nous*, I am fearfully tired of this History. It has stood in the way of everything we have wanted mother to do for the last seven years. We all feel towards these volumes as a family of children would to some favorite adopted child, that filled their places in a mother's heart. Well, if this volume is to linger as long as the others did, I fear we shall not see the end of it before the Fourth of July, the day when all questions of freedom seem to culminate. But it is of little interest to you to know what I, a lukewarm suffrage saint, may think.

To return to again our historians, in the centre of their desk are two ink stands and two bottles of mucilage, to say nothing of diverse pens, pencils, scissors, knives, etc., etc. As these famous women grow intense in working up some glowing sentence, . . . I have seen them again and again dip their pens in the mucilage and their brushes in the ink. Either of these blunders brings them back to the facts of history, where they should be if that blessed word *finis* is ever to be written. *Sub rosa*, it is as good as a comedy to watch these souls from day to day. They start off pretty well in the morning, fresh and amiable. They write page after page with alacrity, they laugh and talk, poke the fire by turn, and admire the flowers I place on their desk each morning. Everything is harmonious for a season, but after straining their eyes over the most illegible, disorderly manuscripts I ever beheld, suddenly the whole sky is overspread with dark and threatening clouds, and from the adjoining room I hear a hot dispute about something. The dictionary, the encyclopedia, the *Woman's Journal, Our Herald, The National Citizen, The Revolution, The Woman's Tribune, The New Northwest, The New Era*—all piled on the floor in one corner—are overhauled, tossed about in an emphatic manner for some date, fact, or some point of law or constitution. Susan is punctilious on dates, mother on philosophy, but each contends as stoutly in the other's domain as if equally strong at all points. Sometimes these disputes run so high that down go the pens, one sails out of one door and one out of the other, walking in opposite directions around the estate, and just as I have made up my mind that this beautiful friendship of forty years has at last terminated, I see them walking down the hill, arm in arm, to a seat where we often go to see the distant hills and lovely valleys, and to watch the sun go down in all his glory. When they return they go straight to work where they left off, as if nothing happened. I never hear another word on that point—the one that was unquestionably right assumes it, and the other silently concedes the fact. They never explain, nor apologize, nor shed tears, nor make up, as other people do; but, figuratively speaking, jump over a stone wall at one bound and leave the past behind them, seemingly with no memory of the hour before.

From "Reminiscences of the Lyceum. VIII— Susan Brownell Anthony," Helen Potter, 1908[7]

The scene of the last installment of my "Reminiscences" was in Philadelphia, the year of our National Centennial Celebration, 1876. That summer I became better acquainted with two of the most notable women of the century, Elizabeth Cady Stanton and Susan Brownell Anthony. . . .

At that time women conspicuously connected with the "Woman's Movement" were subjected to persistent ridicule and caricature, and Susan came in for the largest share of the abuse. . . .

For a woman to speak in public upon any subject, religious or secular, was simply ridiculous, and, by many even thought disreputable.

And to dare to challenge the justice of existing laws, to hold up inane customs for criticism and condemnation was an impertinence so monstrous, so intolerable, as to call for pen and pencil, rioting and clamorous assault to put it down, and stamp it out. Nor was Miss Anthony alone the subject of sneers and abuse; all of the pioneers for the "Emancipation of Woman" came in for a liberal share of that which only the bravest souls could endure.

Mrs. Stanton and Miss Anthony, for over fifty years coadjutors for the uplift of womanhood, can scarcely be memorialized separately. Traveling and lecturing, both within and without the "Lyceum" field; holding meetings and conventions; securing signatures to petitions and hearings before Legislatures; publishing reports, documents and other literature; removing obstructions and misconstructions from their path; surely their lives were not a procession of pleasure excursions but lives of eternal vigilance and incessant work. Work demanding great versatility of talent; work without adequate financial support, in fact, altogether unremunerative; a half century of unparalleled work without even the appreciation and gratitude of a large proportion of the class for whom such rare devotion and self-sacrifice were made.

No record was kept of the number of miles traveled, of the number of speeches made, nor of the big fees earned and never received. No! They had, like all great reformers, taken an unpopular subject and steadfastly carried it forward against all opposition until it commanded the respect and consideration of the highly enlightened people of the civilized world. What the long effort cost in heart and brain the world can never know.

In speaking of Mrs. Stanton, Miss Anthony said: "I always called her the philosopher and statesman of our movement. Every state paper presented to Congress, or the legislatures, in the early days, was written by Mrs. Stanton. She forged the thunderbolts and I fired them. She composed the speeches, while I rocked the cradle for her."[8]

In speaking of Miss Anthony, Mrs. Stanton said, "In thought and sympathy we were one, and in the division of labor we complemented each other. In writing we did better work than either alone. While she is slow and analytical in composition, I am rapid and synthetic. I am the better writer, she the better critic. She supplied the facts and statistics and I the rhetoric and philosophy, and together we have made arguments unanswered."[9]

Mrs. Stanton and Miss Anthony are better known than others in the movement because, as leaders, they have held public attention for more than half a century. Some noble pioneers preceded them, in transient or individual work, and deserve recognition, but it remained for the subjects of this sketch to organize and place it in successful working order before the world. Hosts of capable conscientious persons have enlisted under the standard raised by them, and the work goes on. . . .

Mrs. Stanton, in my opinion, was the most all-round capable and efficient woman whom I have ever known. An exemplary, happy wife and mother (the crowning joy of woman); serenely intellectual and self-poised; unmoved by the hysteria of ignorance, or the malicious pyrotechnics of enemies; learned, logical, consistent and fearless; filled with determinate *justice*; able to cope with a mob, a judge, or a bishop with dignity, precision and effect. A woman well-fitted to champion any cause that appealed to her keen sense of justice. A natural leader. She it was who promptly answered every attack, direct or indirect, from press or pulpit upon the status of woman or affecting her interests. She would have honored the position of a Supreme Judge. . . .

The National Woman's Suffrage Association had established their headquarters in Philadelphia for the summer of the "Centennial," where the suffragists congregated from all parts of the country.[10] Of course the Centennial Fourth of July was the "day of days," with all loyal Americans. The Committee of Arrangements had built a large platform just back of Independence Hall, facing its garden, and arranged a fine program for the occasion, upon which the Suffragists were represented. Mrs. Stanton prepared a "Woman's Declaration of Independence" to follow the reading of the original one which she called "Man's Declaration of Independence," because by that document woman was no more liberated from unjust taxation (without representation, etc.) under man's arbitrary rule, than were the Colonies under British rule. It then became important that the woman's "Declaration" should be read by one who could be heard by the greatest number of an open-air audience.[11]

It was well known that I possessed a voice of extraordinary carrying power, without being forced or disagreeable, so I was invited to read it on that great occasion. On the morning of the Fourth, attired in a plain black silk gown, I reported at "headquarters"[12] somewhat earlier than necessary in order to obtain further instructions as to time, location, etc., of our party.

I found the large rooms crowded with ladies, moving to and fro, making a confusion of many-keyed voices, each evidently intent upon something of vital personal interest. Seeking a friend, or a party of friends, or platform tickets, or information impossible to obtain. A buzz of subdued anxiety pervaded the air. After some effort and inquiry I found Miss Anthony, and, desiring to satisfy their views as a representative, said to her, "Am I attired suitably for the occasion! If not, there is plenty of time to make any change you suggest." She gazed at me vacantly for a moment, and I hastened to add, "to read the 'Woman's Declaration of Independence!'" She flushed with surprise, saying, "Why! didn't they notify you of our change of plan?" I replied, "I have heard of no change of plan!" "It's a shame!" she said. "Mrs. Blank objected to our having an outsider read it; said it would give the impression that the Association had no one capable of reading it, and insisted that one of us should do it! They were to notify you! It's too bad!" Thereupon she took me along to find Mrs. Stanton. Having found her, Miss Anthony said, excitedly, "Do you know Miss Potter has not been notified of the change we made and has come expecting to read our 'Declaration' to-day? I think it was real mean of Mrs. Blank to make such a fuss!" Unmoved by Miss Anthony's excitement Mrs. Stanton answered very composedly, "No, Susan, not mean, but small; one is to blame for being mean, but not to blame for being small. She is as large as she was made." I laughed, and that relieved the tension, and settled it. We all straightway fell into good humor, over the well-known jealousies and bickerings for recognition by Mrs. Blank. It pleased me better not to read it, for now I was free to enjoy the day.[13] Miss Anthony concluded the conference by saying, "Well! Miss Potter shall not lose her seat on the grand stand!" and forthwith provided me with one of the best seats at her command, among the speakers of the day and near their stand.

On the eightieth anniversary of Mrs. Stanton's birthday, Nov. 12, 1895, a notable "Reunion of the Pioneers and Friends of Woman's Progress" was held in the Metropolitan Opera House, New York, to do her honor. It was given under the auspices of the "National Council of Women of the United States," Mrs. Mary Lowe Dickinson presiding. There were sixty-two associations of women in sympathy with the reunion, and over one hundred personal greetings received, among them one from Mrs. Mary A. Livermore and one from Miss Frances Willard, besides many from abroad.[14]

At the hour of meeting an immense audience had assembled and a brilliant scene lay before us. The balconies were draped with flags and emblems; the huge stage was a mass of flowers, decorations and famous ladies; there was a central canopy of ferns, plants and flowers beneath which sat the guest of honor in regal state, and received tributes of esteem and admiration, of gratitude and love, voiced by the most brilliant women of the Nation. . . .

A few days before the reunion, Mrs. Stanton sent for me, and requested me to read her address for her, as she was unable to stand so long, having recently received an injury when alighting from a carriage. I consented, and, that she might be assured that I understood every part of the address, [she] asked me to read it aloud to her, which I did. Miss Anthony was present, and implored, with tears, that a passage in the address be omitted. Mrs. Stanton said, "No! Susan, it is the *truth*, and it has got to be said. No one else dares say it! I may never have another opportunity, and I shall say it." So the text remained uncut and I read it as it was written.[15]

From *Anna Howard Shaw: The Story of a Pioneer*, Anna Howard Shaw, 1915[16]

Mrs. Stanton was the most brilliant conversationalist I have ever known; and the best talk I have heard anywhere was that to which I used to listen in the home of Mrs. Eliza Wright Osborne, in Auburn, New York, when Mrs. Stanton, Susan B. Anthony, Emily Howland, Elizabeth Smith Miller, Ida Husted Harper, Miss Mills, and I were gathered there for our occasional week-end visits. . . .[17]

Most of the conversation in Mrs. Osborne's home was contributed by Mrs. Stanton and Miss Anthony, while the rest of us sat, as it were, at their feet. Many human and feminine touches brightened the lofty discussions that were constantly going on, and the varied characteristics of our leaders cropped up in amusing fashion. Mrs. Stanton, for example, was rarely accurate in giving figures or dates, while Miss Anthony was always very exact in such matters. She frequently corrected Mrs. Stanton's statements, and Mrs. Stanton usually took the interruption in the best possible spirit, promptly admitting that "Aunt Susan" knew best. On one occasion I recall, however, she held fast to her opinion that she was right as to the month in which a certain incident had occurred.

"No, Susan," she insisted, "you're wrong for once. I remember perfectly when that happened, for it was at the time I was beginning to wean Harriot."

Aunt Susan, though somewhat staggered by the force of this testimony, still maintained that Mrs. Stanton must be mistaken, whereupon the latter repeated, in exasperation, "I tell you it happened when I was weaning Harriot." And she added, scornfully, "What event have *you* got to reckon from?"

Miss Anthony meekly subsided.

From "Elizabeth Cady Stanton," Ida Husted Harper, 1902[18]

In 1851 occurred what may well be termed the most important event in Mrs. Stanton's life, her meeting with Susan B. Anthony. The latter was thirty-one years old, electric with the spirit of reform, filled with as holy zeal as ever inspired crusader, fearless, persistent, perfect in physical health, and free to come and go at will. There was an instantaneous, mutual attraction, and before a year had passed a working partnership was formed which was to revolutionize the position of one-half the race during the next forty years, and a friendship was established which was to remain unbroken for half a century. How much of Mrs. Stanton's worldwide fame is due to Miss Anthony cannot possibly be computed. Never two persons more thoroughly complemented each other. Each was strong where the other was lacking, and the two made a perfectly rounded and most effective whole.

It would not be amiss to say that Mrs. Stanton furnished the base of supplies to which Miss Anthony went for the ammunition to rout the enemy. Or that she represented the loom and the warp, Miss Anthony the shuttle and the woof, and by the two was woven the enduring fabric of woman's present position. Mrs. Stanton had no intellectual superior among women, few among men, but she reared seven children to maturity; she was a devoted mother, an unsurpassed housekeeper. It would have been inevitable, during the twenty-five or thirty years of her life while these children were growing up around her, that she would have laid aside in a large degree both writing and speechmaking, had it not been for the relentless mentor who averted this calamity. The reader will find nothing more delicious in history than the accounts in Mrs. Stanton's "Reminiscences" and Miss Anthony's "Life and Work" of the conditions under which were prepared those great state papers and addresses that will go down to posterity. Miss Anthony was not a writer; but as a worker, a planner, a general, a campaigner, she never has been equaled by any woman. She would have a bill prepared for the Legislature, organize her forces, start them out with petitions, and when everything was under headway, betake herself to Mrs. Stanton for a speech. The latter would protest, rebel, but Miss Anthony was inexorable. She would send the writer off to a quiet spot, take upon herself the care of the children and the house, and hold the fort till the speech was finished. Then she would arrange a day for its delivery, and produce the speaker if she had to go and fetch her bodily. Afterward she would appeal to friends for money, have the speech published, and circulate thousands of copies.

This programme was repeated hundreds of times. When the International Council of Women met in Washington, in 1888, Miss Anthony literally compassed sea and land to get Mrs. Stanton over from England, only to find that she had come without any papers suitable for the occasion. Miss Anthony locked her in a room in the hotel and stood guard at the door till she had prepared the brilliant opening and closing addresses which were the leading features of that notable meeting.[19] She really enjoyed writing, however, and when in the spirit of it would spend hours in perfecting the literary style of a single paragraph. She loved best to argue and philosophize, and depended wholly on Miss Anthony for necessary dates and statistics; but between the two were produced innumerable papers which deserve to rank with any in the Government archives,—appeals to the President, Congress, and legislatures, resolutions, addresses for conventions and committees, and in addition numerous articles for magazines and newspapers. For the fifteen years beginning about 1870, when the lecture season was at its zenith, both women were almost continuously on the platform, but during vacations they found time to write the three large volumes of the "History of Woman Suffrage," comprising about 3,000 pages.

Mrs. Stanton had no interest in organization, and hated conventions. She disliked the restrictions of organized work and the responsibility involved in official position,—she wished to be accountable to no one for her utterances. When a convention was imminent, she would write to Miss Anthony: "All I ask is that you will leave me alone in my chimney corner with my goose quill." The latter would go straight forward with the arrangements, advertise Mrs. Stanton as the principal speaker, journey to her home a few days before the date of meeting, pack up her belongings, carry her to the convention, and see that she was reëlected president. The happiest moments of her life were when, at the close of a great speech, she saw her beloved friend greeted with cheers and waving handkerchiefs, and felt that the cause of woman had been moved forward a notch. At the age of eighty, Mrs. Stanton gave her "Reminiscences" to the world, and she dedicated them to "Susan B. Anthony, my steadfast friend for half a century." . . .

Mrs. Stanton was able to disarm every criticism made of the early advocates of woman's rights. She was a wife, a mother, far from angular, beautiful in person, and exquisite in dress. Her voice was rich and musical, and the powerful philosophy and logic of her arguments, with the keen sarcasm of which she was master, were relieved by a fine humor and graceful wit that conquered prejudice and captivated an audience. But it seemed as if no woman ever so deeply felt the disgrace, the humiliation, of her legal and political condition,—certainly none ever so strongly expressed it by voice or pen. In lofty eloquence and noble patriotism many of her speeches may be justly classified as masterpieces, among them "The Degradation of Disfranchisement," "Self-Government the Best Means of Self-Development," and that beautiful classic, "The Solitude of Self." The world may indeed echo the words of Miss Anthony as she gazed on the face of Mrs. Stanton in the grandeur of death: "Oh, this awful hush! It seems impossible that voice is stilled which I have loved to hear for fifty years."

NOTES

1. Quoted in Barry, *Susan B. Anthony*, 157; Stanton, *Eighty Years and More*, dedication page, n.p.

2. Griffith, *In Her Own Right*, 201, 228; DuBois, *Harriot Stanton Blatch*, 245–246, quoted on 15; Ginzberg, *Elizabeth Cady Stanton*, 158–159.

3. "Pankhurst Speech Opens Pocketbooks," *New York Times*, 6 January 1912.

4. DuBois, *Harriot Stanton Blatch*, 247.

5. Opdycke, "Harper, Ida Husted."

6. Lawrence, "As a Mother."

7. Potter, "Reminiscences of the Lyceum."

8. See Anthony, "Tribute from Miss Anthony," for an account that includes all but Potter's memory of Anthony describing her cradle-rocking activities.

9. This is a loose quotation of Stanton, *Eighty Years and More*, 166.

10. The centennial celebration of the nation's birth took place in Philadelphia, where an international exposition opened months before the formal 4 July event, which included a reading of the Declaration of Independence, in Independence Hall. The women's request to deliver their own declaration to the chairman on the stage was refused, so Anthony decided to crash the event and present the text of their declaration to the chairman, uninvited. Afterwards she and her collaborators left the building to read it in the open air.

Following Anthony's reading, the woman suffrage reformers repaired to their own convention. See Lutz, *Created Equal*, 236–238; Griffith, *In Her Own Right*, 166–167; Ginzberg, *Elizabeth Cady Stanton*, 150; *SP* 3:243n4.

11. For the text of the "Declaration of Rights of the Women of the United States," see *SP* 3:234–241.

12. The National Woman Suffrage headquarters were established "outside the Centennial Park, on Chestnut Street" (Griffith, *In Her Own Right*, 167).

13. Susan B. Anthony read the Declaration, shielded by the sun with the umbrella of Matilda Joslyn Gage and attended also by Sarah Andrew Spencer, Lillie Devereux Blake, and Phoebe Couzins. I find no corroborating record for this controversy inspired by Potter's potential declamation: she did, without controversy, for example, deliver impressions of Stanton and Anthony, published her impression of Stanton giving this 1876 Declaration, and in 1895 delivered Stanton's address at the Metropolitan Opera House at the celebration of her eightieth birthday when Stanton was in poor health. As for "Mrs. Blank," Spencer, Gage, Anthony, and Stanton together wrote the Declaration; possibly Spencer and Gage had the greatest stakes in its presentation as a result (Lutz, *Created Equal*, 237–238, 293; Griffith, *In Her Own Right*, 167; *SP* 3:241). For Gage's belief that Anthony discredited her intellectual labors on collaborative suffrage writing before the centennial celebration, see *SP* 3:208–209, 230–231n1, 233n6.

14. An example of Stanton's bad odor at this time, NAWSA refused to sponsor this celebration. Her son Theodore and Anthony secured the National Council of Women instead. Its president, Mary Lowe Dickinson, presided, and thousands attended (Griffith, *In Her Own Right*, 209; Lutz, *Created Equal*, 292; *SP* 5:730). Author, editor, and lecturer Mary Livermore (1820–1905) assumed leadership roles in the AWSA, the Association for the Advancement of Women, the Massachusetts Woman Suffrage Association (which she also founded), and the Sanitary Commission during the Civil War. Before she commenced her successful lecturing career, she served as the editor of the AWSA's *Woman's Journal* (Perry, "Livermore, Mary"). Under the leadership of international temperance reformer and speaker Frances Willard (1839–1898), the Woman's Christian Temperance Union became America's largest women's group; she added to its temperance platform education, woman suffrage, and labor reform.

15. For the full text of Stanton's conclusion, a sustained and sharply anticlerical analysis of the ways in which the canon law, institutionalized religion, and scriptures degrade and disempower women, see *SP* 5:725–730.

16. Anna Howard Shaw, with the collaboration of Elizabeth Jordan, *Anna Howard Shaw: The Story of a Pioneer* (New York: Harper & Brothers, 1915), 240–242.

17. Eliza Wright Osborne (1830–1911), daughter of Martha Coffin Pelham Wright and niece of Lucretia Coffin Mott, married the successful agricultural machinery merchant David Munson Osborne and lived in Auburn, near her mother's home (Palmer, *Selected Letters of Lucretia Coffin Mott*, xlix; Penney and Livingston, *A Very Dangerous Woman*, 85–86). Emily Howland (1827–1929), the daughter of wealthy Quakers Slocum Howland and Hannah Talcott of Sherwood, New York, was reared in the abolitionist tradition and over her lifetime became a patron of education for poor whites and African Americans; in

addition, she was active in temperance, international peace efforts, and woman's suffrage reform (Locke, "Howland, Emily"). "Miss Mills" is likely Harriet May Mills (1857–1935), who, as Ann D. Gordon notes, was the daughter of abolitionist and lecturer Charles de Berard Mills. A graduate of Cornell University, she was a successful lecturer for woman suffrage and the Democratic party (*SP* 6:65n5).

18. From Ida Husted Harper, "Elizabeth Cady Stanton," *American Monthly Review of Reviews: An International Magazine* 26, no. 6 (December 1902): 717–718, 719.

19. Stanton and Anthony initially conceived of an international council for women when they were in Europe together in 1883. In late March 1888, over eight days, fifty-two women's associations in sixteen sessions represented a broad range of women's concerns, with delegates attending from the U.S., England, France, Norway, Finland, Denmark, India, and Canada. Both Stanton's and Anthony's memoirs relate the tale of Anthony locking Stanton in her room for three days at the Riggs House hotel until she had produced her speech (represented at *SP* 5:93–107). Anthony (and Stanton in her addresses) adroitly presented the Council as the celebration of the fortieth anniversary of the 1848 Seneca Falls convention, conceived as the "origins" of woman's suffrage; Lucy Stone and Antoinette Brown Blackwell attempted to counter that portrait at the "Conference of Pioneers" session (see Stanton, *Eighty Years and More*, 413; Harper, *Susan B. Anthony*, 2:636; Lutz, *Created Equal*, 267–270; Griffith, *In Her Own Right*, 192–194; Ginzberg, *Elizabeth Cady Stanton*, 159–161; Tetrault, *The Myth of Seneca Falls*, 145–155).

Schism (1868–1880)

This chapter treats a controversial moment in Stanton's life, one that produced a range of reactions from her contemporaries; in turn, that reception also contributed to the increasingly expansive directions of her advocacy. These selections reflect largely upon the events of 1867 through 1870; and the enormity of their emotional impact upon reformers as well as upon the general public is registered by their duration—as selections from the late 1870s document.

They begin with abolitionist champion, pamphleteer, and newspaper editor William Lloyd Garrison (1805–1879). Garrison's idealistic ethics; keenly developed sense of his own superiority as an antislavery leader; and radical critique of institutional religion, of the foundations of the U.S. government, and of the American political machine instigated both his ascendancy and decline in authority. Stanton published his private letter to Anthony, followed by Stanton's reply, in *Revolution*, to his great anger. Garrison's understandably horrified condemnation of Stanton and Anthony's racist language and association with George Francis Train occurred at a critical threshold in his life, a point of departure Stanton also commented upon sarcastically.

In 1833, at the founding of the American Anti-Slavery Society (AASS), Garrison contributed its statement of principle, the *Declaration of Sentiments*, a model for Stanton's 1848 coauthored document of the same title. The *Declaration* reflected Garrison's larger pacifist vision, in which the "moral suasion" of male and—more controversially—female abolitionists would peacefully transform white Americans' racial prejudices and enable African Americans to assume positions of equality as citizens. Church leaders condemned this idea, which they deemed fanatical, and resulting public tensions rendered abolitionists the victims of deadly mob violence in their homes, streets, and meetings. Confirming Garrison's belief that organized religion and the American government were innately flawed, this crisis only strengthened his support of women's rights. But abolitionists such as Henry Brewster Stanton, who trusted the political process as a means of ensuring African Americans' emancipation and honored societal, governmental, and religious institutions, found Garrisonian positions antithetical. By the time of the AASS 1840 meeting, Garrison's commitment to gender equality and other radical cultural reforms—in this case the election of Abby Kelley Foster, the wife of this chapter's Stephen Symonds Foster, to AASS committee leadership—divided the organization asunder.[1]

Despite his realization of pathbreaking social ideals, Garrison's paternalistic interactions with emerging black abolitionists like Frederick Douglass demonstrate the ways in which racism penetrated even the most visionary white reformers, and they also offer insight into his reception of Stanton and Anthony in the late 1860s. Garrison proved deeply ambivalent about ceding authority when former acolytes branched out as leaders of platforms and organizations that differed from his own. Analyzing Douglass's and Garrison's slow but bitter estrangement, William S. McFeely observes, "The Garrisonians, despite their official secularism, regarded any deviation from their leadership as heresy: theirs was the only way; all others were wrong."[2] McFeely's analysis of this organizational stance, which filtered down from their leader, illuminates the responses of a number of abolitionist reformers to Stanton and Anthony in this chapter. Directly criticizing Garrison for this kind of "prejudice," "passion," and "bad judgment" in her 1869 letter to Susan Howard, however, Isabella Beecher Hooker added, "I realize anew how patient & tolerant reformers should be of each other—the very stuff that makes them reformers, will make them persecutors also if they are not always on their guard."† Indeed, and this chapter makes clear, Beecher eloquently expresses the pained dismay evinced by speakers on both sides of the "schism"—among them, Frederick Douglass, Jane Elizabeth Hitchcock Jones, and Mary Livermore.

Other top-level AASS disagreements put Garrison in a defensive posture and provide additional context for his response to Stanton during and after the Kansas campaign. As woman's suffrage and health reformer Jane Elizabeth Hitchcock Jones (1813–1896) reports with consternation, it was Garrison's and Phillips's public quarrels in 1867 and 1868 and Garrison's subsequent eclipse that Stanton maliciously portrayed in Shakespearian fashion in the 29 January 1868 issue of *Revolution*.[3] To add insult to injury, by publishing and responding publicly to his private letter to Susan B. Anthony, Stanton further provoked Garrison. Despite her frank criticism of Stanton for these actions in 1868, however, Jones praised *Revolution*, and her warm tone in another letter to Stanton may reflect their shared interest in women's physiological education. Although Jones began her reformist career on the abolitionist stage with Abby Kelley Foster, in the 1850s she studied under an

Ohio physician to prepare her to deliver popular and lucrative lectures on anatomy and physiology, using illustrative engravings and a mannequin.[4]

Jones's early abolitionist campaigns may signal an allegiance to the "Boston" woman suffrage activists, but the generous and even-handed tenor of her commentary on Stanton differs from that of their leader, Lucy Stone, in 1868 and 1879. A dedicated antislavery and suffrage activist, Stone (1818–1893) was a farmer's daughter who worked her way through Oberlin College, where she forged strong bonds with her future sister-in-law, Antoinette Brown Blackwell, and developed her interest in woman's rights. Stone was celebrated throughout her career as a gifted and soulful public speaker. Her only living child with Henry, or "Harry," Browne Blackwell (1825–1909), Alice Stone Blackwell, became—like Harriot Stanton Blatch—a second-generation feminist leader. But Stone's refusal in 1879 to contribute for Stanton and Anthony's publications her own biography or information about AWSA reveals humility as well as spleen. As Sally G. McMillen explains, Stone was "totally self-effacing. A number of writers, journalist, and publishers throughout her adult life had approached her, wanting to write about 'one of the most famous women of the world.' She turned them all down." For multiple reasons, then, Stone adamantly refused to participate in the historicizing efforts Stanton and Anthony undertook between 1868 and 1879, when the two women were collecting material for the first volume of *History of Woman Suffrage*.[5]

Theodore Tilton (1835–1907) promoted a different view of Stanton in 1868. Tilton, whose prominent career as an abolitionist, editor, lecturer, and woman suffrage leader would be devastated two years later in the maelstrom surrounding his wife Elizabeth's affair with Henry Ward Beecher, subsequently lived in Paris, a shamed expatriate, but remained friends with Stanton to the end of his life. In his critical but forgiving version of the Train fiasco, Tilton urged the two camps "to make common cause," a prompt he would continue to advocate after "Boston" and "New York" formed AWSA and NWSA.

Like Tilton, prolific author, editor, woman suffrage and health reformer Eleanor Kirk, a pseudonym for Eleanor Maria Easterbrook Ames (1831–1908), appears committed to vindicating Stanton for her allegiance to George Francis Train and free love doctrine. By the age of forty Kirk was twice widowed, and with five children to support she adopted a writer's pseudonym and took a job at the *New York Standard*. Her columns on New York affairs, dress reform, and exercise made her local and then national reputation: by the 1880s they were "in syndication, reaching millions of women through a hundred and fifty newspapers nationwide."[6] Her popular fiction includes *Up Broadway* (1870), a "divorce rights" novel that *Revolution* serialized, and the "sex-egalitarian" utopian romance *Libra: An Astrological Romance* (1896). Not surprisingly, Kirk evidenced a long-standing interest in the lives of working women. She worked with Stanton and Anthony in their postwar Working Women's Association in 1868 and published several manuals intended to help women break into the writer's market. Her companion of forty years, Caroline Le Row, "a Vassar elocution instructor," contributed pieces on education reform to Kirk's woman's rights magazine, *Eleanor Kirk's Idea*.[7]

In her letter to Beecher family friend Susan Howard, Isabella Beecher Hooker (1822–1907) also reflected upon Stanton sympathetically in 1870. The daughter of renowned Presbyterian evangelist Lyman Beecher and his second wife, Susan Porter, from the time of her courtship with John Hooker, Isabella expressed an early interest in the kinds of marriage reforms Stanton proposed for women. In July 1839, for example, she wrote John that biblical injunctions for female submission were "galling to a sensible woman," but unlike Henry Brewster Stanton, John Hooker strongly supported his wife's woman's rights efforts. She would need his support during the Beecher-Tilton scandal, when the entire, powerful Beecher clan exerted every effort to protect one of its own. Under great pressure from her half-siblings, in the midst of the scandal she published *Womanhood: Its Sanctities and Fidelities* (1873) on marriage reform; and she took a principled stand against Henry Ward Beecher when she and John Hooker reached the conclusion that he had indeed engaged in an extramarital affair, even when Beecher family members consulted physicians in order to accuse her of insanity.[8]

Because of his cultural power, Henry Ward Beecher escaped the charge of adultery and the taint of free love in the courts and within his church, but as previously suggested, both NWSA and AWSA suffered from that association in the mind of the general populace. Henry Cuyler Bunner's 1880 "Cartoons and Comments" and Joseph Keppler's centerfold cartoon "A Female Suffrage Fancy" in *Puck* (see fig. 6) demonstrate that both men imagined woman's suffrage as a dangerous force upending traditional gender distinctions, the family, and "appropriate" electoral results. As a result of women's threatening activism, the peaceful domestic scene envisioned in a corner of "A Female Suffrage Fancy" has in Poesque fashion vanished "Nevermore—Nevermore!" and front and center, a bewhiskered wife grinds "Female Deportment" and "Modesty" under her feet, while she casts aside her cookbook in favor of cigars, abandons her children, and drives ugly men at gun-point from the polling stations. The end result of enfranchised women? The election of an incompetent dandy and un-American Francophile: "Charlie de Simple," "A Handsome Fool." Intriguingly, several selections in this chapter expose similarly xenophobic reactions to Stanton's free love and divorce advocacy. The most subtle—presaging NAWSA's total disavowal of Stanton in 1896—include comments at the 1869 AERA convention from Harry Blackwell, Mary Livermore, Lucy Stone, and Phebe Hanaford in which condemnation of "Free Loveism" may be understood as shorthand for criticism of the meeting's presiding officer.

In addition to his duties as editor of the American comic weekly *Puck* (where he worked from 1877 until his death), Bunner (1855–1896) wrote poetry, adult and children's fiction, plays, and comic operas.[9] "Read religiously by tens of thousands, feared and denigrated by those who felt its wrath, *Puck* was one of America's most popular and influential magazines" by 1884, comments Richard Samuel West.[10] As a result, while Bunner's article and Keppler's cartoon serve as representative examples of Stanton's reception in 1880, they also shaped the opinions of *Puck*'s many readers.

From "William Lloyd Garrison Crucifies Democrats, Train, and the Women of The Revolution," William Lloyd Garrison and Elizabeth Cady Stanton, 1868[11]

Dear Miss Anthony:

In all friendliness, and with the highest regard for the Women's Rights movement, I cannot refrain from expressing my regret and astonishment that you and Mrs. Stanton should have taken such leave of good sense, and departed so far from true self-respect, as to be travelling companions and associate lecturers with that crack-brained harlequin and semi-lunatic, George Francis Train! You may, if you choose, denounce Henry Ward Beecher and Wendell Phillips (the two ablest advocates of Woman's Rights on this side of the Atlantic), and swap them off for the nondescript Train; but, in thus doing, you will only subject yourselves to merited ridicule and condemnation, and turn the movement which you aim to promote into unnecessary contempt. The nomination of this ranting egotist and low blackguard for the Presidency, by your audiences, shows that he is regarded by those who listen to him as on a par with the poor demented Mellen, and "Daniel Pratt," the "Great American Traveller."[12] The colored people and their advocates have not a more abusive assailant than this same Train; especially when he has an Irish audience before him, to whom he delights to ring the changes upon the "nigger," "nigger," "nigger," *ad nauseam.* He is as destitute of principle as he is of sense, and is fast gravitating toward a lunatic asylum. He may be of use in drawing an audience; but so would a kangaroo, a gorilla, or a hippopotamus.

It seems you are looking to the Democratic party, and not to the Republican, to give success politically to your movement! I should as soon think of looking to the Great Adversary to espouse the cause of righteousness. The Democratic party is the "anti-nigger" party, and composed of all that is vile and brutal in the land, with very little that is decent and commendable. Everything that has been done, politically, for the cause of impartial freedom has been done by the Republican party. And yet your reliance is upon the former rather than upon the latter party! This is infatuation.

Your old and outspoken friend,
Wm. Lloyd Garrison

Excerpt from Letter to Reverend Olympia Brown, Lucy Stone, c. 1868[13]

My dear Miss Brown

We got your letter, and receipt, at the right time—. I suppose you have seen the official vote in Kansas. 9000[14] is surely doing well—and though in the Spring, I thought we should surely carry the state in the Fall—I am still thankful for the really large vote we got. It will command us respect everywhere in the future, and we are bound to win. . . . Gov. Robinson[15] says, it is sure to be carried in Kansas, [wherever] it is urged on its own merits. But that it must not carry Train or Wood,[16] or Robinson— He says that you, and I, and Mrs. Stanton got the Kansas vote. That Train drew away more Republicans, than he won Democrats—&c. &c.

We are now in the midst of a serious quarrel with Miss Anthony, and Mrs. Stanton, and the Train admixture, from which we are trying to shield our association

We want *them* to have all the credit of the new alliance

Susan said at an executive meeting, the other day—that we were moved by "envy spleen, & hate" &c.

At all events, we shall try and keep the office of our ass. and her paper, separate.

From "Sharp Points," Jane Elizabeth [Hitchcock] Jones, 1868[17]

Parker Pillsbury—*My Dear Friend*: I have delayed writing that I might first read the back numbers of "The Revolution."

. . . you have started a paper that . . . is so entertaining, so spicy, and, with some exceptions, so grand, too in its tone and thought, where shall we find the like? Suffrage is fairly before the world. . . . But what means this new system of ethics of Mrs. Stanton—protesting against the enfranchisement of another man, black or white, until woman is enfranchised? I have not thus learned reform. . . .

I did not propose to discuss the question, especially with Mrs. Stanton; for, however good natured, and humorous, and delightful she is as a friend, I own to a little fear of her sharp points. Her reply to Mr. Garrison was what western people would call "mighty tall talk" to the pioneer of the anti-slavery cause, and doubtless afflicted many souls.[18] The author of *Hannah Thurston* and Mrs. Stanton may tell the world that the abolitionists were a set of tatterdemalions, just as Macaulay held up to ridicule George Fox and his followers; but the harm that results will fall mostly on themselves.[19] For we do our own souls a grievous wrong to undervalue any earnest, intelligent effort in a good cause, especially when its genuineness is stamped with the consecration of the whole man.

From "Mrs. Elizabeth Cady Stanton," Theodore Tilton, 1868[20]

I ONCE watched an artist while he tried to transfer to his canvas the lustre of a precious stone. His picture, after his utmost skill, was dull. A radiant and sparkling woman, full of wit, reason, and fancy, is a whole crown of jewels. A poor, opaque copy of her is the most that one can render in a biographical sketch.

Elizabeth Cady, daughter of Judge Daniel Cady and Margaret Livingston, was born November 12th, 1816, [*sic*] in Johnstown, New York,—forty miles north of Albany. . . .

A Yankee said that his chief ambition was to become more famous than his native town: Mrs. Stanton has lived to see her historic birthplace shrink into a mere local repute, while she herself has been quoted, ridiculed, and abused into a national fame. . . .

In the summer of 1867, the people of Kansas were to debate, and in the autumn to decide, the most novel, noble, and beautiful question ever put to a popular vote in the United States,—the question of adopting a new Constitution whose peculiarity was that it extended the elective franchise not merely to "white male citizens," but to those of what Frederick Douglass calls "the less fashionable color," and to those also of what Horace Greeley calls "the less muscular sex." Mrs. Lucy Stone and Miss Olympia Brown—helped by other ladies less famous, and by several earnest men, including the Hon. Samuel C. Pomeroy,[21] Senator of the United States—made public speeches at prominent places in that State, urging the people to give the new idea a hospitable welcome at the polls. This canvass was as chivalrous as a tournament, and abounded, from beginning to end, with romantic incidents. To hear from the lips of Mrs. Stone (in that delightful eloquence of conversation which she has never surpassed on the platform), a recital of the most serious or the most comical of these, is as pleasant an entertainment as a supper-table chat can well afford. Toward the close of that memorable campaign, Mrs. Stanton and Miss Anthony, like a reserved force, joined themselves to the general battle. Accidentally associated with them (first with Miss Anthony and afterwards with Mrs. Stanton) was Mr. George Francis Train,—soldier of fortune, hero of Fenianism, martyr to creditors, guest of jails, and candidate for the presidency. The "Tribune" has admiringly called Mr. Train "a charlatan and blatherskite."[22] Ampler justice compels me to add that he is, nevertheless, of all mountebanks the most amiable, and of all clowns the most innocent. These women of substance and this man of froth formed in Kansas a coalition which provoked their opponents to smiles, and their friends to regrets. Anxious watchers of the progress of the good cause were apprehensive that the flightiness of Mr. Train's speeches would bring the new question into disrepute. But the history of reforms in all countries, and especially in this, has shown that neither the wildest friends nor the fiercest enemies of a great idea can any more trample it under their feet than if they had trodden on a sunbeam. The result of the vote on the new Constitution was flattering beyond the most sanguine expectation. No wise observer of the signs of the times had looked for the adoption of that radical instrument, but only for a generous minority in its support. The figures stood nine thousand for, and nineteen thousand against. I have never met any student of American politics who was not greatly surprised thus to find that one-third of the voters in any State of the Union were sufficiently advanced in opinion to demand at the ballot-box the political equality of the sexes. If the anti-slavery party in Massachusetts, like the woman's suffrage party in Kansas, had received, on a first trial at the polls, one-third of the votes cast, the early abolitionists would have shouted for joy, and have rung their church-bells for a jubilee. Whether the vote in Kansas was increased or diminished by Mr. Train's harangues, I am unable to say. But it is proper to say that the anti-slavery movement, gathering, as it did, to its annual platforms, many of the greatest as well as some of the shallowest of human brains; and the woman's suffrage movement, constantly repeating, as it does, these same phenomena, thereby furnish to the world a magnificent proof of the universality of those great ideas which thus make known their power upon all classes of human beings, great and small, wise and simple, sane and crazy. God has ordained that the noble army of reformers, while marshaled by the choicest spirits of the age, should give honorable rank also to Tag, Rag, and Bobtail. I can see no reason why the gifted and anointed leaders of great movements should decline to make common cause with any and all who are willing to work for the common end.

After the election in Kansas, Mrs. Stanton, Miss Anthony, and Mr. Train made a slow progress eastward, stopping at the chief cities on their way, and addressing public meetings on woman's rights. These meetings provoked merited criticism on account of the performances of Mr. Train, who amused his audiences with the capers of a harlequin. The previous substantial reputation of the two ladies, as earnest reformers, was, on this account, greatly shaken. And yet their own speeches, on all these occasions, were grave, earnest, and impressive,—always worthy of their authors and of the cause. It was, therefore, supposed that the grotesque partnership would be only temporary, but it proved to be permanent. By the time the three travellers had reached New York, they had projected a weekly journal, which made its appearance at the beginning of 1868, under the topsy-turvying title of "The Revolution"; edited by Elizabeth Cady Stanton and Parker Pillsbury, and published by Susan B. Anthony. Like Jupiter Tonans[23] in the rainy season, this sheet always thunders. It is the stormiest of journals. Its pages, as one turns them over, seem to crinkle, flutter, and snap with electric heats. Examine almost any number of "The Revolution," and it will be found the strangest mixture of sense and nonsense known anywhere in American journalism,—a rag-bag of the most incongruous topics. The articles signed

"E. C. S." and "P. P." are full of force and fire,—seldom commonplace or tame. Mr. Pillsbury has a gorgeous and sombre imagination, which, when it plays about any subject that can bear its strong colors, makes some of his best essays truly magnificent. Mrs. Stanton, who is always in high animal spirits, and who, like a ripe grape, carries a whole summer's sunshine in her blood, fills her most serious articles with fun, frolic, and satire, and, even in her most humorous escapades, shows a rare vein of tenderness, pathos, and eloquence. She so abounds in metaphors and pithy phrases that a characteristic article from her pen is like a Chinese jar of chow-chow,—filled with little lumps of citron, apricot, and ginger, all swimming in a sweet and biting syrup. The political disquisitions of this co-working yet non-assimilating pair are sometimes grand and just, sometimes visionary and absurd, and sometimes outrageous and wicked. . . . But in speaking thus freely of this conglomerate sheet,—a journal, which, on its present plan, can never take a respectable rank among the influential presses of the country,—I must honorably say, on the other hand, that some of the noblest thoughts and utterances pertinent to this day and generation,—ringing words for liberty, justice, and womanhood,—glowing rebukes of false customs, social tyrannies, and degrading conventionalities,—eloquent appeals for a more liberal civil polity, and a more equitable social order,—fervid aspirations toward whatever dignifies human nature and purifies the immortal soul,— these, too, "thoughts that breathe and words that burn,"—are spread week by week upon the pages of "The Revolution," and from no brain oftener than from the fiery, wayward, scornful, sympathetic, and Christian soul of Elizabeth Cady Stanton.

I may now paint her features, and sum up her character.

Mrs. Stanton's face is thought to resemble Martha Washington's, but is less regular and more animated; her hair—early gray, and now frosty white—falls about her head in thick clusters of curls; her eyes twinkle with amiable mischief; her voice, though hardly musical, is mellow and agreeable; her figure is of the middle height, and just stout enough to suggest a preference for short walks rather than for long. In reality, however, she can walk like an Englishwoman,—though, if, during a stroll in the street, some jest sets her to laughing, she is forced to halt, cover her countenance with her veil, and shake contagiously till the spasm be past. The costume that most becomes her (and in which her historic portrait ought to be garmented) is a blue silk dress and a red India shawl,—an array, which, topped with her magnificent white hair, makes her a patriotic embodiment of "red, white, and blue."

Her gift of gifts is conversation. Her throne of queenship is not the official chair of the Woman's Rights Convention (though she always presides with dignity and ease), but is rather a seat at the social board, where the company are elderly conservative gentlemen, who combine to argue her down. I think she was never argued down in her life. Go into a fruit-orchard, jar the ripe and laden trees one after another, and not a greater shower of plums, cherries, and pomegranates will fall about your head, than the witticisms, anecdotes, and repartees which this bounteous woman sheds down in her table-talk. House-keeping and babies, free trade and temperance, woman's suffrage and the "white male citizen,"—these are her favorite themes. Many a person, on spending a delightful evening in her society, has gone away, saying, "Well, that is Madam de Staël alive again."[24]

From *History of Woman Suffrage*, Various Speakers, 1882[25]

The Executive Committee of the Equal Rights Association issued a call for the anniversary in New York, early in the spring of 1869. . . .

The anniversary commenced on Wednesday morning[26] at Steinway Hall, New York. . . . In the absence of the president, Mrs. Lucretia Mott, the chair was taken by Mrs. Elizabeth Cady Stanton, First Vice-President. . . .

STEPHEN FOSTER[27] laid down the principle that when any persons on account of strong objections against them in the minds of some, prevented harmony in a society and efficiency in its operations, those persons should retire from prominent positions in that society. . . . He objected, to certain nominations made by the committee for various reasons. The first was that the persons nominated had publicly repudiated the principles of the society. One of these was the presiding officer.

Mrs. STANTON: —I would like you to say in what respect.

Mr. FOSTER: —I will with pleasure; for, ladies and gentlemen, I admire our talented President with all my heart, and love the woman. (Great laughter.) But I believe she has publicly repudiated the principles of the society.

Mrs. STANTON: —I would like Mr. Foster to state in what way.

Mr. FOSTER: —What are these principles? The equality of men— universal suffrage. These ladies stand at the head of a paper which has adopted as its motto Educated Suffrage. I put myself on this platform as an enemy of educated suffrage, as an enemy of white suffrage, as an enemy of man suffrage, as an enemy of every kind of suffrage except universal suffrage. *The Revolution* lately had an article headed "That Infamous Fifteenth Amendment."[28] It is true it was not written by our President, yet it comes from a person whom she has over and over again publicly indorsed. I am not willing to take George Francis Train on this platform with his ridicule of the negro and opposition to his enfranchisement.

Mrs. MARY A. LIVERMORE: —Is it quite generous to bring George Francis Train on this platform when he has retired from *The Revolution* entirely?

Mr. FOSTER: —If *The Revolution*, which has so often indorsed George Francis Train, will repudiate him because of his course in respect to the negro's rights, I have nothing further to say. But it does not repudiate him. He goes out; it does not cast him out.

Miss ANTHONY: —Of course it does not.

Mr. FOSTER:—My friend says yes to what I have said. I thought it was so. I only wanted to tell you why the Massachusetts society can not coalesce with the party here, and why we want these women to retire and leave us to nominate officers who can receive the respect of both parties. The Massachusetts Abolitionists can not co-operate with this society as it is now organized. If you choose to put officers here that ridicule the negro, and pronounce the Amendment infamous, why I must retire; I can not work with you. You can not have my support, and you must not use my name. I can not shoulder the responsibility of electing officers who publicly repudiate the principles of the society.

HENRY B. BLACKWELL said: In regard to the criticisms on our officers, I will agree that many unwise things have been written in *The Revolution* by a gentleman who furnished part of the means by which that paper has been carried on. But that gentleman has withdrawn, and you, who know the real opinions of Miss Anthony and Mrs. Stanton on the question of negro suffrage, do not believe that they mean to create antagonism between the negro and the woman question. . . . I know that Miss Anthony and Mrs. Stanton believe in the right of the negro to vote. We are united on that point. . . .

Mr. DOUGLASS: —I came here more as a listener than to speak, and I have listened with a great deal of pleasure to the . . . splendid address of the President. There is no name greater than that of Elizabeth Cady Stanton in the matter of woman's rights and equal rights, but my sentiments are tinged a little against *The Revolution*. There was in the address to which I allude the employment of certain names such as "Sambo," and the gardener, and the bootblack, and the daughters of Jefferson and Washington, and all the rest that I can not coincide with. I have asked what difference there is between the daughters of Jefferson and Washington and other daughters. (Laughter.) I must say that I do not see how any one can pretend that there is the same urgency in giving the ballot to woman as to the negro. With us, the matter is a question of life and death, at least, in fifteen States of the Union. When women, because they are women, are hunted down through the cities of New York and New Orleans; when they are dragged from their houses and hung upon lamp-posts; when their children are torn from their arms, and their brains dashed out upon the pavement; when they are objects of insult and outrage at every turn; when they are in danger of having their homes burnt down over their heads; when their children are not allowed to enter schools; then they will have an urgency to obtain the ballot equal to our own. (Great applause.)

A VOICE: —Is that not all true about black women?

Mr. DOUGLASS: —Yes, yes, yes; it is true of the black woman, but not because she is a woman, but because she is black. (Applause.) . . . Woman! why, she has 10,000 modes of grappling with her difficulties. I believe that all the virtue of the world can take care of all the evil. I believe that all the intelligence can take care of all the ignorance. (Applause.) I am in favor of woman's suffrage in order that we shall have all the virtue and vice confronted. Let me tell you that when there were few houses in which the black man could have put his head, this woolly head of mine found a refuge in the house of Mrs. Elizabeth Cady Stanton, and if I had been blacker than sixteen midnights, without a single star, it would have been the same. (Applause.)

Miss ANTHONY: —The old anti-slavery school say women must stand back and wait until the negroes shall be recognized. But we say, if you will not give the whole loaf of suffrage to the entire people, give it to the most intelligent first. (Applause.) If intelligence, justice, and morality are to have precedence in the Government, let the question of woman be brought up first and that of the negro last. (Applause.) While I was canvassing the State with petitions and had them filled with names for our cause to the Legislature, a man dared to say to me that the freedom of women was all a theory and not a practical thing. (Applause.) When Mr. Douglass mentioned the black man first and the woman last, if he had noticed he would have seen that it was the men that clapped and not the women. There is not the woman born who desires to eat the bread of dependence, no matter whether it be from the hand of father, husband, or brother; for any one who does so eat her bread places herself in the power of the person from whom she takes it. (Applause.) . . .

Mrs. LUCY STONE: —Mrs. Stanton will, of course, advocate the precedence for her sex, and Mr. Douglass will strive for the first position for his, and both are perhaps right. If it be true that the government derives its authority from the consent of the governed, we are safe in trusting that principle to the uttermost. If one has a right to say that you can not read and therefore can not vote, then it may be said that you are a woman and therefore can not vote. We are lost if we turn away from the middle principle and argue for one class. . . .

HENRY B. BLACKWELL presented the following resolution:

Resolved, That in seeking to remove the legal disabilities which now oppress woman as wife and mother,[29] the friends of woman suffrage are not seeking to undermine or destroy the sanctity of the marriage relation, but to ennoble marriage, making the obligations and responsibilities of the contract mutual and equal for husband and wife.

MARY A. LIVERMORE said that that was introduced by her permission, but the original resolution was stronger, and she having slept over it, thought that it should be introduced instead of that one, and offered the following:

Resolved, That while we recognize the disabilities which the legal marriage imposes upon woman as wife and mother, and while we pledge ourselves to seek their removal by putting her on equal terms with man, we abhorrently repudiate Free Loveism as horrible and mischievous to society, and disown any sympathy with it.

Mrs. LIVERMORE said that the West wanted some such resolution as that in consequence of the innuendoes that had come to their ears with regard to their striving after the ballot.

Mrs. HANAFORD[30] spoke against such inferences not only for the ministers of her own denomination, but the Christian men and women of New England everywhere. She had heard people say that when women indorsed woman suffrage they indorsed Free Loveism, and God knows they despise it. Let me carry back to my New England home the word that you as well as your honored President, whom we love, whose labor we appreciate, and whose name has also been dragged into this inference, scout all such suggestions as contrary to the law of God and humanity.

LUCY STONE: I feel it is a mortal shame to give any foundation for the implication that we favor Free Loveism. I am ashamed that the question should be asked here. There should be nothing said about it at all. Do not let us, for the sake of our own self-respect, allow it to be hinted that we helped forge a shadow of a chain which comes in the name of Free Love. I am unwilling that it should be suggested that this great, sacred cause of ours means anything but what we have said it does. If any one says to me, "Oh, I know what you mean, you mean Free Love by this agitation," let the lie stick in his throat. You may talk about Free Love, if you please, but we are to have the right to vote. To-day we are fined, imprisoned, and hanged, without a jury trial by our peers. You shall not cheat us by getting us off to talk about something else. When we get the suffrage, then you may taunt us with anything you please, and we will then talk about it as long as you please.

ERNESTINE L. ROSE:[31] We are informed by the people from the West that they are wiser than we are, and that those in the East are also wiser than we are. If they are wiser than we, I think it strange that this question of Free Love should have been brought upon this platform at all. I object to Mrs. Livermore's resolution, not on account of its principles, but on account of its pleading guilty. When a man comes to me and tries to convince me that he is not a thief, then I take care of my coppers. If we pass this resolution that we are not Free Lovers, people will say it is true that you are, for you try to hide it. . . .

SUSAN B. ANTHONY repudiated the resolution on the same ground as Mrs. Rose, and said this howl came from those men who knew that when women got their rights they would be able to live honestly; no longer be compelled to sell themselves for bread, either in or out of marriage. . . .

Mrs. PAULINA W. DAVIS[32] said she would not be altogether satisfied to have the XVth Amendment passed without the XVIth, for woman would have a race of tyrants raised above her in the South, and the black women of that country would also receive worse treatment than if the Amendment was not passed. . . .

Mr. DOUGLASS said that all disinterested spectators would concede that this Equal Rights meeting had been pre-eminently a Woman's Rights meeting. [Applause.] They had just heard an argument with which he could not agree—that the suffrage to the black men should be postponed to that of the women. . . .

THE PRESIDENT, Mrs. Stanton, argued that not another man should be enfranchised until enough women are admitted to the polls to outweigh those already there. [Applause.] She did not believe in allowing ignorant negroes and foreigners to make laws for her to obey. [Applause.]

Mrs. HARPER (colored)[33] asked Mr. Blackwell to read the fifth resolution of the series he submitted, and contended that that covered the whole ground of the resolutions of Mr. Douglass.[34] When it was a question of race, she let the lesser question of sex go. But the white women all go for sex, letting race occupy a minor position. She liked the idea of working women, but she would like to know if it was broad enough to take colored women?

Miss ANTHONY and several others: Yes, yes.

Mrs. HARPER said that when she was at Boston there were sixty women who left work because one colored woman went to gain a livelihood in their midst. [Applause.] If the nation could only handle one question, she would not have the black women put a single straw in the way, if only the men of the race could obtain what they wanted. [Great applause.] . . .

ERNESTINE L. ROSE said . . . This Society calls itself the Equal Rights Association. That I understand to be an association which has no distinction of sex, class, or color. Congress does not seem to understand the meaning of the term universal. . . . I ask the same rights for women that are extended to men—the right to life, liberty, and the pursuit of happiness; and every pursuit in life must be as free and open to me as any man in the land. [Applause.] . . . I suggest that the name of this society be changed from Equal Rights Association to Woman's Suffrage Association.

LUCY STONE said she must oppose this till the colored man gained the right to vote. . . .

Mrs. STANTON: The question is already settled by our constitution, which requires a month's notice previous to the annual meeting before any change of name can be made. We will now have a song. [Laughter.]

Mr. BLACKWELL said that he had just returned from the South, and that he had learned to think that the test oath required of white men who had been rebels must be abolished before the vote be given to the negro.

He was willing that the negro should have the suffrage, but not under such conditions that he should rule the South. [At the allusion of Mr. Blackwell to abolishing the test oath, the audience hissed loudly.]

Mrs. STANTON said—Gentlemen and Ladies: I take this as quite an insult to me. It is as if you were invited to dine with me and you turned up your nose at everything that was set on the table.

Mrs. LIVERMORE said: It certainly requires a great amount of nerve to talk before you, for you have such a frankness in expressing yourselves that I am afraid of you. [Laughter and applause.] If you do not like the dish, you turn up your nose at it and say, "Take it away, take it away." [Laughter.] I was brought up in the West, and it is a good place to get rid of any superfluous modesty, but I am afraid of you. [Applause.] It seems that you are more willing to be pleased than to hear what we have to say. [Applause.] Throughout the day the men who have attended our Convention have been turbulent. [Applause.] I say it frankly, that the behavior of the majority of men has not been respectful. [Applause.] . . .

After a song from the Hutchinson Family, who had come from Chicago to entertain the audiences of the Association, the meeting adjourned.[35]

**Excerpt from Letter to Isabella Beecher Hooker,
Henry Browne Blackwell, 1869[36]**

Private

BOX 299 P.O [*sic*] NEW YORK
DEC 1. 1869

Dear Mrs Hooker

I hope you will regard as confidential the long and perhaps tedious history which I tried to give you, the other night, of our controversies & tribulations of the past two and a half years—

Believe me, I have *no desire* to undermine your confidence in Susan B., or Mrs S. —no wish to stir the ashes of unhappy controversies which I heartily wish forever buried—

But, in justice to Lucy & to the Cause, I wished to show you that there are *two sides* to this unhappy division & that, whatever may be the opinion of our New York friends, & the exceptional *intensity* of Lucy's views & convictions, she is *not* animated by malignity, nor desire of leadership—but solely by love of the Cause—

For the rest, I fully agree with you that *no one* must be *proscribed*; that we must let everyone work in his own way, but *not* put in the position of *leader-ship* any who are unwise, or incompetent leaders.

I am *thankful* that your brother is in that position—that we have now a leader who will not repel the most *orthodox*, nor the most *liberal* advocates of the cause—a man who enjoys the respect and esteem of *all*.[37]

The real object of the new organization is a society in which *all can work*, without compromising individual convictions or extraneous subjects, for the one object—*woman's Suffrage*—a society so representative that it can never be controlled by any person, clique, newspaper, or locality.

Now then—since you wisely desire *not to take sides* & since you are already one of the advisory counsel of Miss Anthony's organization—why not make your Ct. organization auxiliary to the Am Ass[n] & thereby make Mr Burton one of our Vice Presidents & yourself a member of our *Executive Committee*.[38]

By your tastes, principles & social position, you belong to our phase of this Movement—you can help keep it *American* in spirit & I will help you to do so. . . .

We are about to print a circular with the Constitution & names of officers— *May I print those of Mr Burton & yourself as the officers for Ct?* Please, say yes & oblige

Very truly yours
Henry B. Blackwell

Excerpt from Letter to Susan Howard, Isabella Beecher Hooker, 1870[39]

HARTFORD JANY. 2. 1870

Dear Susie[40]

. . . But I must not enlarge—for Susie—the rest of your letter has so stirred me up I shall have to inflict a long letter I fear on those topics—altho' I have neither time nor strength to do it—I should not attempt anything of the kind just now, were it not that I hope good may come of it in various ways—& when I have written & see how I come out, I will tell you one or more of the ways.

In the first place let me say, for your comforting that the plan for changing name of the Revolution has failed—chiefly because, Miss A. was advised so strongly against it by publishers & other gentlemen friends, I was not willing she should do it, simply to secure us as Editors (Corresponding or Assistant). That would lay upon us a responsibility & anxiety in making the new thing go, that we were not able to assume—so I also advised her not to change & we remain simply contributors, according to our pleasure & under no pledge whatever. My intention is to do for the paper all that I should have done, but I feel immensely relieved to be under no pledge & free from official responsibility. But as to the general principle that I should avoid all connection with that paper & refuse to write for it because the views of its Editor & Publisher are in some respects not quite my own, I cannot adopt it, nor do I think it can be reasonably defended. When brother Henry was invited to preach in Theodore Parker's assembly, I thought it one of the grandest opportunitis [sic] of his life & should have been pained and surprised had he refused it.[41] But here is my opportunity to preach Christ & his dear gospel of freedom & responsibility to five thousand people every week if I please—& I am urged to do it, with no limitations of any kind. Now suppose that anti christian words are to be found in that same paper— (I do not often find them there, not so often as I do in most of the so-called religious papers—)—how important that these be met & overcome if possible by my higher truths—my prayerfully considered expositions of Bible teaching. And this is just what the prospectus invites—what Susan & Elizabeth earnestly desire. Pray read that column carefully & tell me wherein the Revolution proposes or invites a wicked or undesirable practice—I heartily approve every word of the Prospectus & I think there are not many men or women in the country that would be capable of putting forth so generous an advertisement as that—so nice & discriminating especially after receiving such criticism & abuse as these two women have done. . . .[42]

But now we come to Mrs Stanton & her peculiar views—which are far more trying to meet than any thing Susan says or does, because the subject is so difficult to handle—& out of that difficulty comes many a misunderstanding because of the unwillingness of all parties to speak plainly & without circumlocution. I wrote Mrs Stanton before I ever saw her—for an exposition of her views & she sent me a pamphlet which I now enclose to you—saying they were there embodied. She has also said that they were substantially those of Robert Dale Owen as set forth by Horace Greely [sic] in one of his books.[43] I have always hoped to find time to read Owen as he probably gives a more clear & philosophic statement than Mrs Stanton has ever had time to do. She, I think has written & spoken from the promptings of a great, loving, motherly heart & it is plain that she has always had the interests of children in mind even more than parents—& out of the desire to protect them from the wretched inheritances they too often receive from uncongenial & discordant parents she has come to look upon easy divorce as a blessing & a necessity. But to say that she ever advocated this, as a means of *personal gratification* to woman or man is simply to insult her in my opinion—& yet that is what free love means if it means anything—& my indignation is aroused every time I hear this word used so loosely as it is coming to be.

This whole question of divorce & the proper relation & duties of husband & wife is the most profound that has ever come before the civilized world—it is up now & will not disappear from the public eye till it has been thoroughly probed & when it is finally & rightfully settled we may begin to look for the millennium—but not before. Meantime the good & faithful ones—Christ's own children will differ & differ & dispute & grow hot & angry—& anathematize each other, just as they did about slavery—& out of it all will come emancipation not only of women but hosts of little children—who will some day rise up to call blessed some of the early apostles who have suffered crucifixion as it were on their behalf. My [rule] then is—to watch the *life & conduct* of reformers—& [when] that is satisfactory, to listen to their opinions with respectful attention—to overthrow them in fair argument if I can—& to treat them uniformly with friendly courtesy. So long as a woman is faithful to every family duty—is just, tender & truthful I honor her in my heart & will listen to her words patiently—and when she adds to this a life of heroic service in the cause of truth & righteousness as Mrs Stanton has done & is attacked by enemies I will stand by her, at any cost—& however injudicious at times may be her utterances.

When I see as I do now from Mr Garrison's own conversation & letters what a man of prejudice—of passion of bad judgment he is & always must have been, I realize anew how patient & tolerant reformers should be of each other—the very stuff that makes them reformers, will make them persecutors also if they are not always on their guard.

And this is just the place where Lucy Stone seems to fail—insomuch that I am more & more afraid to listen to her—& feel driven away from her. Her husband told me in the course of a long conversation on the "differences"— that Mr Train went to Kansas on the invitation of one Wood a republican to lecture to whomever would hear on *Woman Suffrage* among other things; (Wood's mother was a Quaker—which accounted for his heresy it seems).

Mr Blackwell & Gov. Robinson & two or three others who were conducting the W. S. campaign thought it might be well for Susan to accompany Train & so get more democratic votes—while at the same time she could perhaps keep *him* straight on the negro question—Train being then against negro suffrage. *They accordingly advised & promoted her Kansas trips with Train* & she went as General Agent of the Equal Rights Assotn. & with their full approval on that whole Kansas campaign. Now I could hardly believe my ears when Mr Blackwell quietly told me this, in the beginning of the story—& so I waited a while & then asked him if I understood him rightly in saying thus & so—he said I did & then went on to show me that the thing didn't work well—that they thought they lost more republican votes for W. Suffrage by Train's advocacy than they gained democratic & were disgusted with the experiment. But Susan & Mrs Stanton did not agree with them—they thought the 9000 votes for W.S. a great gain—almost a victory—& were confident that Train had helped to gain it—& moreover they wanted to continue the coalition & lecture all the way home—& in New Eng. This was the *breaking spot* between them & the beginning of Lucy's embittered feeling—& according to Mr B. they all got angry & had hard times together after that—so that it was easy to find fault with Susan's management & ways of spending money &c &c—even in places where she had before been allowed to work in her own way & had escaped criticism.[44]

I could easily see, from all this story, how Mr Blackwell & his wife might have tolerated Train out there & hoped to make him useful to their two causes, negro suffrage & woman Suf. under the guidance of such a worker as Susan B—& yet how they might shrink from introducing him to the eastern public—but I cannot think they were honorable in throwing the whole blame on Mrs Stanton & Susan, when they themselves initiated the enterprise & only found by experiment that it was an undesirable one—according to their judgmt.

So much for that— Now worse than this, Mrs Lucy—who has known Mrs Stanton & worked with her & approved her for years without a suggestion of disapprobation so far as I can learn, *since that break* & because she dreaded sharing the odium that accompanied the Train campaign (east) has begun to accuse her of holding free love doctrines—while it is certain that Mrs S. entertains no new views—none that Mrs Lucy had not heard from her previously.

If there have been conversations between them & exchange of *speculations* on these most difficult questions in the days when they were agreed I hold it a breach of trust for Mrs Lucy to report these now, without asking permission & it is very certain that nothing in Mrs Stanton's life or writings warrants the charges she now makes. To illustrate the spirit of Mrs S. & her friendliness to Mrs Lucy I am going to send you by express a volume that I have borrowed for the purpose—please read the life of Mrs Stanton by Tilton (it is evidently something of an autobiography) & then her own notices of *Lucy Stone* & the other prominent reformers.

I chanced to read these for the first time just after receiving your letter—& I got great comfort from them I do assure you. I said to myself—if it is "cleaning Augean stables" to associate with such women as these let me turn hostler at once[45]—I cannot be in much better business—I do hope you . . . will read these—the one about Mrs Lozier too—& then when you hear reports of "street talk" remember what you have read & say in your *hear[t]*, at least, "I dont believe it." . . . [46]

Dear Susien [*sic*] you are in a hard place & I am not urging you to try to defend any body—but I do wish you could read & think & pray & keep your own heart warm & tender towards us who are called to a heavy warfare—& then some truth will work in to the minds & hearts of those about you without invitations of any sort. I hope you will take the Revolutn. for my sake & read it in your chamber. . . .

. . . On looking over your letter I am amazed at the words of Lucy Stone to Henry—I send you the constution [Constitution] & Officers of the National Suf. Assc. & wish the names might be pointed out of loose women or free lovers. Our object is "purely suffrage"—so much so that it is quite probable if the new Society finds *delegate* members to work well—& a Ex-Coun. [Executive Council] of 15 scattered *all over the U.S. an efficient working body*, we shall join them—sending delegates of our own & helping to elect officers—& ten to one Susan & Mrs S. will be elected to some somewhere—& then where will Mrs Lucy be—will she have to get up another Society & another?—for depend upon it wherever the work is most effic[i]ently prosecuted there will these old workers be found till the end comes—& the more they are accused of their associates the greater odium will the whole cause have to carry—since they are identified with it. It is like leaving foreigners without the ballot & thinking you have settled the question of their harmfulness to the country. They are here & disfranchisement will not annihilate them—but fraternizing will educate & gradually make them an integral part of the body politic. . . .

But enough—I shall tire you out—I only wish my dear brother could be persuaded to hear some of these things—not because I wish to wean him from his new alliance & friendships—but because he could be much more useful to them & to the whole cause by understanding the counter currents. Nothing could be more trying to me than to be driven to these investigations—but I shirked as long as I dared—& now I would gladly save him any such necessity by giving him briefly as possible the results. I am inclined to think it is well that he accepted that office—if he does not allow himself to be warped & set against other workers he can do great good there, by restraining & giving wise Counsel—& they will heed him because they will fear to lose him—& God speed the day when we may all join hands & prepare to go over the walls together. Oh Susie—*few men* know what this battle means—but many women, wives & mothers know & *feel* it all—feel it for their sisters if not for themselves—I am one of them—& I stagger under the weight of my load.

yrs. in love I.B.H.

From "Two Women of the Present," Eleanor Kirk [Eleanor Maria Easterbrook Ames], 1870[47]

There is nothing on earth more difficult than to draw truthful, and at the same time satisfactory and interesting, pen-pictures of one's personal friends. To depict virtues without flattery, to touch upon faults without offense, is almost an impossibility. Mrs. Stanton and Miss Anthony are personal friends of the writer, and to her the dearest and best of the sex they have striven so long and so successfully to benefit.

ELIZABETH CADY STANTON.

This woman is a stumbling-block and rock of offense to many of the opponents not only of Woman's Suffrage, but of women's rights in general. Certainly she fails to fill their idea of a "strong-minded woman," which is a being deficient in all the gentler and more tender qualities of her sex. The fact is, Mrs. Stanton has that rare mixture of masculine and feminine traits which when possessed by a man is called genius! but which in a woman is not apt to be dignified by the critics with so complimentary a name.

"Don't talk to me about Mrs. Stanton," said a hard-headed, hard-hearted man of the world not long since, who boasts that his wife is quite as much his property as the horse, dog, or establishment he had bought with an *inherited* fortune. "A woman who will go roaring round the country in the style she does, can not be possessed of the least womanliness or love for her children. She has children, I hear?"

"Yes, *sir, seven* of them," we replied proudly, and with a little sniffing of the air, which in a farmer's horse would be called "fractious."

"What kind of children are they?"

"They will not suffer by comparison with yours," was the rather curt reply.

"I have a genuine horror," he continued, "of females who are not domestic. My idea of a perfect woman, nobly planned, is a pleasant face, a bright eye, a graceful figure with a good sized waist, arrayed in clean, well-fitting calico set off by spotless linen—with a broom in her hands."

For the edification of this man, and that of the world at large, allow me to say that Mrs. Stanton has a pleasant face, a good figure, a sizable waist—sometimes wears calico, with the immaculate adornments he has a liking for, and is said to be as thorough and systematic a "sweepist" as she is "talkist."

Let us imagine an old fogy of the most fossilized sort being persuaded to listen to one of this lady's lectures. He walks into the hall, under protest of course, and is fully prepared to be disgusted and repelled by a bony, hard-featured, defiant woman whose every look will be a thrust, and every word and gesture an offense to his ideal of what is ladylike and becoming. As he sits awaiting with prophetic dread the entrance of this virago, behold a plump rosy woman, apparently about forty-five years of age, comes with gentle dignity to the front of the platform; a woman whose every look and gesture proclaims her "to the manner born"—whose natural pride in the good blood she bears in her veins gives her a dignity and queenly presence that many a taller woman might envy; a lady with handsome, round, regular features, a winning smile, and a beautifully shaped head crowned with curls of snowy white; nothing about her but her earnest, steady, keen eyes to show that she is strong-minded. Our fossil is first amazed—next bewildered—then fascinated—then convinced—not exactly of the doctrine of woman's suffrage, perhaps—but at any rate that a woman to be an advocate of that doctrine need neither be a fright nor a fury.

Intellectually, Mrs. Stanton is sharp and clear, cutting with Alexandrian sword through the hard knots of argument that many men waste so much time and patience in untying. But the sharpness does not in the least infect her manner, that is rounded, and softened, and polished to a degree rare even among women who are acknowledged *"reines du salon."*[48] Although her mind is what is generally called masculine, there is nothing in the least mannish about her; in her speech, gestures, general appearance, and dress she is only pure womanly. She is what we might imagine one of the old Roman matrons to be—Cornelia, for instance.[49]

About her lecturing there is a sure magnetism; she takes captive her audience, not by her reasoning and dignified speech alone, though both are rare, but by her actual presence as well, so much so, indeed, that she would doubtless possess the lawyer-like power of convincing an audience of what she was not entirely convinced herself.

Mrs. Stanton is a natural diplomat, and as President of this Republic she would never fail for want of executive and manipulating power.

Socially, this lady is even more pleasing than on the platform. Her lively sallies, sharpened by a wit that flickers like heat lightning through her conversation, making it brilliant without being scorching, have made converts to the cause of woman's suffrage from among a social class which its sterner and more rigid advocates could never reach. As she informed a recent audience, she has been married thirty years, during which her quiver has been gradually filled with fine sons and daughters. To be a mother of sons, is a blessing to a strong-minded woman. It naturally modifies her judgment of a sex to which her theories place her in an antagonistic position. It has had this effect upon Mrs. Stanton by her own confession.

There has been considerable fault found with this lady's management of her children. Her boys were allowed to jump, and shout, climb fences and trees, tear their clothes, stub their toes, and bark their shins, without the least reproof from their mother. The girls were actually driven out to walk and run, and were even allowed the privilege of jumping and climbing fences with their brothers.[50] It is said that a New York landlord, whose house the Stantons occupied for some time, determined on several occasions to invite Mrs. Stanton to find other premises. It was extremely aggravating, when he called, to see the boys coming down stairs, one after another, astride the banisters, and to hear the girls on the second floor executing a double shuffle, while the glasses on the elaborate chandeliers shook and rattled in apparent sympathy.

"I will not let this opportunity pass," he would say to himself; "this family must find other quarters. But," to use his own words, "just then Mrs. Stanton would come in smiling, and extend her plump little hand, comment upon the day, the general news, and make herself so agreeable, that upon my honor I hadn't the heart to say a word. Sometimes she would remark, when a bang and a whoop somewhat more startling than the preceding noises would issue from the stair-way or room above, 'What a noise those children are making! but they do take so much comfort, Mr. ——.' What *could* a man do under such circumstances? She made me respect her, for I knew that those children were not instructed to deceive me. There was no slinking into corners because the landlord had called."

Mrs. Stanton's writings are characterized by the same logical force and clearness, the same *esprit*, and the same choice and dignified diction. As editor of the *Revolution*, she has exerted a great influence over public opinion, the spicy little sheet having created no little consternation in the camp of the ultra-conservatives.

There may be a little too much of the "gay Greek" in the reckless way in which she overrides all criticism, and insists upon woman's right to do whatever she pleases, even to violating the rules of grammar, because she had no hand in making them; but if she is a little excessive in her claims, her manner of making them is so sparkling and graceful that she will be readily forgiven. There is a slight inconsistency about her in one respect, as there is indeed about most persons. With all her professed irreverence for prerogatives, she is not entirely democratic, the most hateful of aristocracies to her being that of sex.

As a wife, Mrs. Stanton, like another wife to whom reference is often made, is above suspicion, although her advocacy of the right of uncongenial married partners to divorce has caused the unjust aspersion that she is a free lover.[51] Indeed, that term is becoming exceedingly comprehensive nowadays, and would include, according to many, all women who claim in any degree the right of self-protection from abusive husbands. On this subject Mrs. Stanton is more than eloquent. It is safe to predicate that the remainder of her days will be more blessed, if possible, than those that have preceded them, on account of the peculiar sacredness of her future work. She sees with that accurate, straightforward, far-seeing vision which has always characterized her judgment, that the political rights of her sex are almost won. She has piloted the bark of woman's suffrage into calm and easy sailing, and can now intrust the helm to the hands and brains she has so successfully educated, while she seeks this new avenue of labor—the education of wives, and the alteration of our divorce laws.

Mrs. Stanton is as resolute and independent as she is brilliant and logical. When asked on one occasion by a person whose conscience was in rather a fussy condition, how she could consent to receive money from George Francis Train for the purpose of carrying on the *Revolution*, she replied: "Mr. Train, in my estimation, is much purer than many men who abuse him. He may be fanatical in some respects, but as far as I know, he is an honest man. Still, that is neither here nor there. If the Prince of Darkness himself should come to me and say, 'Mrs. Stanton, here is money which you may devote, if you please, to the enfranchisement of woman,' I should say, 'Devil, I thank you.'"

As a mother, Mrs. Stanton is wise, thoughtful, and loving, and is like Solomon's wise woman in looking to the ways of her household.[52] Whether she knows how to darn stockings, that most highly lauded and strictly exacted of feminine accomplishments, is a question that must be left to the imagination of the reader, for concerning this point the writer is not informed. In the words of the immortal Rip, "Here's to her health, and her family's! May they live long, and prosper!"[53]

Excerpt from Letter to Harriet Jane Hanson Robinson, Lucy Stone, 1879[54]

[Regarding Harriet Jane Hanson Robinson's request that Stone contribute to the *History of Woman Suffrage*][55]

I do decline any and all participation in the Suffrage history which Mrs Stanton, and Susan Anthony are preparing. . . .

I must therefore beg you not to mention the subject to me again, I am more than content to be left entirely out of any Suffrage history those ladies may publish. I can readily understand how much they must prefer to write their own Statement of their connection with Geo. Francis Train, Mrs. Woodhull, Laura D Fair and the Mormons, and it is easy to see that they will be glad to get you, and other women, who had only regret for their action in connection with those persons, to appear with them in history.

From "Cartoons and Comments, [Henry C. Bunner?], 1880"[56]

If the aged but volatile Susan B. ever settles down into the silence of satisfied ambition, we may look for some startling changes in the social constitution of this country. When the women have those alleged "rights," which Susan B., and Mrs. Cady Stanton, and the lovely Lilly [*sic*] Devereux Blake[57] have so long jointly and severally yearned for—*then*, it is promised us, we shall see the purification of politics through the gentle feminine influence of the new crop of voters. Frankly, we don't believe it. It takes a good deal more than sweetness and light to purify politics in this sweet land of moral liberty. The experiment has been tried, more than once; and as a general thing it resulted in making the experimenter a subject for purification. . . .

We view with a vast apprehension the prospect of female suffrage. With us, it is more a question of etiquette than anything else. How are we to adjust our ideas to the changed conditions of society? What are to be the rules and regulations of the electioneering business, when the ladies begin purifying? We want to understand all about it. For instance, how will they manage about the drinking question? It ought to be possible to hold an election without liquor; but, as a matter of fact, it isn't. And if you want to purify politics, you must go right in, and tackle the politician in his native lair. There may be more women than men in the United States; but what chance will that miserable majority have against the skilled ballot-stuffers of the sterner sex? They must needs win the assistance of these practiced politicians, if they want to purify with any solid results. Thus, you see, it will come down again to the regular old-fashioned feminine influence, exerted in a slightly different manner, on a new class of men. Lovely woman, after all, will have to deck herself in robes of beauty, will have to wreathe her lips with smiles, and coy and coquet just as she has done for the past dozen-or-so thousands of years, if she wants to get the assistance of the men whom she can no more fight than the toughest band of Amazons that ever lived could fight a company of U.S. Regulars, working a Gatling gun.

And here arises another perplexing problem. Will the unpurified politicians consent to be cajoled by the new type of charmers? The coarsest of "heelers" is susceptible to the sweet magic of woman's charms; but it is probable that he will be conservative enough to prefer the old style of woman to the new. It is doubtful if his veins will run "all crinkly, like curled maple," when he stands at the bar alongside of a trousered Doctor Mary Walker of the future, who gulps down her gin-and-water, and remarks, with husky dignity: "Tell yer, shir, thish coun'ry's got to be pu[f]ried, pu-pu-furipied—an' we'sh jush er fellersh ter do it, now you bet. Jake, obli'sh me by hangin' zhat up!"[58]

It is too disgusting to talk about, the whole shameless lunacy. Purify Politics, indeed!—these ranting women who have not even been able to purify their own organization from the fatal association of free-lovers and spiritualists! Yes, indeed, it is within the power of women to purify our political system; but the duty lies with a very different class of women. We shall have no more swindling politicians, no more thieves in high places, no more unfaithful servants, when men in general understand that their wrong-doing will cost them the love, the respect and the companionship of their wives, their daughters, their sisters and their mothers. *There* is the opportunity for the women of America to be as Spartan as they please, and do good in the pure and beautiful way in which Nature meant them to go about their business.

NOTES

1. Stewart, "Garrison, William Lloyd."

2. McFeely, *Frederick Douglass*, 175.

3. The 1867–1868 arguments about how to best use funds bequeathed for African Americans during Reconstruction "brought a barrage of criticism down upon Garrison," explains Henry Mayer, "in which the terms 'Iscariot' and 'Arnold' were frequently used" (*All on Fire*, 611–612, quoted on 612).

4. According to Brodie, Jones made five thousand dollars in three years of lecturing (*Contraception and Abortion in 19th-Century America*, 129–130; *SP* 2:243, 244n1).

5. McMillen, *Lucy Stone*, 222–225, quoted on 222.

6. Collins, "How to Pitch a Magazine (in 1888)."

7. Ibid.; Hedrick, *Harriet Beecher Stowe*, 357; Kessler, *Daring to Dream*, 261.

8. Campbell, *Tempest-Tossed*, 130, quoted on 35.

9. Lynch, "Bunner, Henry Cuyler." At this time, Bunner was also the probable author of "Cartoons and Comments" (West, *Satire on Stone*, 233–243).

10. West, *Satire on Stone*, 1.

11. William Lloyd Garrison and Elizabeth Cady Stanton [E.C.S.], "William Lloyd Garrison Crucifies Democrats, Train, and the Women of The Revolution," *Revolution*, 29 January 1868.

12. Like Train, Pratt and Mellen were frequent presidential aspirants. Eccentric itinerant lecturer and writer Daniel Pratt (1809–1887) claimed to have walked across most of the United States during his lecture circuits and asked to be addressed as "The Great American Traveller." He was well known on college campuses, speaking on the solar system and the human mind. The Boston chemist, abolitionist, and writer Dr. George Washington Mellen was routinely mocked in Boston, Chicago, and New York newspapers for his appearance at abolitionist meetings and his presidential campaigns, up through the mid-1870s; according to Henry Brewster Stanton, he died in an insane asylum ("New-England Anti-Slavery

Convention," *New York Daily Times*, 2 June 1855; "Pendleton's Presidential Pilgrimage," *Chicago Tribune*, 23 December 1875; Ruchames, *The Letters of William Lloyd Garrison, Volume II*, 727n9; Stanton, *Random Recollections*, 70; Horowitz, "Pratt, Daniel").

13. Lucy Stone to Reverend Olympia Brown, 6 January [1868], Olympia Brown Papers, A-69/M-133, Folder 129, courtesy of the Schlesinger Library, Radcliffe Institute, Harvard University.

14. Women suffrage went down to defeat 19,857 to 9,070, while black suffrage was also defeated, 19,421 to 10,483 (Dudden, *Fighting Chance*, 130).

15. Charles Robinson (1818–1894) was the brother-in-law of Stone's brother Bowman Stone. The passage of the Kansas-Nebraska Act (1854) enabled territories like Kansas to settle the slavery question through popular sovereignty. Trained as a physician, the Free Soil Robinson played a pivotal rule during Kansas's violent progression to free-state statehood, a time known as "Bleeding Kansas." He served as the state's first governor and, after the Civil War, a University of Kansas regent and president of the state historical society (Dudden, *Fighting Chance*, 109; Rawley, "Robinson, Charles").

16. Kansas state senator Samuel Newitt Wood supported woman suffrage but alienated supporters of African American male enfranchisement by blocking legislative amendments that excluded female suffrage; during the Kansas referendum he established a newspaper, the *Chase County Banner*, in which he did not directly oppose African American men's enfranchisement but did make "undeniably anti-black comments" there. Wood's "irritating combination of high ideals and expedient short-cuts" worried woman's suffrage advocates (Dudden, *Fighting Chance*, 120–122, 109).

17. Jane Elizabeth [Hitchcock] Jones, "Sharp Points," *Revolution*, 9 April 1868.

18. Stanton's acerbic wit was in full force in this piece, an article prefaced by Garrison's letter to Susan B. Anthony of 4 January in *Revolution*. Perhaps most stinging is her characterization of Garrison in the guise of Hamlet's Act II conversation with the ghost in Shakespeare's *Hamlet*:

> For a third of a century slavery was one of the most important subjects on the theatre of American affairs. In that great drama, Mr. Garrison acted a leading part. This letter shows that he, full of the illusions as well as of the actualities of the scene, lags superfluous on the stage, seemingly unconscious of the fact, that the curtain has fallen upon the last act, that the lights are extinguished, and the audience gone to their homes.
>
> In respect even to the *débris* of negro agitation, Mr. Garrison is as dead as the "royal Dane." We suspect he thinks so himself; for, we have not heard of him for years at any of those anti-slavery convocations where he used to forge thunderbolts and gather laurels. He should be content to remain in his sepulchre, and not "revisit the glimpses of the moon," and by diatribes like the above endeavor to frighten live people from their appropriate sphere.
>
> "Rest! rest, perturbed spirit!" (Garrison and Stanton, "William Lloyd Garrison Crucifies Democrats")

19. American novelist and poet [James] Bayard Taylor is the author of *Hannah Thurston* (1863), a novel satirizing American social reformers. Seventeenth-century English

preacher George Fox founded the Society of Friends, or Quakers; after the publication of his two-volume *History of England* (1848) nineteenth-century historian, essayist, and politician Thomas Babington, Baron Macaulay, was criticized by a number of religious sects for his treatment of their role in the progression of British history and culture.

20. Tilton, "Mrs. Elizabeth Cady Stanton," 332–333, 354–357, 358–359.

21. Samuel Clarke Pomeroy (1816–1891) was a leader in establishing Kansas as a free state and was twice elected a U.S. senator, despite charges during his career of election bribery and fraud. He was also actively involved in and attempted to profit from procurement of Native American lands in Kansas for settlers and the railroad but was a consistent supporter of suffrage for women and African Americans (Plummer, "Pomeroy, Samuel Clarke").

22. The *New York Tribune* described Train as "the vagabond charlatan and blatherskite" in a piece critiquing his repugnant views of slavery ("G. F. Train—C. M. Clay").

23. "Tonans," or "Thunderer," is a titular epithet associated with Jupiter.

24. Born in France to Swiss parents, the internationally influential author and salonnière Anne-Louise-Germaine de Staël-Holstein, or Germaine de Staël (1766–1817), was well known for her scintillating conversation and political acumen.

25. Stanton, Anthony, and Gage, *History of Woman Suffrage*, 2:378–379, 381–383, 388–390, 391–392, 396, 397–398.

26. The "anniversary" meeting of AERA commenced on 12 May 1869.

27. Abolitionist Stephen Symonds Foster (1809–1881) denounced Republicans for their inconsistent support of full rights for African Americans after the Civil War. He shared the feminist and abolitionist activism of his wife, Abigail Kelley Foster.

28. Train, "Letter from Geo. Francis Train." Train's rambling letter begins with a summary of its subject matter. Its initial words read, "THAT INFAMOUS FIFTEENTH AMENDMENT." Thereafter, he praises female doctors as professionals, claims that women are better at keeping secrets than are men, and defends mothers like Stanton, mothers-in-law, and stepmothers. Train also condemns abortions and characterizes "THAT INFAMOUS FIFTEENTH AMENDMENT" as a "two-faced" "farce."

29. Blackwell refers to activism centered on married women's property rights and divorce laws—reforms that would seek to enable married women to own property and their own wages, for example, or to gain custody of their children in the case of divorce. Since 1860, Stanton had declared marriage merely a civil contract, rather than a divinely sanctioned union unbroken until death. Many regarded her idea as a direct attack on marriage and family and an embrace of free love. Blackwell's motion attempts to protect the AERA from such aspersions and, more subtly than Symonds Foster, condemns Stanton as unfit to lead and represent reformers—an inference repeated in the anti-free-love commentary (by others) that follows.

30. Universalist minister, author, and suffrage activist Phebe Ann Coffin Hanaford (1829–1921) served on *The Woman's Bible* revising committee. Her marriage to homeopathic physician Joseph H. Hanaford was incompatible, although they never divorced. She was active in both NAWSA and AWSA. In 1877 she maintained a principled defense

of her companion, Ellen Miles, the source of contention for some congregational members, and ultimately formed a new congregation of supporters. The relationship of forty-four years endured until Miles's death in 1914 (Cody and Barber-Braun, *A Mighty Social Force*, 147, 227–242, 369).

31. Of Polish birth, freethinker and feminist lecturer Ernestine Louise Siismondi Potowski Rose (1810–1892) rejected her parents' Judaism because of its subordination of women; she left Poland in 1827 and associated in the United States with utopian socialist Robert Owen, also marrying another of his followers, William Ella Rose. Rose was active in efforts to reform New York's property and divorce laws and married women's legal rights, as well as temperance, abolition, and woman suffrage (Miller, "Rose, Ernestine").

32. Abolitionist, woman suffrage reformer, editor, and women's health lecturer Paulina Kellogg Wright (1813–1876) with Ernestine Rose campaigned for married women's property rights in the 1830s. Her first husband, Francis Wright, joined her during this time in abolitionist activism. After his death in 1845, Davis delivered lectures to women on anatomy and physiology, using a mannequin to demonstrate. A leader in the woman suffrage movement, Davis worked closely with Stanton and Anthony and also established the periodical *Una*, passing the editorial work to Caroline Healey Dall in 1855. After her second marriage to widower Thomas Davis, the couple settled in Providence, Rhode Island (Lederman, "Davis, Paulina Kellogg Wright").

33. Poet, novelist, and political activist Frances Ellen Watkins Harper (1825–1911) was born in Baltimore to free parents. In 1860 she married Fenton Harper, who died in 1864. Their only child died two years before Harper. She lectured on women's and African Americans' enfranchisement; her fiction and verse also treat the plight of African American women, in slavery and during Reconstruction; and she was one of the founders of the National Association of Colored Women (Locke, "Harper, Frances Ellen Watkins").

34. Read in the Wednesday morning session, the fifth resolution is as follows, "*Resolved*, That any party professing to be democratic in spirit or republican in principle, which opposes or ignores the political rights of woman, is false to its professions, short-sighted in its policy, and unworthy of the confidence of the friends of impartial liberty" (Stanton, Anthony, and Gage, *History of Woman Suffrage*, 2:385).

35. The Hutchinson Family Singers turned their reformist interests in temperance, abolition, and woman's suffrage into musical campaigns. They wrote reformist lyrics to the popular tunes of black minstrelsy and church hymns, producing the original American "protest song," and were wildly popular, especially in the 1840s. They frequently sang at conventions such as this one (Gac, *Singing for Freedom*).

36. Henry B. Blackwell to Isabella Beecher Hooker, 1 December 1869, ALS 4 pp., New York [NY], Isabella Beecher Hooker Collection, courtesy of the Harriet Beecher Stowe Center, Hartford, CT.

37. Henry Ward Beecher was elected the first president of AWSA after it was formed in November 1869.

38. Isabella Beecher Hooker established the Connecticut Woman Suffrage Association (CWSA) in October 1869; in one of her several attempts to unify the Boston and New York

suffrage groups, she ensured that the organization remain independent of either entity. The Reverend Nathaniel Burton was Hooker's minister; he and his wife, Rachel, were also personal friends of the Hookers, occasionally boarding in their home, and later becoming neighbors. Burton's younger brother, Henry or "Eugene," married Hooker's daughter Mary after their engagement in 1863. Burton shared the Hookers' interest in woman suffrage and was elected as the CWSA's first president (Campbell, *Tempest-Tossed*, 102; White, *The Beecher Sisters*, 98).

39. Isabella Beecher Hooker to Susan Howard, 2 January 1870, ALI 18 pp., Hartford, Isabella Beecher Hooker Collection, courtesy of the Harriet Beecher Stowe Center, Hartford, CT.

40. Susan Raymond Howard (1812–1906) and her husband, John Tasker Howard (1808–1888), a wealthy Brooklyn couple, were good friends of Henry Ward Beecher and his siblings. John purchased the building for Beecher's first Plymouth Church and suggested that Henry would be a good candidate to lead the church. The couple even named one of their children "Henry Ward Beecher Howard." John—no fan of the woman suffrage movement—angrily contacted John Hooker after Isabella wrote to Susan, accusing Stanton of the free love charges that Susan apparently also broached with Isabella. This same month John and Susan Howard's son Joseph, editor of the *New York Sun*, informed John Hooker that Henry Ward Beecher's affair with Elizabeth Tilton was common knowledge in Brooklyn, information that may have accentuated the pious Howards' sensitivity and defensiveness in regard to "Free Loveism" (*Some Memories of John Tasker Howard, 1808–1888, and His Wife Susan Taylor Raymond, 1812–1906* [n.p.: 1909]; Applegate, *The Most Famous Man in America*, 2, 202–203, 207; White, *The Beecher Sisters*, 173; Campbell, *Tempest-Tossed*, 128).

41. In *A Discourse of the Transient and the Permanent in Christianity*, a May 1841 ordination sermon, Transcendentalist and Unitarian minister Theodore Parker (1810–1860) denied the spiritual authority of Jesus of Nazareth and his miracles, as well as the "infallible inspiration of the Bible": "It seems difficult to conceive any reason why moral and religious truths should rest for their support on the personal authority of their revealer, any more than the truths of science on that of him who makes them known first or most clearly," he urged, adding, "Christianity . . . is absolute, pure morality; absolute, pure religion; the love of man; the love of God acting without let or hindrance" (Myerson, *Transcendentalism*, 351, 358). As a result of this sermon and with few exceptions he was denied pulpit exchanges with other Unitarians; moreover, his radical stances on abolition and woman's rights offended many. In 1845 a large group of potential parishioners asked him to preach for them, but because of his notorious reputation, they were able to rent a space only in the Melodeon Theater in Boston. There, Parker would preach his radical theology, built around his notion that the church could "organiz[e] the American Idea" of principled life and action (Grodzins, *American Heretic*, 460–467, quoted on 467).

42. See, for example, the first issue of *Revolution*. Citing four primary subjects for the paper (politics, religion, social life, and new commercial and financial policies), the prospectus advocates in politics "Educated Suffrage, Irrespective of Sex or Color; Equal Pay to Women for Equal Work; Eight Hours Labor; Abolition of Standing Armies and

Party Despotisms; Down with Politicians—Up with People!" For religion it espouses
"Deeper Thought; Broader Idea; Science not Superstition; Personal Purity; Love to Man
as well as God." For social life the prospectus advocates "Morality and Reform; Practical
Education, not Theoretical; Facts not Fiction; Virtue not Vice; Cold Water not Alcoholic
Drinks or Medicines"; it further eschews "Quack Advertisements." Its long list of finan-
cial concerns includes these: "America no longer led by Europe. Gold like our Cotton
and Corn for sale. Greenbacks for money. An American System of Finance. American
Products and Labor Free. Foreign Manufactures Prohibited. Open doors to Artisans and
Immigrants" (*Revolution*, "The Revolution; The Organ of the National Party of New
America").

43. Scottish-born freethought radical, editor, congressman, and author Robert Dale
Owen (1801–1877) was an active proponent of fertility control and liberal divorce laws.
With fellow Scottish freethought author and reformer Frances Wright (1795–1852), he ed-
ited the *Free Enquirer*. He published his views on divorce in its pages, and his divorce
legislation made Indiana the "'divorce capital' of the nation" (Passet, *Sex Radicals and the
Quest for Women's Equality*, 200n7). Hooker likely refers to Horace Greeley and Robert
Dale Owen, *Divorce* (1860), or Greeley, *Recollections of a Busy Life . . . Also, a Discussion
with Robert Dale Owen* (1868).

44. For the special meeting convened by AERA officers, without Stanton and Anthony,
and subsequently repeated and apparently concocted charges of financial irregularity during the Kansas campaign, see Barry, *Susan B. Anthony*, 186–187; SP2:153, 163n5; Dudden,
Fighting Chance, 141, 247n61.

45. A reference to Hercules's fifth labor—cleaning the stables of King Augeas.

46. Hooker refers to Theodore Tilton's "Mrs. Elizabeth Cady Stanton" (excerpted
in this volume) and Stanton's "The Woman's Rights Movement and Its Champions in
the United States." In the latter essay, Stanton extolls Stone's extemporaneous speaking
abilities, early leadership in the woman suffrage movement, education, career as an abolitionist, marriage protest, and recent activism in Kansas. Speaking of her refusal to take
husband Henry Browne Blackwell's name, Stanton observes, "I honor her for her steadfast
principle." The Reverend H. B. Elliot, however, rather than Stanton, wrote "Woman as
Physician," the chapter in *Eminent Women of the Age* on the activism of physician, suffrage
leader, and lecturer Clemence Sophia Lozier (1813–1888), who established the first medical
college for women in New York (*Eminent Women of the Age*, 332–361, 362–404, 392–394,
quoted on 393).

47. Eleanor Kirk, "Two Women of the Present," *Phrenological Journal and Packard's
Monthly* [old series 51; new series 2, no. 1] (July 1870): 57–59.

48. "Salon queens."

49. Cornelia (c. 190–102 BCE) was a daughter, mother, and wife of respected political
figures—notably the mother of the populist "Gracchi," Tiberius and Gaius (both killed for
their radicalism)—and a renowned woman in her own right. Through the Christian era,
writers extolled her "as a model of Roman motherhood" (Dixon, "Cornelia").

50. Typically, Stanton's parenting was depicted positively in the press; she related stories of her children's notoriously wild antics in her lectures largely to highlight her own

maternal acumen and advice. The period of renting in the New York area would begin in 1862, when Stanton sold her Seneca Falls home and moved to Brooklyn to join Henry Brewster Stanton, who had taken a position as deputy collector at the New York Custom House in 1861 (Ginzberg, *Elizabeth Cady Stanton*, 106). Her three eldest boys, Neil, Kit, and Gat, ranged from twenty to seventeen in 1862 and occasionally lived with their parents. Her younger children, Theodore, Maggie, Hattie, and Bob, ranged in age from eleven to three then. In May 1863 Stanton wrote Elizabeth Smith Miller to confirm that Miller's sons had arrived for a visit and to report that the cousins were constantly active and enthralled with professional baseball (*SP* 1:486–487). However, a more serious event that likely reflected poorly on Stanton's parenting occurred in 1862, when Neil, clerking for his father in the Custom House, accepted a bribe.

51. When rumors circulated about the infidelity of Pompeia, the wife of Julius Caesar, Caesar divorced her, "saying that although he knew nothing of the affair, 'Caesar's wife must be above suspicion'" (*Oxford Dictionary of Reference and Allusion*, s.v. "Caesar's wife").

52. See Proverbs 14:1: "Every wise woman buildeth her house: but the foolish plucketh it down with her hands."

53. In the early 1860s renowned American author and actor Joseph Jefferson III (1829–1905) adapted a dramatic script of Washington Irving's *Rip Van Winkle*; first staged in New York in 1866, it became a blockbuster hit through the end of his life (McArthur, "Jefferson, Joseph, III").

54. Lucy Stone to Harriet Jane Hanson Robinson, 4 March 1879, copy in the hand of Lucy Stone, Papers of Harriet Jane Hanson Robinson and Harriette Lucy Robinson Shattuck, A-80/M-110, Folder 58, Schlesinger Library, Radcliffe Institute, Harvard University, Cambridge, MA.

55. Harriet Jane Hanson Robinson (1825–1911) was a Lowell (MA) mill worker, author, and suffragist; she married antislavery journalist William Robinson and was a former AWSA ally. Harriot Stanton Blatch wrote the chapter in *History of Woman Suffrage* on AWSA and Stone's efforts. At this time Anthony had won over Robinson to NWSA, and in letters through 1882 she instructed Robinson in effective strategies to bring other AWSA leaders into the NWSA fold (Kerr, *Lucy Stone*, 208, 279n8).

56. [Henry C. Bunner?], "Cartoons and Comments," *Puck*, 14 July 1880, 336.

57. Novelist and New York suffrage leader Lillie Devereux Blake (1835–1913) was a close friend of Stanton's.

58. Bunner quotes from James Russell Lowell's "The Courtin'," whose sweethearts, Huldy and Zekle, marry; Lowell tapped into postbellum nostalgia for "the quaintness . . . of a bygone, nearly legendary culture" during an era in which "urban and technological realities" butted up against older "agrarian ideals" (Burns, "Yankee Romance," 74). Lowell's late 1860s revisions heightened the traditionally gendered qualities of the courting couple (Voss, "The Evolution of Lowell's 'The Courtin','" 50). Author, physician, woman suffrage and dress reformer Mary Walker (1832–1919) commonly wore the "Bloomer" costume and male attire; she was arrested repeatedly for this "offense." For twenty years the *National Police Gazette* publicized her efforts at dress reform in ways that directly influenced public

opinion in the late 1870s and early 1880s. It "published items about her and made fantastic stretches of imagination to connect her to any form" of ostensible feminine deviancy. "Because Mary chose to dress in pants rather than a skirt, her body became an accepted object of public scrutiny and mockery, with depictions of her as a hybrid male-female" (Harris, *Dr. Mary Walker*, 170).

The *Woman's Bible* Controversy (1896)

The selections in this chapter reflect upon Stanton's late November 1895 publication of *The Woman's Bible* and span a relatively brief period—between January and May 1896. Although the book generated great controversy, tangible and long-standing precedents for Stanton's religious critique existed. In the 1880s the publication of a widely promoted (and then reviled) Revised New Testament (1881), the increasing proliferation of biblical exegeses (including Voltaire's satirical *Commentary*, a text Stanton read in 1882), and Frances Willard's *Woman in the Pulpit* (1888) all foregrounded Stanton's serious interest in *The Woman's Bible* as a viable intellectual project.[1]

Willard's biblical commentary offers a unique lens with which to analyze such assumptions. After assuming the leadership of the powerful Woman's Christian Temperance Union (WCTU) in 1879, Willard encountered a troubling reality: male Protestant church leaders who had previously welcomed her as a popular lecturer "consistently resisted any exercise on her part of independence or power" in this new role. *Woman in the Pulpit* details her initial and public exploration of that problem. In its pages, Willard sought to highlight the ways in which churchmen cherry-picked (men's translations of) biblical passages subject to literal interpretation; through that selective process they restricted women from undertaking leadership positions in the church, she argued, calling additionally for women's interpretations of scripture. In the foregoing one sees common objectives in Stanton's and Willard's attempts to prompt civic conversations about the apparent tensions between organized religion and women's autonomy. Why did only Stanton's endeavor provoke a maelstrom within NAWSA, of whose members WCTU constituted a significant number?

Importantly, although *Woman in the Pulpit*—and Willard's other efforts to shake up male church hierarchy—aroused reactionary protests, her impeccable religious credentials and cultural influence remained secure. "Willard epitomized American Protestant Christianity," explains Ruth Bordin, who also emphasizes the similarities between the intent of Willard's and Stanton's books. "Her constituents contested her when she pushed them too hard in directions they found uncongenial, but few of them hated her and none dared denounce her."[2] It must be conceded, however, that despite the fact that both women investigated the ways in which organizational religion subordinated women and both hoped that new exegetical approaches would stimulate public debate, Stanton alone refuted the divinity of Jesus of Nazareth and regarded the Old Testament as barbaric mythology, positions with which Willard felt deep discomfort. "The Protestant hierarchy was hardly pleased by *Woman in the Pulpit*," Bordin reiterates emphatically. "It was aghast at" Stanton's project. The initial idea of *The Woman's Bible* appealed to Willard, and she briefly joined the revising committee before understanding its radical scope. But in December 1895, at the WCTU's quarterly meeting, delegates formally disavowed Stanton, the committee, and her book. Nonetheless, the relationship between Stanton and Willard remained cordial and respectful of their shared interests in the cultural and political restrictions of women's independence.[3]

The selections in this chapter from "The Washington Convention," from Susan B. Anthony's "Remarks" to NAWSA delegates (both in January 1896), and from Jean Brooks Greenleaf's "Letter" (in May 1896) underscore the extent to which Anthony had lost control of the leadership she had carefully selected to secure the vote. Even Greenleaf (1831–1918), the current president of the New York State Woman Suffrage Association and a friend of Anthony's, seemed mainly interested in correcting Horace L. Green's mischaracterizations of Carrie Chapman Catt three months previously.[4] More pointedly dismissive of Stanton, however, at the Washington convention the majority voices of conservative and pragmatic NAWSA activists listened, unmoved, to Anthony's pleading *cri de coeur*—despite the best efforts of a few outlier radicals like Charlotte Perkins Stetson, later Gilman, whose fiction and nonfiction prose would articulate an impassioned feminist vision in the twentieth century. Stanton, despite her outsized self-satisfaction, was undoubtedly also stung by Avery's scathing assessment of her publication's literary and intellectual merit. She reprinted the text of Anthony's appeal as an appendix to the second volume of *The Woman's Bible* (1898), entitled "'The Woman's Bible' Repudiated," along with a characteristically mordant repurposing of scripture: "'The Truth shall make you free.'—*John viii., 32.*"[5]

Anticipating Stanton, in his March 1896 *Free Thought Magazine*, editor and publisher Horace L. Green (c. 1828–1903) adapted biblical references to defend her "martyred truth." Moreover, in this number and in other issues,

> multiple contributors within the freethought community engaged in a spir-
> ited debate about Stanton and *The Woman's Bible*. That they were mainly
> defending Stanton herself, however, seems clear, because, as Kathi Kern
> maintains, most critics seemed not to have read the book.[6] Nonetheless, in
> terms of assessing her reception at the century's turn, their opinions held
> weight, for the *Free Thought Magazine*, along with the *Truth-Seeker*, consti-
> tuted "the two leading liberal organs" at this time.[7] Green, who founded the
> *Free Thought Magazine* in Ithaca, New York, in 1882, published it for twenty-
> one years there and in Chicago until his tragic death, an apparent suicide,
> in 1903.[8]

From "The Washington Convention," *Woman's Journal*, 1896[9]

The twenty-eighth annual convention of the National-American W.S.A. opened Thursday morning, Jan. 23, 1896, in the Church of Our Father, Washington, D.C., the president, Miss Anthony, in the chair. . . .

MRS. AVERY'S REPORT.

In the absence of the corresponding secretary, Mrs. Rachel Foster Avery, her report was read by Miss Isabel Howland.[10] It said, in part: . . .

During the latter part of this year, the work of our Association has been in several directions much hindered by the general misconception of the relation of the organization to the so-called "Woman's Bible." As an Association we have been held responsible for the action of an individual (an action which many of our members, far from sympathizing with, feel to be unwise) in issuing a volume with a pretentious title, covering a jumble of comment (not translation, as the title would indicate), without either scholarship or literary value, set forth in a spirit which is neither that of reverence or inquiry. If the organization were not in so many quarters held responsible for this work, I should feel it out of place to mention it here; but I should be untrue to my duties as secretary of this Association did I fail to report the fact that our work is being damaged. I recommended that we take some action by resolution to show that the Association is not responsible for the individual actions of its officers when acting unofficially and as individuals simply.

"Remarks of S[usan] B[rownell] A[nthony] to the National-American Woman Suffrage Association," Various Speakers, 1896[11]

EDITORIAL NOTE: This, the main debate about the *Woman's Bible* took place at a public session in the afternoon of 28 January 1896. Lillie Blake tried to find a compromise during an Executive Committee meeting on 25 January 1896, proposing that criticism of the *Woman's Bible* be struck from Rachel Avery's report while "the part stating that the Association had no connection with it be allowed to remain." SBA made strenuous objection. The two parts of Avery's attack were equally objectionable, she said, and "[f]or the association to pass this disclaimer will be but the beginning of an inquisitorial censorship to which there will be no end." Blake withdrew her motion. This report of the debate on January 28 is the most complete, and it served as the chief source for the version of SBA's remarks in the official report of the proceedings. A peroration from the official report is appended to the source text, set off by angle brackets. (*Report of the Twenty-eighth Annual Convention, 1896*, pp. 29 [*sic*], *Film*, 35:304ff.)[12]

[28 JANUARY 1896]

The interest of the closing afternoon centered in the report of the Resolution Committee.[13] The resolutions were discussed, amended in various particulars, and finally adopted as given below. Resolution 8, referring to the Woman's Bible, was the subject of sharp discussion.[14] As soon as it was before the Convention it was moved by Mrs. Colby and seconded by Mrs. Thomas[15] of Maryland that it be laid upon the table. The motion was lost. Mrs. Stetson[16] moved to amend by striking out all after "religious opinions," thus dropping off all reference to publications. She thought the Association should not take cognizance of the action of individual members. Mrs. Avery said that anything done by any member which seemed to strike at the organization should be taken notice of. She had found no greater obstacle to the work of organizing than the general public misconception of the relation of this organization to the Woman's Bible. This is the blow from which we are suffering. The organizers write that a great deal of time and strength is wasted in having to make explanations and doors are closed in the faces of the suffragists. Mrs. Colby spoke in favor of the amendment. Mrs. Hallowell[17] thought it was not right to particularize in this way. Mrs. Simmons[18] of South Dakota moved that the words, "with the so called Woman's Bible," be stricken out. This was seconded by Major Merwin.[19]

[175]

Mrs. Whitney[20] of St. Louis thought the Woman's Bible had done harm, but that we could educate people to understand that we were not responsible for it. This resolution commits us to a policy of negation.

Mrs. Blake opposed the second amendment, agreeing with a point made by Mrs. Colby that if harm had been done this resolution would not neutralize it, because it would not be known. She said one of the great objections brought forward by opponents of woman's emancipation is that women are priest ridden and hidebound in their views. If this resolution is carried it will be used against us confirming this belief.

Mrs. Johns[21] said that many of us were in entire sympathy with Mrs. Stanton. But if those who oppose our disavowing anything were doing field-work and finding doors slammed in their faces; people saying that they would not have anything to do with your organization as long as it had anything to do with the Woman's Bible, they would change their opinion.

Miss Keyser[22] of New York said she had been engaged in organizing, and she had never had such an objection offered. When people had spoken to her about it she had replied she swore by Mrs. Stanton as a suffragist and not as a theologian. Mrs. Stryker[23] of Kansas said, so soon as we make a disavowal of this work, we shall raise such opposition as we have never met before. We should have courage to stand to-day and ignore such objections. Miss Lewis[24] of North Carolina and Miss Yates[25] both spoke of the difficulty that the "Woman's Bible" had placed in the way. Major Merwin opposed the resolution. He remembered when it was said of the woman suffragists that they were all free lovers and that men all wore long hair. Suppose the Association had passed resolutions about this, what absurd position it would to-day seem to have occupied. Mrs. Diggs[26] said it was the wisdom of life to know when to make exceptions. She thought this was the exception and ought to be taken cognizance of in a resolution. She did not suppose Mrs. Stanton would object to our telling people what she had often said herself that this "Woman's Bible" was an individual work. Mrs. Addison[27] of Kansas said she had had this objection to meet in her work.

Mrs. Catt said that the report had gone out all over the country that this matter had come up in the Association, and if we do not pass the resolution it will stand that we are responsible. The "Woman's Bible" has been seriously injurious to the work of organizing. We all know that if Mrs. Stanton had produced something that had increased our membership we would all have been glad to declare that she was an officer of our association and that we wanted to share the honor with her. The people in a district in the southern part of Illinois had been writing all the year about organizing there. As much work was done there as was done in any of the States that were organized, and everything was ready. After the "Woman's Bible" was published the report came from this district that they did not dare to take an organizer and we had to withdraw. Every organizer has reported that they met the obstacle of the "Woman's Bible" everywhere. No lecturer who has not been in the field since December 1 has any right to say that it has not injured us. I have had hundreds of letters expressing this. I should feel sorely discouraged about organization and that we cannot do what we have planned if this resolution is not carried. The condition will be that we shall be considered to have endorsed the "Woman's Bible" and we shall be put back many years.

Miss Hatch[28] thought we should not hurt Mrs. Stanton by passing it but we might the organization, and she would prefer that we maintained a dignified silence and let the whole thing drop.

Mrs. Cary[29] said in Brooklyn they had never found that the "Woman's Bible" had done them harm. Mrs. Chapman[30] of Brooklyn called for Miss Anthony who said in substance as follows:

The one distinct feature of our Association has been the right of individual opinion for every member. We have been beset at every step with the cry that somebody was injuring the cause. You have endorsed me and I was born a heretic. I consider it great waste of time, and I have told Mrs. Stanton so, to descant on the barbarisms of 6,000 years ago. When people then did a cruel and brutal thing, they claimed to do it by command of God, and so it has been since. I always distrust people who know so much about what God wants them to do to their fellows. All the way down the history of our movement there has been the same contest on account of religious belief. Just forty years ago one of the most beautiful spirited men on our platform said, "You had better never hold another convention than let Ernestine L. Rose[31] stand on your platform," because that Polish woman who always stood for justice and freedom did not believe in the verbal inspiration of the Bible.[32] Did we banish Mrs. Rose? Now a lot of new people come up and go over the same old ground. The question is whether you will sit in judgment on a woman that has written views different from yours. If she had written your views you would not object. There was a person once, in the early days, who wanted us to pass a resolution that we were not free lovers, and I was not more shocked then than I am to-day at this.[33] It looks like the reviving of the old censorship. We have been growing larger and broader and I thought we had got away from this. When Lucy Stone[34] did not take the name of her husband, many claimed it injured the cause and Olympia Brown[35] said once, she had to spend much of her time in explaining that she was legally married. Suppose we had passed resolutions against a woman not taking her husband's name. Thank God! we had strength not to do it. To pass such a resolution is to set back the hands on the dial of reform. I would say to the organizers, tell them we have all sorts of people in the Association and that a Christian has no more right on our platform than an atheist. When this platform is too narrow for all to stand on, I shall not be on it. I have endured many things in the convention that I thought would harm the cause.[36] Who is to set up a line? Neither you nor I can tell but Mrs. Stanton will come out triumphant and that this will be the greatest thing ever done in woman's cause. Lucretia Mott[37] at first thought Mrs. Stanton had injured the cause of woman's rights by insisting on the demand for woman suffrage, but she had sense enough not to pass a resolution about it. When in 1860 Mrs. Stanton made a speech before the committee in favor of a bill making drunkenness a cause for divorce, many people thought she had killed our cause.[38] Just think of it. You ought to be able, girls, to stand this and go on with your work and say this has nothing to do with Mrs. Stanton's views on the Bible. I should be pained beyond expression if we are not broad enough to drop this.[39] We need not mind what the newspapers say about it. They are only talking to say something, and not because they care about the Bible. I have yet to see the first editorial word from an honest soul that takes the position that the Bible was directly inspired. You might just as well give up resolving or your hands will be full. Are you going to cater to the whims and prejudices of people that don't like this or that? The two women that stood by Lucy Stone in keeping her own name were Mrs. Stanton and myself. Who are these people who are troubled about this? They are people that have not thought. If you fail to teach women a broad catholic spirit, I would not give much for them after they are enfranchised. If they are going to do without thinking, they had better do without voting. They are not yet indoctrinated in the broad principles of this Association that knows no creed line. We draw out from other people our own thought. If, when you go out to organize, you go with a broad spirit you will create and call out breadth and toleration. You had better organize one woman on a broad platform than 10,000 on a narrow platform of intolerance and bigotry.

<I pray you all, vote for religious liberty to each and all, without censorship, without inquisition. This resolution adopted will be a vote of censure. It cannot mean less.>[40]

The resolution was favored by Mr. Blackwell and Rev. Anna Shaw,[41] after which three votes were taken by roll call. The two amendments were defeated and the resolution adopted by 51 to 41 according to the count of this writer but the official record shows 53 to 40.[42]

The corresponding secretary's report was then taken from the table and was adopted, save the paragraph criticizing the "Woman's Bible." Unfinished business referred to the executive session, Wednesday morning.

"Elizabeth Cady Stanton Convicted of Heresy," Editorial Department [Horace L. Green?], 1896[43]

At the late "National Woman Suffrage Convention," held at Washington, D.C., Mrs. Elizabeth Cady Stanton, the oldest and most prominent woman suffrage advocate in America, was tried and convicted of heresy and punished, not by burning or imprisonment, but by resolution, passed by a majority of ten. The prosecuting attorney was one Mrs. Catt, an appropriate name for such proceedings. The indictment upon which Mrs. Stanton was convicted charged her with being the author of "The Woman's Bible"—or in other words, attempting to improve on "The Word of God." The resolution was to the effect that Mrs. Catt, Mrs. Blackwell, and the other pious members of the association did not desire to be held responsible for the heresies of Mrs. Stanton.[44] No one had ever asked them to be responsible. No one had ever thought of holding them responsible. No one suspected any of them of having the courage, the honesty or the ability to accomplish the work that Mrs. Stanton had done in behalf of Liberty and Humanity. It was generally understood that the Blackwells and Catts and the smaller fry—the recent converts who voted for the resolution—were a set of bigots who were constantly on their knees begging favors of the church, and that they all greatly enjoyed reading in the Holy Bible that their grandmother Eve was made out of one of Adam's smallest ribs—that they all admired the saying of St. Paul, who declared that if women desired to know anything they must ask their husbands at home.

But we suspect that this resolution will not entirely annihilate Mrs. Stanton's world-wide reputation, as the most advanced woman in America, and the acknowledged leader of the Woman's Suffrage Movement. As to the Woman's Bible, it will only increase its sale.

This is not the first instance in this world where a great reform leader has been arraigned, tried, convicted, and punished by a set of ignorant, bigoted, mental Lilliputians, who had not the intellectual capacity to comprehend the great work that their convict was engaged in. We will here cite a few noted historical examples:

Some nineteen hundred years ago there was born in Bethlehem of Judea a child who became a radical reformer. Who, like Mrs. Stanton, believed that the Bible the people of that day all swore by as the only word of God needed to be revised, and he took the liberty to improve upon it—to make it accord more nearly with Liberty, Justice and Truth. The old version said: "Thou shalt love thy neighbor and hate thy enemy," but Jesus changed this orthodox statement and made it read: "Love your enemies, bless them that curse you, do good to them that hate you, and pray for them which despitefully use you and persecute you." The orthodox Bible of that day taught the doctrine of revenge: "An eye for an eye and a tooth for a tooth," but Jesus revised that cruel doctrine and made it read: "Resist not evil, but whosoever shall smite thee on thy right cheek turn to him the other also." In fact nearly all of Christ's "Sermon on the Mount," now so much admired, consists of the revision or restatement of the then old Bible.[45] But it appears that there were a class of bigots at that period who did not desire to be responsible for Christ's heresy, and we read that they "took counsel against Jesus to put him to death."[46] Passing resolutions had not come into fashion at that time; they punished him by nailing him to a cross.

A later instance of this kind of heresy that Mrs. Stanton has recently been convicted of is that of Giordano Bruno. He did a little revising of the Bible. He denied that the Bible, when properly construed, taught the doctrine of Transubstantiation and of the Immaculate Conception, and like Mrs. Stanton, he endeavored to put a more humane, scientific and reasonable construction on "God's Word," but he found a large number of people who did not wish to be responsible for such vilification of the Holy Scriptures and, as up to that date, punishment by resolution had not been invented, they decided that the only way to save their reputations was to burn Bruno at the stake and scatter his ashes to the four winds of heaven. And so on the seventeenth day of February, 1600, the Blackwells and Catts and their bigoted associates of that ignorant day kindled a fire around the body of the brave and noble iconoclast and looked on with ecstasy as they saw his quivering flesh burn to embers.[47]

But to come down to more modern times. A few years ago there was in Boston a great preacher. His name was Theodore Parker. He was at one time the editor of the *Scriptural Interpreter*, a paper in which he was engaged in doing the very same kind of work that Mrs. Stanton has been doing—trying to make the Bible a little more reasonable—as it were, re-editing some portions of it. Like Mrs. Stanton, he considered the Bible the product of Man and not of a God. This grand man knew from his inmost soul that injustice was wrong, and he could tolerate it in the Bible no more than in any other book. And when he came to preach his ordination sermon in Boston in 1841 on "The Transient and Permanent in Christianity," in vulgar parlance, he "let the cat out of the bag"—that is, he denied the special authority of the Bible and of Christianity, and asserted there was but one true religion, and that was the "absolute religion," the religion of Humanity—love to God and love to Man. This alarmed the clergy and laity of the Unitarian sect, and as crucifying and burning at the stake were not then in vogue, punishment by resolution was introduced in their stead. It was resolved, as in the case of Mrs. Stanton, by the godly Unitarians that they would not be responsible for such abominable infidelity as Theodore Parker was preaching in Music Hall in Boston.[48]

The three above briefly stated examples of persecution, for about the same identical crime that Mrs. Stanton has been convicted of, are sufficient to illustrate what we desire to establish: that such trials and convictions prove the truth of the new Gospel of Evolution,—that progress is the eternal law of the universe and can not be prevented or stayed by persecution. The advocates of a great truth may be nailed to the cross, or burned at the stake, or resoluted out of "respectable orthodox society," but as it was with the martyr John Brown,[49] their souls go marching on, and future generations are sure to do them justice. Jesus Christ was killed upon the cross, but he, in spirit at least, rose from the dead. Bruno was burned at the stake, but ever since he has been more alive than ever he was before the day of his death. Parker was anathematized by his Christian brethren, for defending the liberty of mankind, and his natural body now lies buried under the silvery skies of Italy, but as he stated in his last moments, there is another Theodore Parker in America who is carrying forward the works of reform inaugurated by the great Free Thought preacher in his lifetime.[50]

Whether people believe in what Jesus is reported to have taught or not, there are few living in civilized countries but know something of the story of his life, and no reasonable person can doubt but that he was a man much in advance of the day and generation in which he lived, and that he was an honest reformer trying to make the world better. The parable of the Good Samaritan establishes that claim if it be conceded that he was the author of it. Now we inquire: Where can you find persons who would be proud to trace their genealogy back to the persons who put Jesus to death?

Giordano Bruno, whose body was burned in the city of Rome on the seventeenth day of February, 1600, by Christian bigots for the crime of endeavoring to give the world a better religion, is not dead. His soul has been marching on ever since. And on the ninth day of June, 1889, the Free Thinkers of the civilized world united in erecting a magnificent statue on the precise spot where his body was burned, amid the unbounded enthusiasm of some 30,000 spectators, to the joy and satisfaction of every lover of liberty on this planet and to the dismay of its enemies.[51] Can you, reader, refer us to any such honor that has recently been paid to the bigots who kindled the fire that destroyed his precious and valuable life?

There is no minister of this country, living or dead, more revered than is the memory of the great humanitarian preacher, Theodore Parker. The Unitarians who cast him out of their fellowship while he was living can not now honor him enough. They have really made a saint of him and few of them visit Italy without making a pilgrimage to his grave. His sermons and addresses that were anathematized by Unitarians at the time they were delivered are now issued by the Unitarian publishing houses, and you can not find a Unitarian in America that will admit for one moment that any of his ancestors were the enemies of Theodore Parker. It would seem that Parker's Unitarian persecutors never had any children.

So we say to Mrs. Stanton and her many friends: Have no fears, past history proves conclusively that the future will do this brave, honest woman full justice,

> "For Humanity sweeps onward; where to-day the martyr stands,
> On the morrow crouches Judas with the silver in his hands;

Far in front the cross stands ready and the crackling fagots burn,
While the hooting mob of yesterday in silent awe return
To glean up the scattered ashes into History's golden urn."[52]

"Mrs. Greenleaf's Letter," Jean Brooks Greenleaf, 1896[53]

ROCHESTER, NEW YORK,
MARCH 24, 1896.

Editor of the Free Thought Magazine:

DEAR SIR: —A few days since I received a copy of the *Free Thought Magazine*, with a marked article entitled "Elizabeth Cady Stanton Convicted of Heresy," which I have read with care and no little interest. Will you permit me to say a few words respecting it?

That what I have to say may not be misunderstood, I will state that, in respect to the resolution in question, I stand with Miss Susan B. Anthony, "irrevocably and unalterably opposed to it." I think the subject should never have been introduced in the Convention; that it was no business of ours, as an association, whether Mrs. Stanton, or any other woman, wrote or did not write a Bible, or whether we personally liked or disliked the Bible in question. It was, it appears to me, a grave mistake, but it was not made by church-bound women. Mrs. Catt, to whom you allude, is not a "bigot constantly on her knees begging favors of the church." Indeed, her theological position is altogether different from the one pictured. But she is a practical woman and has found in her work of organization, as have those working with her, that there are those—a by no means limited number— who *did* hold the association responsible for the issuance of the Woman's Bible, and that such belief was a stumbling-block in the way of organization; especially was this true in the south and west.[54] It was thought best, therefore, by some of the officers of the association, to make a public repudiation of the publication. It seems incredible that such a course should have been deemed necessary, especially by the liberal-minded women who did it. Had these women borne the opposition that the pioneers of our cause encountered, the roars of the present lion in the way would not have stricken them with such terror.

But Mrs. Stanton is not injured. No one has forgotten the debt of gratitude that all women owe to her. Those who object to her Bible will continue to object. Those who esteem it highly will do so and live. It is simply out of the association, as indeed it always was. Time will place the crown of the victor where it belongs, and bring the day when liberty of thought will be recognized, because the fetters of old superstitions of sex and creed have passed away.

Most respectfully,
JEAN GREENLEAF BROOKS.

NOTES

1. Kern, *Mrs. Stanton's Bible*, 72–73, 71; DuBois, *Woman Suffrage & Women's Rights*, 165, 174n22.

2. Bordin, *Frances Willard*, 160–163, 172.

3. Ibid., 173; *SP* 6:5n4, 206–208.

4. *SP* 6:140–141n2.

5. Stanton and Revising Committee, *The Woman's Bible, Part II*, 217.

6. *Mrs. Stanton's Bible*, 174; for Kern's full assessment of this reception, see *Mrs. Stanton's Bible*, 172–222.

7. Brandt, "Free Thought in Oregon," 192. Brandt emphasizes the cultural impact of these two magazines and ostensibly of their editors. "Since most liberal organizations were very small and disorganized," she remarks, "these two exceptions to the rule gave freethinkers hope that real power might yet be achieved" (203n90).

8. Green and his wife were found dead in their bed, with their gas oven running. The couple was said to be in poor health and in financial distress ("Free Thinker and Wife Are Suffocated in Bed," *Chicago Daily Tribune*, 31 October 1903).

9. "The Washington Convention," *Woman's Journal*, 1 February 1896.

10. The independently wealthy woman suffrage reformer Rachel G. Foster (1858–1919), later Avery, began her service as corresponding secretary in 1881. The niece of Emily Howland, Isabel Howland (1859–1942), was most active as a woman suffrage advocate in New York (*SP* 5:4n1, 6:169n1).

11. *SP* 6:14–24. Editor's note: "*Woman's Tribune*, 1 February 1896; *Proceedings of the Twenty-eighth Annual Convention of the National-American Woman Suffrage Association Held in Washington, D.C., January 23rd to 28th, 1896*, ed. Rachel Foster Avery (Philadelphia, n.d.), 93."

12. Editor Ann D. Gordon's editorial note in *SP* 6:14–15. Gordon is the author of the editor's notes quoted in subsequent endnotes for this chapter.

13. Ibid., 6:19n1. Editor's note: "Each state's delegation to the convention selected one of their number to serve on the Resolutions Committee, making in this year a committee of thirty-three members. See *Report of the Twenty-eighth Annual Convention, 1896*, pp. 17–18, *Film*, 35:304ff."

14. Ibid., 6:19n2. Editor's note: "'That this Association is non-sectarian, being composed of persons of all shades of religious opinion, and that it has no official connection with the so-called "Woman's Bible," or any theological publication.' (*Report of the Twenty-eighth Annual Convention, 1896*, p. 91.)."

15. Ibid., 6:19n3. Editor's note: "Mary Henrietta Bentley Thomas (1845?–1923), a Quaker from Sandy Spring, Maryland, served as president of the Maryland Woman Suffrage Association from 1894 to 1904. She also contributed the state chapter to volume four of the *History of Woman Suffrage.* (Lawrence Buckley Thomas, *The Thomas Book, Giving the Genealogies of Sir Rhys ap Thomas, K.G., the Thomas Family Descended from Him, and of Some Allied Families* [New York, 1896], 60, 200; Federal Census, 1900; Sandy Spring Museum; *History,* 4:695–700; *Friends' Intelligencer* 80 [1923]: 150; Maryland State Archives, Vital Records Indexing Project, Death Record Index, 1910–1951.)."

16. Ibid., 6:19n4. Editor's note: "Charlotte Ann Perkins Stetson (1860–1935), later Gilman, was already known as a writer, thinker, and strong lecturer before she published her most famous work, *Women and Economics* (1898). She qualified as a delegate from California at this convention, though she had left the state in 1895. (*NAW*; *ANB*.)."

17. Ibid., 6:19n5. Editor's note: "This was meant to be Caroline Hallowell Miller (1831–1905), widow of the attorney and teacher Francis Miller, who had charge of a school for girls in Sandy Spring, Maryland. An active member of the National association in the 1880s, she gained a reputation as an excellent speaker. Through local, state, and national societies, she pursued suffrage until the end of her life. (*Woman's Journal,* 16 September 1905; *Friends' Intelligencer* 62 [1905]: 575; *History,* 3:254–55, 956; 4:20, 72, 114, 147, 263, 267, 296, 695, 697, 1100.)."

18. Ibid., 6:19n6. Editor's note: "Anna Rebecca Johnson Simmons (1848–1936) was a member of the Resolutions Committee. A graduate of Cornell College in Iowa, she accompanied her husband, Thomas Simmons, to Dakota Territory in 1884 or 1885, when he was sent to organize a Methodist Episcopal church in Faulkton. The National-American sent Anna Simmons into Missouri as a lecturer in 1895, and from that year to 1900, she presided over the South Dakota Equal Suffrage Association. In the twentieth century, she worked more closely with the state and national Woman's Christian Temperance Union. (*SEAP*; *History,* 4:791; C. H. Ellis, *History of Faulk County, South Dakota, Together with Biographical Sketches of Pioneers and Prominent Citizens* [Faulkton, S.D., 1909], 298, 303–4; South Dakota Death Index.)."

19. Ibid., 6:19n7. Editor's note: "James Burtis Merwin (1829–1917), delegate to the convention from Missouri, was a noted temperance advocate and former editor of the *American Journal of Education,* a journal he founded in 1867. (*ANB*.)."

20. Ibid., 6:20n8. Editor's note: "Victoria Geraldine Conkling Whitney (c. 1857–?), a delegate from the Missouri Equal Suffrage Association and a member of the Resolutions Committee, would soon be at the center of a dispute between rival suffrage associations in the state. She was brought to Missouri from Ohio by her widowed mother in the 1870s. An early start as a teacher culminated in a year as a professor at the Missouri School of Mines in Rolla. There she met Professor Geordie Z. Whitney, a graduate of Oberlin College and the University of Michigan. After their marriage in Boston in 1886 and several cross-country trips in search of good health, the Whitneys settled in Springfield, Missouri, just before G. Z. Whitney's death in May 1889. In her widowhood, Victoria Whitney trained for the law, helped by older brothers who practiced law in Missouri and Kansas. By one account, she was first admitted to the bar in Kingman, Kansas, where Lucius Conkling practiced.

Reports of her birth vary widely; the year given here is derived from her marriage registration that gives her age as twenty-nine. (Anne André Johnson, *Notable Women of St. Louis, 1914* [St. Louis, 1914]; *The History of Pettis County, Missouri, Including an Authentic History of Sedalia* [N.p., 1882], 581; *Rolla New Era*, 1, 22 September 1883, 28 March 1885, 19 May 1888; Registration of marriage, Boston, April 1886, vol. 372, p. 50, Massachusetts Archives; Will of Geordie Z. Whitney, Greene County Archives and Records Center, Springfield, Mo.; St. Louis city directory, 1896; with research assistance from Melody Lloyd and Sherry Mahnken, Missouri University of Science and Technology.)."

21. Ibid., 6:20n9. Editor's note: "Laura Lucretia Mitchell Johns (1849–1935) was recruited into the Kansas Equal Suffrage Association in 1884, not long after her move to Salina from Illinois, and she won election as president of the association in January 1887. Johns retained that position until 1895. In the meantime, her loyalties and duties grew more complex: she simultaneously served for several years as superintendent of the franchise for the Kansas Woman's Christian Temperance Union and organized the Kansas Woman's Republican Association. Johns worked for many years as an organizer for the National-American association, heading this year into Idaho as part of an amendment campaign. Johns and her husband left Kansas for California in 1911. (*American Women*; *Woman's Who's Who 1914*; Amy A. Mitchell, 'Reminiscences of Laura Lucretia Johns,' typescript, Alma Lutz Papers, NPV; 'Laura M. Johns,' *Chronicle Monthly Magazine* 2 [September 1894]: 3–5; Michael Lewis Goldberg, *An Army of Women: Gender and Politics in Gilded Age Kansas* [Baltimore, 1997], 72–74, 88.)."

22. Ibid., 6:20–21n10. Editor's note: "Harriette Amelia Keyser (1841–1936) worked with the Church Association for the Advancement of the Interests of Labor, founded by the Episcopal Diocese of New York, when she entered the New York City suffrage movement during the amendment campaign of 1894. She had supported herself in many ways, including a long stint as a stenographer for executives of the Western Union Telegraph Company. A close ally of Lillie Blake and the New York City Suffrage League, Keyser came to this convention representing the league's Political Study Club. (*WWW4*; Erma Conkling Lee, comp., *The Biographical Cyclopaedia of American Women* [1925; reprint, Detroit, 1974], 2:211–16; *New York Times*, 11 October 1936; *1894. Constitutional-Amendment Campaign Year*, 197–98.)."

23. Ibid., 6:21n11. Editor's note: "Althea Briggs Stryker (1860–?), of Great Bend, Kansas, at this date, was a Populist with ambitions as an orator. She worked in the amendment campaign of 1894 and remained active in the equal suffrage association. Her husband, William Stryker, won election as a Populist to be Superintendent of Public Instruction, serving from 1897 to 1899. One story telegraphed to papers outside the state claimed she 'was a prominent populist long before her husband was publicly known.' By 1900, the couple had moved to Wellington, Kansas, to publish a newspaper; by 1901, the husband was an editor in Tulsa, Oklahoma; and by 1910, he had been married for six years to a new wife. (Federal Census, 1900, 1910; Kansas Census, 1895; *Men of Affairs and Representative Institutions of Oklahoma, 1916: A Newspaper Reference Work* [Tulsa, Okla., 1916], unpaginated, s.v. 'Stryker, William'; *Wichita Daily Eagle*, 1 June 1893, 3 March 1895; *Kansas City Daily Journal* [Mo.], 8 January 1897; *Oswego Daily Times*, 12 February 1897.)."

24. Ibid., 6:21n12. Editor's note: "Helen Morris Lewis (1852–1933), a native of South Carolina, was North Carolina's pioneer in woman suffrage organizing and active with Laura Clay in her Committee on Southern Work. She served on the Resolutions Committee at this convention. Though growth of her state suffrage society was weak, she returned as a delegate to the convention in 1898. (William S. Powell, ed., *Dictionary of North Carolina Biography* [Chapel Hill, N.C., 1991], 4:58–59.)."

25. Ibid., 6:21n13. Editor's note: "Elizabeth Upham Yates (1857–1942) of Maine was one of the National-American's busiest lecturers and organizers and a member of this meeting's Resolutions Committee. A trained elocutionist, she went to China in her early twenties as a missionary for the Methodist Episcopal church. Returning to the United States five years later, Yates became a lecturer for the Woman's Christian Temperance Union before making her mark in the suffrage movement. It is likely that she first joined Lucy Stone's New England Woman Suffrage Association; she was speaking for that society around Boston in 1890 and 1891. After making her debut as a scheduled speaker at the National-American's convention in 1893, Yates found herself in heavy demand. She took part in the Kansas amendment campaign of 1894, traveled as a lecturer for the National-American across the South and the Northeast in 1895, and spent months working in the California amendment campaign of 1896. In the twentieth century, Yates settled for many years in Rhode Island, where she presided over the state suffrage association, enrolled as a special student at Brown University, and ran for lieutenant governor. (*American Women; Woman's Who's Who 1914; History*, 4:passim; *Historical Catalogue of Brown University, 1950 Edition* [Providence, R.I., 1951], 570; *New York Times*, 25 December 1942.)."

26. Ibid., 6:21n14. Editor's note: "Annie LePorte Diggs (1848–1916) of Kansas was already a national figure among Populists and a leader of the state suffrage association. She served as its president in 1899. (*NAW; ANB*; Goldberg, *An Army of Women*, passim. See also *Papers* 5.)."

27. Ibid., 6:21–22n15. Editor's note: "Kate Rowen Addison (1863–?) of Eureka, Kansas, was elected president of the state's equal suffrage association in 1895 and served four years. In her efforts to rebuild the society after the defeat of 1894, Addison published the *Kansas Suffrage Reveille* as the association's organ. Growing up in Iowa, she was the daughter of a former evangelical preacher turned insurance agent who served in the state senate and whose political connections won him consular posts for fourteen years in the Falkland Islands and Chile. Her husband, George W. Addison, whom she married in 1882, was a dealer in livestock. By 1900, the Addisons had moved to Kansas City, Missouri, and still resided there in 1920. (Federal Census, Greenwood County, Kan., 1900, Kansas City, 1910, 1920; Kansas Census, Greenwood County, 1895; B. P. Birdsall, ed., *History of Wright County, Iowa, Its People, Industries and Institutions* [Indianapolis, 1915], 395–97; *Woman's Who's Who 1914*.)."

28. Ibid., 6:22n16. Editor's note: "Lavina Allen Hatch (1836–1903), a former school teacher, was a founding member and officer of the National Woman Suffrage Association of Massachusetts, the rival to Lucy Stone's Massachusetts Woman Suffrage Association. Both groups were auxiliaries of the National-American. Hatch also wrote the group's history for the *History of Woman Suffrage*. (Julia Ward Howe, ed., *Sketches of Representative*

Women of New England [Boston, 1904], 114–17; *Woman's Journal*, 4 April 1903; *History*, 4:750–54.)."

29. Ibid., 6:22n17. Editor's note: "Cornelia Hull Cary (1841–1907) was a leader of the Brooklyn Woman Suffrage Association and active for many years in the National-American. A Brooklyn native, she studied art as a young woman and taught art at the Pratt Institute before her marriage in 1871 to Isaac Harris Cary, a businessman active in local politics. (Henry Grosvenor Cary, *The Cary Family in America* [Boston, 1907], 105; *New York Times*, 22 December 1907; *Woman's Journal*, 4 January 1908.)."

30. Ibid., 6:22n18. Editor's note: "Mariana W. Wright Chapman (1843–1907), a Brooklyn Quaker, led the borough's suffrage association and became president of the New York State Woman Suffrage Association at the end of 1896, holding that post until 1902. A state delegate to this convention, she was made a member of the Resolutions Committee. (*Quaker Genealogy*, 3:67; Inventory of the Family Papers of Mariana Wright Chapman, 1808–1983, PSC-Hi; *New York Times*, 12 November 1907.)."

31. Ibid., 6:22n19. Editor's note: "Ernestine Louise Siismondi Potowski Rose (1810–1892), one of the first women to petition for reform in the laws regarding married women's property, was a freethinker and a powerful speaker on the antebellum woman's rights platform. Born in Poland and married in England, Rose arrived in New York in the 1830s. After the Civil War, she and her husband settled in England. (*NAW; ANB*. See also *Papers* 1–4.)."

32. Ibid., 6:22n20. Editor's note: "In the official report of this sentence, SBA is made to say 'plenary inspiration.' Whether that corrects SBA's mistake or Clara Colby's mistake cannot be known. (*Report of the Twenty-eighth Annual Convention, 1896*, p. 92.)."

33. Ibid., 6:22n21. Editor's note: "Mary Livermore offered a resolution to that effect at the American Equal Rights Association meeting in May 1869. See *History*, 2:389."

34. Ibid., 6:22–23n22. Editor's note: "Lucy Stone (1818–1893) and her husband, Henry Browne Blackwell (1825–1909), known as Harry, shared editorial duties at the Boston *Woman's Journal* until Stone's death and controlled the powerful executive committee of the American Woman Suffrage Association until it united with the National in 1890. (*NAW*, s.v. 'Stone, Lucy'; *ANB*, s.v. 'Blackwell, Henry Browne' and 'Stone, Lucy.' See also *Papers* 1–5.)."

35. Ibid., 6:23n23. Editor's note: "Olympia Brown (1835–1926), an ordained Universalist minister, was pastor of the church in Racine, Wisconsin, and the state's leading suffragist. She married John Henry Willis in 1873 and, like Lucy Stone, retained her maiden name. (*NAW; ANB*. See also *Papers* 2–5.)."

36. Ibid., 6:23n24. Editor's note: "In the official report, this sentence reads: 'I have known many things said and done by our orthodox members that I felt exceedingly harmful to our cause.' (*Report of the Twenty-eighth Annual Convention, 1896*, p. 92.)."

37. Ibid., 6:23n25. Editor's note: "Lucretia Coffin Mott (1793–1880) helped to plan the woman's rights convention at Seneca Falls in 1848. Although ECS said nothing of Mott's opposition to the demand for suffrage in accounts of the meeting, Theodore Tilton, in a biography of ECS, commented that Mott 'attempted to dissuade' ECS, and Laura Curtis Bullard, writing later, had Mott say, 'Lizzie, thou wilt make the convention ridiculous.'

(*NAW*; *ANB*; T. Tilton, 'Mrs. Elizabeth Cady Stanton,' in James Parton, *Eminent Women of the Age* [Hartford, Conn., 1868], 347; L. C. Bullard, 'Elizabeth Cady Stanton,' in *Our Famous Women. An Authorized Record of the Lives and Deeds of Distinguished American Women of Our Times* [Hartford, Conn., 1884], 614.)."

38. Ibid., 6:23n26. Editor's note: "The *Tribune* gives this year as 1836 in error; other reports use 1860. But SBA scrambles several different sensations ECS caused with her ideas about divorce. She first mentioned divorce for drunkenness in a letter she sent to a women's temperance meeting in Albany in January 1852, in *Papers*, 1:191–93. A year later, she elaborated the idea in an appeal sent to another meeting in Albany, in *Film*, 7:513–14, and SBA described the uproar that appeal caused, in *Papers*, 1:217–19. The year 1860 came to mind because ECS brought resolutions about divorce reform to that year's National Woman's Rights Convention, in *Papers*, 1:418–31, causing an uproar in the press and among reformers. She did not, however, speak to the legislature about divorce that year. She spoke at a judiciary committee hearing on divorce on 8 February 1861, in *Film*, 9:1101–9."

39. Ibid., 6:23n27. Editor's note: "Ida Harper made significant revisions and additions to SBA's remarks in *Life and Work of Susan B. Anthony*, 2:853–54, in *Film*, 35:441. One sentence that only she discovered falls here: 'This year it is Mrs. Stanton; next year it may be I or one of yourselves, who will be the victim.'"

40. Ibid., 6:23n28. Editor's note: "Harper's version of the conclusion is still more dramatic: 'I pray you vote for religious liberty, without censorship or inquisition. This resolution adopted will be a vote of censure upon a woman who is without a peer in intellectual and statesmanlike ability; one who has stood for half a century the acknowledged leader of progressive thought and demand in regard to all matters pertaining to the absolute freedom of women.' (*Anthony*, 2:854.)."

41. Ibid., 6:23n29. Editor's note: "Anna Howard Shaw (1847–1919), physician, minister, and popular orator, entered the suffrage movement through the American Woman Suffrage Association and the patronage of Lucy Stone and Henry Blackwell, but her infatuation with SBA drew her away. At this meeting she was reelected vice president at large of the National-American Woman Suffrage Association. (*NAW*; *ANB*.)."

42. Ibid., 6:23n30. Editor's note: "According to the official published results [*sic*], the final vote was fifty-three to forty-one. (*Report of the Twenty-eighth Annual Convention, 1896*, p. 93.)."

43. Editorial Department [Horace L. Green?], "Elizabeth Cady Stanton Convicted of Heresy," *Free Thought Magazine* 14, no. 3 (March 1896): 183–187.

44. Green may refer to Antoinette Brown Blackwell, or, with a typo, to Henry Browne Blackwell, who—as seen in the previous selection—moved to accept the resolution of NAWSA disavowal. Green misunderstands the notable leader of woman suffrage and world peace Carrie Chapman Catt (1859–1947); in the words of a recent biographer, "organized religion held little interest for her and she found the antifeminism of most churches exasperating"; her stance on *The Woman's Bible* was governed by pragmatic objectives. Catt's strategic acumen, which she displayed during her lifetime on a national and international scale, was remarkable. As NAWSA president, Catt's two-pronged "winning plan," which pushed for women's enfranchisement at the state and federal constitutional level,

would usher in the Nineteenth Amendment in 1920. By that time she had "enfranchised thirty-five million women and doubled the black vote; she had organized women in thirty-six countries all over the world" (Van Voris, *Carrie Chapman Catt*, 9, 90, 3).

45. Here and above, Green refers to Matthew 5.

46. Matthew 27:1.

47. In 1562, Italian philosopher, lecturer, and author Giordano Bruno (1548–1600) fled the Dominican Order he had entered after being accused of heterodoxy; he lectured and taught in England and Europe for nearly twenty years before he was seized and imprisoned by the Inquisition in 1592. Influenced by Copernican science, Bruno and his pantheistic philosophy were deemed heretical, and he was burnt at the stake on 17 February 1600. John Owen's *The Skeptics of the Italian Renaissance* (1893) interpreted Bruno's life and writings within the freethought tradition and is apparently the source of Green's commentary on Bruno's theology and death. See *Oxford Dictionary of the Christian Church*, s.v. "Bruno, Giordano"; Owen, *The Skeptics of the Italian Renaissance*, 89–90, 264–265, 327–329.

48. Unitarian minister, abolitionist, Transcendentalist, and social reformer Theodore Parker (1810–1860) developed a theological platform that established "divinity" in humanity and in acts of social justice. During his tenure at Harvard Divinity School he edited the seminary's journal, *Scriptural Interpreter*, an early outlet for his interest in critical scriptural interpretation. In his *The Relation of Jesus to His Age and the Ages* (1844), Parker predicted that while "Jesus . . . is the greatest person of the ages . . . [and] taught the Absolute Religion—Love to God and Man[,] that God has yet greater men in store I doubt not" (17). See also Bowden, "Parker, Theodore."

49. Abolitionist John Brown (1800–1859) was executed on 2 December 1859 for his October 1859 raid on the Harpers Ferry federal arsenal. In the wake of his death, Transcendentalist reformers and abolitionists memorialized Brown as a Christ-like martyr. As David S. Reynolds indicates, international commentary, like that of French novelist Victor Hugo, concurred. "The execution of John Brown revealed America to be the greatest oxymoron in the world. In this unthinkable act, Hugo wrote, the world witnessed 'the champion of Christ . . . slaughtered by the American Republic,' 'the assassination of Emancipation by Liberty'" (*John Brown, Abolitionist*, 402–408, quoted on 409).

50. Parker died in Florence, where he had traveled for his health. From the time of the first biography produced by original scholarship, John Weiss's *Life and Correspondence of Theodore Parker* (1864), this anecdote circulated about his last days and prophetic commentary (Collison, "Theodore Parker," 219). "I have something to tell you," he is said to have confided to a visitor, "there are two Theodore Parkers now. One is dying here in Italy, the other I have planted in America. He will live there, and finish my work" (Weiss, *Life and Correspondence*, 2:438).

51. The *New York Times* reported in February 1889 that American freethinkers, led by Robert G. Ingersoll, T. B. Wakeman, Daniel G. Thompson, and Thomas Davidson, had raised four hundred dollars in support of the erection of Bruno's memorial statue in Rome. On 10 June 1889 the *Chicago Daily Tribune* described the unveiling of the statue, the work of sculptor Ettori Ferrari, the previous day ("In Memory of Bruno," *New York Times*, 21 February 1889; "A Statue to Giordano Bruno," *Chicago Daily Tribune*, 10 June 1889).

52. An excerpted stanza from James Russell Lowell's antislavery poem "The Present Crisis," first published in the *Boston Courier* in December 1845. Faith Barrett and Cristanne Miller emphasize the poem's immense shorthand symbolism for reformers through the 1860s, an assertion borne out and extended by its similar reprinting in the *Chicago Daily Tribune*'s 1889 article, 'A Statue to Giordano Bruno' (Barrett and Miller, *"Words for the Hour,"* 29n3).

53. Jean Brooks Greenleaf, "Mrs. Greenleaf's Letter," *Free Thought Magazine* 14, no. 5 (May 1896): 334–335.

54. Kern points out that "some anecdotal evidence bears out Catt's assertion that the *Woman's Bible* was harming the cause," due in large part to Southern clergy and deep "religious conservatism in the region" (*Mrs. Stanton's Bible*, 185).

Not "A Person of One Idea"

The Aging Radical (1884–1897)

As the preceding chapter demonstrates, in her final decades Stanton's activist vision could not be contained by NAWSA's march toward women's enfranchisement. The selections in "Not 'A Person of One Idea': The Aging Radical" detail that increasing scope. In her 1884 portrait, Laura Curtis Bullard (1831–1912) underscores Stanton's continuing evolution as a reformer with an expansive social platform. In her view, a time in which the world was "outgrowing itself" or, in Stanton's words, "moving," required this catholic approach. However, Bullard also identifies one of the reasons that Stanton's name may fail to resonate today with the force it commanded in her own time. Not only was the bulk of her authorial production ephemeral—appearing in widely scattered newspapers and periodicals and delivered orally by her (or more frequently in these decades by others)—but also her still-compelling physical presence ensured its greatest reception.

Bullard was well qualified to understand the ephemeral nature of journalistic production. Moreover, her recent recovery from near extinction evidences the ways in which scandals and political crises can also produce literary and historical oblivion,[1] as her wry recollection of Stanton's one-time advice for her to "submit to the inevitable" while "looking on the bright side of things" also suggests. A successful novelist, journalist, editor, and woman's suffrage worker after the Civil War, Bullard nonetheless found her reputation in shambles during the Beecher-Tilton scandal. A long-time friend to Stanton and Anthony, Bullard was active in NWSA from its inception, serving as its first corresponding secretary, and she was a contributor to and then editor of *Revolution* before she bought the paper from Anthony in July 1870. Bullard was also friendly with Elizabeth Tilton, who served as *Revolution*'s poetry editor, and with Elizabeth's husband, Theodore; and it was to Bullard and Stanton that Theodore had revealed the details of his wife's affair with Henry Ward Beecher in the fall of 1870. But in January 1871, the New York papers publicly accused Bullard of committing adultery with Theodore. Elizabeth and Theodore Tilton denied these charges, but rumors and innuendo continued to swirl, up through the civil trial in 1875; as Denise M. Kohn argues, Bullard's "reputation had become caught in the personal and professional battle between [Theodore] Tilton and Beecher." After these events, Bullard removed herself from the foreground of reform, and although she continued to publish occasionally thereafter, by the time of her death, the *New York Times* identified her as a "widow and daughter" only.[2]

Although Adelaide Johnson's relationship with Stanton was of shorter duration than the enduring friendship Stanton and Bullard enjoyed, her two-week, 1891 diary observations on the aging radical and record of their conversations enable us to appreciate the extensive variety of Stanton's pursuits and her increasingly transcontinental influence at this time. A woman of eclectic interests in her own right, Johnson (1859–1955) was a sculptor, Spiritualist, periodical author, and thoroughgoing reformer who participated actively in the National and International Councils of Women, NAWSA, and the National Woman's Party. As in the case of Stanton's bust, Johnson's sculptures of figures that contributed to the movement exemplify her principled expression of artistic activism; and she introduced to the general populace uniquely tangible symbols of woman's rights.[3] Indeed, Laura R. Prieto argues persuasively that Johnson's and other female artists' influential "visual culture" played an important role in the resurgence of the woman suffrage movement at the turn of the twentieth century.[4] After studying her craft in St. Louis, Dresden, and Rome, Johnson established studios in Europe and America, keeping a home studio in Washington, DC, while she attempted to raise funds to sculpt female reformers. Johnson's dream of establishing a museum for the busts of the pioneering figures in the woman suffrage movement did not come to pass, but her seven-and-a-half-ton monument in white Carrara marble, the group sculpture of Stanton, Anthony, and Lucretia Mott entitled *The Woman Movement* and later renamed *The Portrait Monument*, now sits in the Capitol Rotunda in Washington, DC (see fig. 14). It was unveiled there on Anthony's birthday, 15 February 1921, attended by family members of the memorialized figures. Jane Addams of Hull House fame delivered the primary address.[5] "The monument was not made for entertainment," Johnson explained, "but as an immortal record of the mightiest thing in the evolution of humanity that has taken place since the dawn of mind in the brute, for the revolution embodied in the woman movement represents the potentiality if not yet the dawn of ethics in the human race."[6]

During the sittings Johnson describes in this selection, she made an initial clay bust preparatory for display at the Columbian Exposition in 1892. After viewing the exhibit there, May Wright Sewall praised Anthony's bust, adding, "Mrs. Stanton does not seem to me so good, but her excessive fat would, I know, make it very difficult to model her portrait."[7] Anticipating such responses, the vain Stanton demanded that Johnson reduce the size of her neck and chin. A related curiosity from this sitting is Anthony's possible jest or actual suggestion that Stanton's in-progress sculpture resembled Wendell Phillips, who had died in 1884. Stanton's potential resemblance to the balding and somewhat long- and narrow-visaged Phillips seems unlikely. Instead, Anthony's observation may recapitulate—as these diary entries do also—Johnson's real challenge during these sittings. She strove to create an art that would invigorate reform; in this case she aimed to render with both accuracy and vital symbolism the unwieldy physical attributes of a woman whom she revered as a women's rights hero and icon.

Scottish-born John Swinton (1829–1901) is the third activist evoking Stanton's popularity among liberal reformers. An antebellum abolitionist, after the war he established a reputation in New York City as a labor journalist, committed socialist, and newspaper publisher; Swinton rose steadily through the ranks of all three of these related fields. He served at different times as chief of the editorial staffs of both the *New York Times* and the *New York Sun*. Swinton's sympathies for labor extended to the plights of African American workers, particularly in the South, and also for the execrable industrial working environment for women and children. Asked whether human rights extended to women in 1886, Swinton declared, "When we speak of the rights of man, those of women are implied every time, truly and fully—her right to life, liberty, and the pursuit of happiness."[8]

From "Elizabeth Cady Stanton, Laura Curtis Bullard, 1884"[9]

Do you know Mrs. Elizabeth Cady Stanton? was the first question put to me by Madame George Sand, when I met her a few years ago in Paris.[10] "Yes, I know her well," I replied. The famous Frenchwoman inquired minutely concerning my distinguished friend—her personal appearance, her views and purposes, her style as a writer and speaker, and her method of reformatory agitation. As I then found it no easy matter, even during a long and free conversation, to answer all these queries, so now I find it still more difficult to make a fit record, in a few pages, of the busy career and varied labors of a lady who, in addition to the cares of a large family, has been the originator of one of the chief public movements of our times, and who has also been an active participant in many kindred reforms. For although Mrs. Stanton is best known as the leader of the agitation for woman suffrage, she is not "a person of one idea," but has been among the foremost of the many zealous laborers, both American and English, who have striven for the abolition of slavery—for temperance—for a working day of eight hours—for the suppression of usury—for the co-education of the sexes—for co-operative industry—and last, but not least, for international arbitration and peace. In fact, a complete biography of this representative woman would include a history of the political, social, and religious thought of the last two generations. Moreover, not even such a history could reflect a faithful image of such a life's work; for Mrs. Stanton's public efforts have taken the evanescent form of lectures, speeches, resolutions, protests, criticisms, and editorials—all growing out of the events of the day, and which it is not possible to reproduce at a later period in their original vitality, however accessible they may be in the archives of the various movements which have called them forth. But though her finest intellectual productions have been of an ephemeral type, like those of any other speaker or journalist, yet in her representative capacity as the head and front of a movement peculiarly her own—a novel reform whose novelty seems never to wear out—Elizabeth Cady Stanton, now in her green and sunny old age, is still what she has been for the last thirty years—an object of affection to one class of her countrywomen, of aversion to another, and of curiosity to all. . . .

Mrs. Stanton's views on other topics than woman's rights are briefly these: As to her political preferences, she feels that she has little to choose between the Republican and the Democratic parties, since she is disfranchised by both. As to her social theories, she holds to the sacredness of marriage (like all other good women); but when an unhappy marriage destroys the ideal family relation, and when the children born of such a union are the innocent and wretched victims of the vices or mistakes of their parents, she believes (as John Milton did) in a wise freedom of divorce.[11] As to political economy, she has a doctrinaire's devotion to free trade, to co-operative industry, and to the rights of labor as opposed to the tyranny of capital—though her chief interest in these questions is because, as she says, "Woman is the great unpaid laborer of the world." As to religion, like many another person brought up under the Calvinistic system, she first passed through a long period of mental suffering in a vain attempt to solve problems which lie beyond the finite mind, and at last abandoned what she calls "a theology inconsistent with enlightened reason, and inadequate to the wants of the soul." . . .

It is always pleasant to know something of the personal appearance of a distinguished man or woman; but, as a rule, nothing is more illusive and shadowy than a verbal description, and nothing more vague than the impression made by such a portrait upon one who has never seen the subject of it. I will try, however, to tell what manner of woman Mrs. Stanton is. First, then, she is noticeably fine looking: in any crowded assembly she would command attention, and people would wish to know who she was. She is above the medium height; rotund of figure; fair of complexion; with bright, fearless, and sparkling blue eyes, and a rosy, wholesome mouth, filled with fine white teeth, which she shows in her frequent smiles; for she is pre-eminently a mirthful, sunny-tempered woman, abounding in—

> "Quips and cranks and wanton wiles,
> Nods and becks and wreathed smiles."[12]

Her features are all regular, and her white hair, which curls naturally, is so abundant and beautiful that many a young girl might envy its quality and profusion. She has often been likened in looks to Martha Washington. Her manners are genial and courteous, and she has the rare gift of putting everybody at ease who comes into her presence; while she herself is equally at home in the simplest cottage in the far West, or in the fine residences of the nobility of England, where she has been cordially welcomed. She is a democrat, pure and simple, and values individuals according to their just deserts, quite apart from their social surroundings. She does not despise a man because he is rich (as some radicals do) any more than she looks down on one because he is poor. She ignores every mere external consideration in her estimate of people, and weighs their moral and intellectual worth, judging them accordingly. She is a woman of scientific and philosophic tastes; but still more she is a practical worker for humanity; and she loves her fellow-beings as if they all were near of kin to her. Her temperament is sweet and buoyant, and she has borne all the vicissitudes of a life full of labors and duties most cheerfully. She once said to me, "Submit to the inevitable, for it is the true philosophy of life"; and she has acted on her own theory—not only submitting, but submitting gracefully. "The ills of life," she says, "are sufficiently hard to bear without adding to them the wear and tear of discontent and rebellion." . . .

. . . She regards sickness as a crime, since it is an evidence of a violation of some physical law; and I have heard her say that she hoped and believed the time would come when people would be as much ashamed to admit that they had headache or indigestion as they would be to admit that they had committed theft or told a lie. Her own health is so perfect, and her spirit so joyous, that she seems like a woman who has never had an ache to endure, or a grievance to redress. I have seen some women who excelled her in animal spirits, but never one who possessed an equal measure of habitual cheeriness in all situations.

It is from this hopefulness of nature—this habit of looking at the bright side of things—that she borrows her impetuous methods of appealing to the public mind. She is always seeing the goal, not as afar off, but as near at hand. Years ago, Mr. Mill said to me that while he admired Mrs. Stanton greatly, he thought she was sometimes premature in her public utterances; and he added that after he had written his book on the "Subjection of Women," he retained it in his writing-desk for twenty years before venturing on its publication.[13] Mrs. Stanton, on the other hand, has said, "The time is ripe for the expression of any thought as soon as the person is found who is ready to utter it." It is a favorite idea with her that "There is no use in saying what people are ready to hear." On making the acquaintance of Daniel O'Connell, during the Repeal excitement, she asked him if he really expected to secure a repeal of the Union. "Oh, no," he replied, "but I claim *everything*, that I may be sure of getting *something*."[14] This has ever since been *her* method likewise. Thus, during our national discussion of the fourteenth amendment, which provided the franchise for the freedmen, she insisted that the same amendment should be so interpreted as to secure the like privilege to women. But what seems radical to-day becomes conservative to-morrow. Mrs. Stanton has long since outlived (as Lucy Stone has done) the early criticisms which denounced both these women as visionaries and fanatics. The world has a good habit of outgrowing itself, and is thereby getting better and better.

From "Record of Sittings: Mrs. Stanton," Adelaide Johnson, 1891[15]

Morning sept 25th 1891

I have had the first sitting with Mrs Stanton and she certainly is lovely as well as wonderful Miss Anthony came for a moment stood at the window and said the bust looked like Wendell Phillips. Mrs Stanton has talked of books and thoughts and things and her idea for formulation now is "The Solitude of Self,"[16] which corresponds to mine "The desolation of the Individual" she told me of Stepniak a Russian Prince nihilist[17] and her visit to Howard Castle the home of lady Carlisle[18]

afternoon

Miss Anthony has been in they have been talking over reminiscences Mrs Stanton told me of the first time she made a speech on the divorce laws how it was accepted the reply of Wendell Phillips &c in the N.Y. Legislature[19] She is so quaint and wonderful This is friday but the Bust was begun before then the time has come for the womans day to be changed to one of good omens rather than ill. . . .

My Birthday Sat Sept 26th 1891

The day has been full and wonderful Mrs Stanton talked reminiscences all day this morning She told me of Lucy Stone and her little black bag with valuable? documents. This afternoon Miss Anthony the blessed came in and sat with us and they talked and read letters also the responses to a public call concerning the superstition of 13[20] Mrs S told me of her experience with George Francis Train how he carried them through several states and so many things

One of the most amusing is that she insists upon my making "Susans chin," only a little rounded out. The work does not make much show to day, but it grows gradually and will be glorious when finished . . .

Mrs Stanton also told me of the attempt to wear the Bloomer costume Miss Anthony Mrs Miller and herself.

. . . Sept 27th 1891

At Miss Anthonys Home

This morning Mrs Stanton and I went to the Studio while Blessed Miss Anthony and the rest went to church. I find every faculty held to the last degree trying to retain the words of wisdom and goodness from these great Souls and minds until I can digest them. Which in addition to the natural anxiety concerning the Bust makes my load heavy though precious and ever inspiring To day Mrs Stanton has talked much of Carl Pearson's work in which he shows that woman is and has been the chief factor in civilization and she has given her great thought of the cause and occasion of the dark Ages after the Matriarchate or the last Struggle for the Supremacy of the Masculine when they killed us off physically when we think of 400 maidens being burned at once as witches and but one wizard and so on through all that state.

When she told me how she answered the Bishop who prated of "womans disabilities," the first mentioned was our gift of motherhood she showed how it gave us added power and made us superior to them. Then he said our dress was surely a disability but she said we are not born with a dress on so that is something we can drop at any time and do when the occasion demands Then she said our skirts are emblems of diginty [dignity] You and the Judges of the supreme court upon all great occasion wear them.[21]

Then in the afternoon she said here they want us to fight after we have given them the whole army and served ourselves as nurses, did you ever hear such Tyranny and was ever more demanded of any race of slaves so words of wisdom are falling every moment heaven help me to gather some of the crumbs from this bountiful feast . . . Blessed day.

Sept 28th 1891.   Anthony Home

Another wonderful day has passed here Stanton has been telling reminiscences her experience with the babies the one of the telegraph operator was very interesting and when the young mother told her what the nurse told her about the liver being soft like Cartillage [*sic*] and they must be bound up she asked if it were reasonable that God should make kittens and puppies so they would stick together and leave babies to the mercy of bandages? . . .[22]

Tuesday Sept 29th 1891.

The day has been rather dark as the Bust has not grown as I had hoped for I am growing impatient or rather anxious to see it approach completion. Mrs Stanton was late to day and has felt inclined to sleep much. I had a nice talk with Miss Anthony and asked her to day what she would prefer of herself a standing or sitting statue and she promptly replied

Sept 29th 1891 continued

standing

Wednesday Sept 30th 1891

We had a good time this morning dressing Mrs Stantons hair as that was to be my special work to day, but finally it was accomplished and looked beautiful. This morning Mrs Stanton told me of their experience in Washington when they went to hear Mr Patten answer the W.S. Convention— when they went up and Miss Anthony said "Mr Patten I do not know what to say to you, but if I were your mother I would spank you" The [news] papers took it up and sounded the cry the country over that Miss Anthony and Mrs Stanton had stopped him in the midst of his Sermon—and that Miss A had actually spanked him. . . .[23]

Thursday Oct 1st

A heavenly day this has been and we have worked faithfully dear Mrs Stanton has slept more than usual. The work progresses slowly, but surely. . . .

October 2nd Friday. 1891

This morning I took the large picture of Mrs Stanton over and have been working on the expression of the Mouth to get it like it. We have had several visitors to day. . . . I walked down in the city with Miss Anthony before tea after tea I took Mrs Stanton for a little walk and now as usual here I shall retire early.

October 3rd Saturday 1891

To day Mrs Stanton did not sit at all she wrote the call for the coming Suffrage convention. . . .

Sunday. Oct. 4th 1891

I worked all morning on the hair[24] Mrs Stanton wrote with Miss Anthony and did not come over after dinner they both came, but I

Oct 4th continued

I had unfortunately just spoiled the mouth so I spent my time on that during the afternoon then came home to write letters . . .

Monday Morning October 5th 1891

Mrs Stanton thought before coming over this morning that she would not be able to sit at [sic] but blessed Susan dragged her over and she was so wide awake the morning passed like a moment. she told me of her eldest born, his devotion to her how he passed away while she was on the other side of the water . . .[25] Then she insisted upon my cutting the clay away from the neck making it not so heavy I am wondering what Miss Anthony will say . . .

Tuesday Oct 6th 1891

This has been a cold day—have spent most of my time on the hair of the Bust to day. Mrs Stanton has slept nearly all day . . .

Wednesday Oct. 7th 1891

A pouring rain day bitter cold. I went to the Studio and tried to work but found that with the darkness cold and dampness it was useless so came back and wrote until dinner after dinner the whole family . . . went over to see the Bust. The general impression was good although it is unfinished and dear Miss Anthony said it was much improved which was more to me than all the rest . . .

"Letter to Elizabeth Cady Stanton," John Swinton, 1897[26]

48 WEST 93D ST. NEW YORK
DECEMBER 29, 1897

My dear Mrs. Stanton—

I dreamed of you last night, —dreamed that I saw you standing upon a huge rock, in a boundless desert, discoursing upon righteousness and the judgment to come, — dreamed that you were in the prime of life, and spoke loftily, — dreamed that, as I had dropped [off] all my clo' in the farthest corner of the Vast Esplanade, you approached and covered me with a red horse blanket, — dreamed that your daughter told me that, as I had not paid attention to your discourse, she would furnish me with a stenographic report of it, — dreamed that a dancing girl in short skirts had manifested the Spanish bolero just before you stood on the end of the shivering rock, — oh, how I dreamed about you!

This makes me think that I ought to try to find out where you live, and make a call on New Year's.

If I can find out, I, or we, shall, at least, rap on your door.

In admiration
John Swinton

NOTES

1. Kohn, "Introduction," x.

2. Ibid., xiv–xv, xxi–xxiii, quoted on xxiii, xxviii; *SP* 3:97–98n2. Kohn also discusses Bullard's ostensibly unhappy marriage to Enoch Bullard and scholars' views on whether the Bullard-Tilton rumors were grounded in truth ("Introduction," xiii–xiv, xxiii, xln16).

3. Burton, *Adelaide Johnson*, 9–13.

4. Prieto, *At Home in the Studio*, 167.

5. For a detailed overview of the National Woman's Party's extended battle with Congress to display the sculpture, see Tetrault, *The Myth of Seneca Falls*, 187–190.

6. Quoted in Burton, *Adelaide Johnson*, 61.

7. Ibid., quoted on 40.

8. Quoted in Winter, "Swinton, John."

9. Bullard, "Elizabeth Cady Stanton," 602–603, 618–619, 620–621, 622–623.

10. The French novelist, playwright, autobiographer, and political writer George Sand, a pseudonym for Aurore Dudevant (1804–1876).

11. British poet, political pamphleteer, and theological writer John Milton (1608–1674) examined the reform of divorce laws in *The Doctrine and Discipline of Divorce* (1643). In this anticlerical attack on the ostensibly sacred nature of marriage bonds he emphasized the dissonance of maintaining a marriage between incompatible partners (Campbell, "Milton, John").

12. Bullard excerpts John Milton's "L'Allegra," published in *Poems Upon Several Occasions* (1673).

13. The woman's rights publications of British philosopher and economist John Stuart Mill (1806–1873), particularly *The Subjection of Women* (1869), profoundly impacted Stanton's thinking, as did the anonymously authored essay of his wife, Harriet Hardy Taylor, "The Enfranchisement of Women" (1851).

14. See Stanton, *Eighty Years and More*, 89–90, for her conversation with the Irish nationalist leader Daniel O'Connell (1775–1847).

15. Adelaide Johnson, Record of Portrait Sittings, Adelaide Johnson Papers, MSS27821, Box 71, courtesy of the Manuscript Division, Library of Congress, Washington, DC.

16. Stanton delivered "The Solitude of Self" to the House Judiciary Committee in Washington, DC, on 18 January 1892 and again that evening to NAWSA's convention. She republished it in the *Boston Investigator* in 1901 (*SP* 5:423–424).

17. The exiled radical Sergei M. Kravchinskii (1851–1895) was an influential Russian revolutionary determined to overthrow his country's autocracy. He assassinated N. V. Mezentsev, "chief of Russia's political police, the Third Section," in August 1878 before avoiding capture in Europe and then America. Using the pseudonym S. Stepniak, he disseminated influential books and lectures that convinced Western humanists that "the Russian nihilists, a term used frequently in Europe and England to describe all Russian revolutionaries, were actually Western-style liberals"; he arrived in New York in December 1890 and conducted a successful American lecture tour (Good, "America and the Russian Revolutionary Movement, 1888–1905," 275–277, quoted on 275, 276).

18. A good example of Stanton's transatlantic woman's rights networking in the 1880s and 1890s, in July 1891 while in England, Stanton spent a week at Castle Howard with Lord and Lady Carlisle. Rosalind Frances Stanley Howard, Countess of Carlisle (1845–1921), was a leading figure in the Women's Liberal Federation. See *SP* 5:380n1; and for Stanton's account of this visit, see Stanton and Blatch, *Elizabeth Cady Stanton as Revealed in Her Letters, Diary, and Reminiscences*, 2:275–278.

19. It was after Stanton's address on divorce at the tenth National Woman's Rights Convention in 1860 that Wendell Phillips moved to suppress Stanton's resolutions, considering them inappropriate and off-topic for a suffrage convention (*SP* 1:427–428).

20. Playwright, author, editor, and archivist of the Thirteen Club Jacob R. Abarbanell (1862–?) dispersed a circular to one hundred "leading women of the country" for their view of the superstitious fear of seating thirteen at table and of superstitions in general. The Thirteen Club, founded in New York in 1882, sought to dissolve superstition—the "handmaid of ignorance"—with science, "the advance of civilization," and "reason and

commonsense." Abarbanell published twenty-nine replies—including those from Stanton, Anthony, Lillie Devereux Blake, Frances C. Willard, Clara Barton, and Grace Greenwood—prefaced by his commentary in the May 1891 issue of *Belford's Magazine* (*Abbeville Meridional*, National News Section; Abarbanell, "The 'Thirteen' Superstition among the Fair Sex," 801–804, quoted on 801, 804; *Who's Who in New York City and State*, s.v. "Abarbanell, Jacob R.").

21. Stanton related the same incident about her encounter with Bishop Arthur Cleveland Coxe in her address to members of the Seidle Society on 12 July 1889. See *SP* 5:205–208.

22. These anecdotes are staples of Stanton's addresses and lectures about marriage and children. See, for example, in this volume Stanton's lecture in "Marriage and Maternity: The Public 'Mother of the Gracchi'" and Clara Bewick Colby's selection in "Death and Legacy of Elizabeth Cady Stanton"; Stanton, *Eighty Years and More*, 115–118, 124–126.

23. Stanton narrates an event from January 1885, in which William Weston Patton, president of Howard University, delivered "Women and Skepticism," a sermon illustrating the idea that "unsexed" women become agnostic or immoral, using as illustration figures such as free love lecturer Victoria Woodhull, Scottish feminist and abolitionist Frances Wright, British feminist and author Mary Wollstonecraft, and British novelist George Eliot. See *SP* 4:402–403.

24. Lori D. Ginzberg suggests that Stanton "hated" her completed bust, "for 'the curls looked just like bananas'" (*Elizabeth Cady Stanton*, 177).

25. Daniel "Neil" Cady Stanton died while Stanton was in England. Writing in her diary on his birthday, she wrote, "Had he lived, he would have been forty-nine, nearly half a century. And yet it seems so short a time since he was a baby—my first one—in my arms" (Stanton and Blatch, *Elizabeth Cady Stanton as Revealed in Her Letters, Diary, and Reminiscences*, 2:272).

26. John Swinton to Elizabeth Cady Stanton, 29 December 1897, Elizabeth Cady Stanton Papers, MSS41210, Box 1, courtesy of the Manuscript Division, Library of Congress, Washington, DC.

Death and Legacy of Elizabeth
Cady Stanton (1902–1903)

On 22 November 1902, nearly a month after Stanton's death, the "News and Comment" section of the *Duluth News-Tribune* declared, "The brain of Elizabeth Cady Stanton is causing controversy—even yet." Helen Hamilton Gardener (1853–1925), whose tribute to Stanton the following year would also include an extended discussion of Stanton's wish to be cremated after donating her brain to the Neurology Department at Cornell University, had ignited a public argument with the Stanton family, led by Harriot Stanton Blatch, in the newspapers.[1] Department head Professor Burt G. Wilder's collection included the brains of Harvard and Cornell professors Chauncey Wright and James Edward Oliver; and indeed fifteen years previously Gardener had written Stanton about Cornell's scientific analyses of brain size and secured the necessary paperwork, prompting Stanton to write on the reverse of Gardener's note and using a playful nickname, "You must save my brain for Heathen Helen's statistics."[2] Stanton had already been buried, so in one sense the point was moot, but Gardener and Blatch each held a stake in what the public understood about this bequest. "This bizarre incident raised an issue that would eventually become crucial to the meaning of Harriot's life," observes Ellen Carol DuBois: "Who possessed Elizabeth Stanton, now that she no longer belonged to her self?"[3]

This question was much on the minds of two of the women whose selections follow. If Gardener highlighted Stanton's freethought and scientific interests, making her a secular "Mother Superior," Clara Bewick Colby (1846–1916) depicted her as the "everyday" lyceum-story mother and woman's rights mentor. For this reason her selection amplifies Johnson's abbreviated summaries of these stories, helping us appreciate their significance for reformers, lyceum attendees, and intellectuals. Unlike Gardener and Johnson, Colby was herself a mother, so she may have gravitated naturally to this literal maternal emphasis in her depiction of Stanton as an activist; but that focus also reflects her own objectives for her life work—the publishing of the *Woman's Tribune*. As Kristin Mapel Bloomberg avers, Colby's professional "vision" was for a "newspaper that could bind together all women—including rural and working-class women who were too often left out of national political discussions."⁴ Women of all demographics, she may have imagined, could unite through their common love for their children. Importantly, however, both Gardener and Colby wrote at a time when they had good reason to imagine that Stanton would not be remembered as they would have wished; these posthumous portraits represent dedicated attempts to shape their dead leader for history.

By contrast, May Wright Sewall's somewhat mystified reception of Stanton in 1902 is less calculated. As she herself declares, Sewall—not unlike many of Anthony's "nieces"—had experienced little contact with Stanton in her final years. Educator, woman suffrage reformer, and clubwoman May Eliza Wright Sewall (1844–1920) was active in her Indiana suffrage organization as well as in NWSA, but perhaps her greatest achievements as an activist were international in scope. She was a founding member of the International Council of Women (ICW) and the American National Council of Women, serving as the former's president from 1899 to 1904. Notably, her prominence and success with such international positions render Sewall's lack of familiarity with Stanton poignant. Despite Stanton's influential contributions to the transcontinental woman's rights movement in the 1880s and early 1890s, for Sewall the former NWSA and NAWSA leader was both unfamiliar and even opaque.⁵

From "Tribute of May Wright Sewall. President International Council of Women," May Wright Sewall, 1902⁶

It was my great privilege to come into personal contact with Elizabeth Cady Stanton when I was myself but recently out of college, and at what might be called the beginning of my active life. I had my first personal knowledge of Mrs. Stanton in June of 1876 at the Arch street headquarters of the National Suffrage Association. The impression produced by her rare personality has not been erased; and as in the intervening years, I have from time to time met her, each meeting has revived it; each meeting, I may say, has accented the two strongest elements of that impression. When I first saw her, Mrs. Stanton was discussing the "Woman's Declaration of Independence," which she had prepared, as is well-known, with a view of trying to have it read with the original Declaration of Independence, on the fourth day of July of that Centennial year. A group of men and women were gathered about her, including, I remember Lucretia Mott, Susan B. Anthony and several other of the pioneers of the great movement. The sonorous tones and the earnest manner with which Mrs. Stanton urged the fulmination of the New Declaration, filled me with a kind of awe; her eloquence and logic were irresistible. I was, however, not more impressed with these than with what seemed to me the curious incongruity of her own witty interruptions of herself, as she read and commented upon the document. Her own attention seemed to be frequently diverted from the main point, namely, the public issuance of the "Declaration," by her enjoyment of the dismay and disgust which would fill the minds of opponents; and particularly of the anxiety which she apparently thought was already torturing the minds of the officials in charge of the preparations for the Centennial celebration of the great Fourth, to whom application had been made for the official representation of women on that occasion. This combination of serious purpose, statesmanlike grasp of great principles, and devotion to humanity, with a pure love of fun and mischievous delight in the prospect of being able to interrupt the solemnity of a national ceremonial puzzled me. How any woman could be so strong, so wise, so courageous, was hardly more astonishing than how a mature woman could be so much like a little child in love of fun and mischief. Has not that combination baffled and charmed all of us who have had the privilege of anything like an intimate acquaintance with the woman who has gone from us?

"Elizabeth Cady Stanton," Helen H. Gardener
[Alice Chenoweth], 1903[7]

Three years ago Mrs. Stanton asked me, in case she should go into the silence before me, if I would speak for her—at her grave. I have come here tonight, in part, to keep my promise to the dead. She agreed to do the same for me should I go first. When she died I was unfortunately traveling hundreds of miles away, and did not know at once that the end had come.

When I learned, by wire, I did my best to fulfill my promise, but circumstances combined to prevent, and I am glad of this opportunity to say for her some of the things which she particularly wished me to say.

First of all, she wished it known that she died, as she had lived, a fearless, serene agnostic. Her philosophy kept her sane and sweet. No fear for her soul, no dread of any future life, prevented her from using all of her splendid energies to better conditions in this world. She worked for the welfare of the race, here and now, and believed that any possible future could and would take care of itself.

In pursuance of this idea it was her earnest wish that her tireless brain, when she should be done with it, should go to Cornell University, that it might serve science and mankind in helping to arrive at the truth, after death, as it always had done in life.

She knew that the brain of no great woman had ever been examined. She knew that the brains of all womankind had been judged and weighed and measured by that which science had learned about woman through its hospital subjects, its paupers, its "unknown" dead. She knew that this was wholly unfair to woman.

She knew that the brains of men were judged by no such inadequate records; but that they had their great ones carefully preserved, and sacredly held, to show the use and benefits of education, of opportunity, of the development of his kind. She knew that in science, in art, in law, in politics, in literature, in philosophy, man had his representatives in brain weights, measurements, qualities and forms; that upon these great ones man builds his theories and conclusions as to what is desirable, possible or remarkable for him.

She felt that a brain like hers would be useful for all time in the record it would give the world, for the first time—the scientific record of a thinker among women. She knew that many men of distinction had willed their brains to Cornell in our country, or to the great universities of England and Germany, which, like Cornell here, have asked to become custodians of these sacred trusts to science in the interest of humanity.

She felt that the record of her life and work, in so far as it might be stamped in that splendid brain of hers, should be a part of the fine heritage of all women. She wished to leave it to the world as her last and holiest gift. Even as her gentle voice might come back to us if preserved by science on the waxen cylinder of a graphophone, so might she leave to us, in the very texture of the brain itself, in the indelible handwriting of Nature, the record of her lofty intellectual life—the message of her unceasing battle for the highest in all things, not only for herself, but for humanity.

She knew that her work was not for woman only. Every blow she struck for woman was really a blow for man, quite as truly, were he only wise enough to recognize the fact. The day is not so far distant when he will recognize it—and then will the name of Elizabeth Cady Stanton stand side by side with those of Washington and Lincoln in the reverence of her countrymen and of the wise and good in every land and clime. For her vast influence, already stamped on the thought and bettered laws of her time, has not stopped in America, in England, in France nor in Germany. Its waves and echoes have reached the Orient, and the little brown women of India and the dainty, patient Japanese maidens have also felt some of the results of the liberty and justice that she and her co-laborers have sent to them. And in the years that are to come, when the mothers of the race shall, for the first time on earth, be reckoned as self-respecting, self-directing human units, with brains and bodies that are sacredly their own, even these little women of the Orient when they set their incense tapers alight before their household gods will burn the sweetest one to her—their gentle-faced deliverer from the bondage of inequality before the law and abject slavery to silly and degrading superstitions.

And the men, also, will rise up and call her blessed, for freeing them, however much against their will, from the degradation of a lifelong bondage in marriage with an inferior, a chattel, a plaything of their leisure hours, and for giving them instead the opportunity to know the blessedness and sacred joy of a real companionship with an equal, a comrade, a soul-mate in the mother of their children.

She died as she wished to die, in the full possession of her splendid powers. Three years ago, when the eloquent voice of her friend and mine, that great and splendid soul, Robert G. Ingersoll, was stilled forever, she said to me: "Sad as it is to lose him, I am glad that he went just as he did. I hope it may be so with me—and with you. I do not want to live a day after I fail to be able to do good work." Her wish was wholly fulfilled. Only three days before she died she wrote that second lawyerlike article on the divorce problem which she contributed to the symposium on that subject in the *New York American*—the only note struck in the discussion, with one possible exception, up to that time, that was clear, frank and untrammeled by fear of public opinion and ancient superstitions.[8]

Her thought had always the luminous quality. Every topic her brain touched was lighted as by a torch of reason. She did not write with one eye on her paper and the other on the public pulse—she proposed to help regulate that pulse herself, and she believed absolutely in the power of sincerity, frankness and truth.

Yet she never forgot to be gracious. Her social quality was fine. She had the tact of a diplomat—and when I say "tact" I do not mean duplicity. But, while many reformers or specialists lose adherents by forever and at all times clinging to their specialty and advancing it in season and out of season, she never made that mistake.

Well do I remember laughing with her at the tactlessness of a certain well-known lady who, at a great social function, where we were all guests, persisted in riding the suffrage hobby straight through, from oysters and olives to the walnuts and wine. Not so with Mrs. Stanton. She often captured her audience before she made her speech—before her listeners knew of her belief. The scintillation of her ready wit, the philosophy of her outlook, the charm of her diction, on any topic under discussion, made her a delightful hostess or guest at any banquet. A fine conversationalist, she could meet the ablest man on his own grounds and entertain or vanquish him with the serene self-poise of supreme self-respect without egotism. She was never aggressive in method. That was one of her chief charms.

Hers was a many-sided character. It is not especially difficult to seem to be great if one is possessed of but one idea. It is not so easy to be a many-sided person and keep one's poise in them all.

One of the most versatile of women she was, therefore; and yet, for so many years her tongue and pen led the contest in this and other countries for what is commonly called the rights of woman—that is, for woman's right to stand as a unit among other units of the race—so it happens that her name naturally is fixed in the general public mind as belonging to that step of progress alone.

Indeed, in one of the most intelligently appreciative editorials I have yet seen on her life and death, which editorial appeared in a leading New York daily paper, she was spoken of as "a woman with one idea—suffrage—to which she had held, steadfastly, for fifty years."

This might be said of many of her associates, perhaps, either in praise or criticism; but a woman of one idea was precisely what Mrs. Stanton was not. Hers was a wonderfully well-rounded mentality, poised and strong on every side. Fearless and truth-loving, sincere and frank. But she did not allow her frankness to degenerate into rudeness. Her truth-loving never led her to disregard the feelings and rights of those who did not agree with her. She never mistook a loud voice and a sharp retort for argument, or for proof of the justice of her position.

She wished her body to be cremated. This, also, was because of her firm conviction of the right and value to the living, of this method of disposing of the dead.

She hugged to her breast no superstitions that prevented her from thinking first and always of the highest good to the living—to those who come after. Many of her constituents in the suffrage work deeply deplored her activity in free religious lines; but she calmly replied that woman would never be fit for freedom, nor understand its benefits and bearing until she ceased to hold to her bosom the primary cause of her degradation—her religious superstitions, which bind her to the degraded status assigned her as "the will of God" in all accepted "revelations." So long as she really believes (or pretends to do so for policy's sake) that Jehovah created her to serve man as his subordinate, she can be only half-hearted in her demand for either legal or social equality, and she can use only half of the legitimate arguments in her own defense. She spikes her own guns and throws away most of her powder. She weakens her case from the start and utterly begs her question. She leaves her antagonist in full possession of the field and allows him to plant her batteries to suit himself. She must have the courage to go to the root of the difficulty if she expects to gain her point.

So, for the past few years, much of Mrs. Stanton's time and literary energy have been spent in an effort to bring women up to this vantage ground—in a contest against religious superstitions, rather than against purely political ones, which she perceived had their basis and origin in the religious ones. Like Wendell Phillips, in the anti-slavery work, she believed in striking at the root, rather than in breaking of the branches of a fundamental wrong in the hope to eradicate it. She was deeply blamed by some of her old associates for putting out what she called "The Woman's Bible." That is to say, she gathered together all of the passages in the Bible which related especially to woman, and interpreted them (as man had done with all of them relating to himself—and to woman, also) in the light of modern thought.

For eighteen years past it has been my good fortune to be a close friend of this wonderful woman. I have hundreds of letters from her on the work of this "Woman's Bible," and on other topics, and I believe I may claim to know her aims and intent in it as well as any other person. In fact, I was one of the original "revision committee," and while the usual objection made to it by her critics is that it is too radical, my own objection was, always, that it was not radical enough! But to neither criticism did she give heed. She had her own ideal and plan and she went steadily about it without fear and without bigotry.

In 1887 she wrote me from England thus: "Think of it, she (referring to a fine suffrage leader) says she wishes to break down the material slavery of woman. If she wanted to get the Turkish women out of the harem, would she begin with arguments on republican government? No, indeed; she would know that they are held in sexual slavery by the power of their religion—and so are we. If women were emancipated from their religious superstitions they would understand their interests in the things of this life more readily. But believing that all things here are regulated by the finger of God, the Bible written by him, expressing his will, how can you rouse them to a desire for or belief in their social and political freedom until you first show them that all these things are the outgrowth of man's thought and selfishness, largely based upon his own superstitions and ignorance of Nature's laws, and resulting in woman's degradation and subjection? Do write whenever you have time. We enjoy your good, wholesome common sense. You, at least, never aim at one thing and try thereby to hit another."

Gladstone was called "the grand old man" because it was believed by many of his constituents that he had the faculty of always seeing and dealing with any new subject or difficulty wisely and ably.[9]

I always called Elizabeth Cady Stanton "My Mother Superior," but she may well be known as "the grand old woman," for upon almost every social and political question of her time, her voice and pen expressed her clear and lucid thought in luminous language, and never once did she fail to face toward the light; never once did her steady eye look away from Justice, Freedom and Fair-dealing for all.

She asked no privileges and opposed those who did.

What she sought for herself, she sought, also, for others. She did not believe that mistakes, however hoary, were sacred. She believed in progress—in rectifying the blunders of the past. The last bubble punctured by her keen pen was done, as I say, only three days before she died. It was in the interest of a clean, wholesome, happy home life—in the interest of honest, loving parenthood, in the interest of a child-life spent in an atmosphere of harmony and freed from one of pretense and domestic warfare—a plea, in short, for the right of children to be born of love and reared in its pure light. It was the last protest of this clear, fearless brain against the sophistries of those who hold that it is for the dignity and honor of woman and home that a mistake should be made perpetual— that the "Almighty" has joined together two who hate each other and on this theory they must continue to live out the farce to the bitter end. Her last printed utterance was an able protest against this absurdity, and was an honor to both head and heart of one who, seeing clearly is not afraid to express her thought even though she be (as she was in this case) the only champion whose bugle note did not quaver behind the mists and fogs of past ideas and lose its values in the defective acoustics of rock-bound superstitions.

Harriet [*sic*] Stanton Blatch, worthy daughter of this splendid mother, writes me of her last hours: "None of us knew mother was so near her end 'til Sunday really (the day she died). She had been suffering from short-ness of breath lately, from time to time, and from that cause felt under the mark. On Saturday she said to the doctor, very emphatically, 'Now, if you can't cure this difficulty of breathing, and if I am not to feel brighter and more like work again, I want you to give me something to send me pack-horse speed to heaven.'" And I can just see the twinkle in her eye when she said it.

Her daughter continues: "Two hours before her death (on Sunday) she said she wished to stand up. She was sitting in her arm chair in the drawing-room, not dressed, but in her dressing-gown, and with her hair all arranged as usual." In those beautiful white puffs, like a halo around her massive head—how well we all know and love them! "She had told her maid earlier in the day to dress her hair, and when it was finished she said: 'Now, I'll be dressed.' But I dissuaded her, seeing she was weary. The trained nurse (who had only been summoned an hour earlier), and the doctor, when she asked to stand, helped her to rise and stood on either side of her. I placed a table for her to rest her hands on. She drew herself up very erect (the doctor said the muscular strength was extraordinary) and there she stood for seven or eight minutes, steadily looking out, proudly before her. I think she was mentally making an address. When we urged her to sit down she fell asleep. Two hours later, the doctor thinking her position constrained in her chair, we lifted her to her bed, and she slipped away peacefully in a few minutes." And so passed from our sight and touch that splendid-all-embracing per-sonality. Could any death be more ideally beautiful—more what she would have wished? I can see her now, standing there in her last hours, with that delicate halo of soft, white curls around her death-touched face, pleading once again the cause of the mothers of the race, before an imaginary audience of sons and fathers of those who have lost in her their most eloquent, far-reaching voice.

For in her the world has lost its greatest woman, its noblest mother, its clearest thinker. She embraced in her motherhood all who were under the ban of oppression; she thought for the thoughtless of whatever sex, she was great enough to be honest with her own soul, and to walk in the light of the sun, hand in hand with the naked Truth! And in this she stood almost alone.

Other women there are and were, who walked side by side with her on certain planes, it is true. But none kept perfect step. Not one matched her in all-around ability, in versatility, in the capacity to be supremely clear and strong in every field of thought, in every line of progress.

Elizabeth Cady Stanton stood absolutely alone—a unique personality. In the "Solitude of Self" she walked like a Queen, a Philosopher, a Sage.

Others there were and are, perhaps, whose beautiful motherhood equals hers in that it glorifies home and makes of their children monuments to their domestic virtues. Others there were and are, perhaps, whose public work in some special lines for the betterment of their sisters, or for the race, place them on the same pedestal; and I am sure that none of us can ever speak the name, or picture the beautiful face of Mrs. Stanton without at the same time bowing the head of reverence and gratitude to that lifelong friend and co-worker of hers, our beloved, revered and glorious benefactor, Susan B. Anthony.

Possibly a few other women of our enlightened age have matched Mrs. Stanton, in brilliancy of thought and diction on economic, social or philosophical lines. A few there are who have turned their attention to the study and practice of law and have equalled her in legal acumen. A few who have worked in other special fields, as teachers, as preachers, as editors, as philanthropists, as students of natural science or sociology, may have burned as bright and steady lights as she. But there is not today, there never has been in all this world, a woman who for clearness and scope of vision, for fearlessness without self-assertion, for a splendid rounded personality and power in all the great topics, in all the varied fields of life, kept time and step with this powerful, this sweet, this beautiful woman, whom it was our privilege to know and revere—who worked day and night for us. For fifty long years she labored that we might "inherit the earth," and come into our natural right to live our own lives guided by the light of love and reason. And then she went bravely and sweetly out into the Unknown, still facing the light, still hoping for the race—hoping that the higher light that had touched and glorified her, might touch and gild the future for us all, and give to manhood and womanhood that loftiest crown of glory, the mutual confidence and respect of those who stand as equals before the law, asking from each other only that which they freely give to each other—absolute justice and absolute truth.

And so, at last, this majestic woman who faced opposition, misconception, abuse, if need be, with a smile and with the serene and glorified patience of one who has found life's deeper meanings, and climbed the heights and sounded the depths, reached that calm philosophy that can come only to the souls that walk in the light of Nature's profoundest secrets. Thus filled with honors and with years this majestic soul has passed into the infinite silence with the simple dignity and courage that encompassed her whole life, and we can only lay upon her grace the reverent tribute of our gratitude and tears, and softly say, Farewell!

*Delivered Nov. 13 at "Friends' Meeting House," Washington, D.C., at "Stanton Memorial meeting."

From "Side Lights on Life of Elizabeth Cady Stanton," Clara Bewick Colby, 1903[10]

[November 12, 1815–October 26, 1902]

Seldom has it been granted to a human being to be the foremost representative of an impulse that has modified conditions throughout the civilized world, but this we may claim for Elizabeth Cady Stanton. Mrs. Stanton did not originate the "woman's rights" movement. This had been growing from the dawn of history just as fast as the exigencies and limitations of social evolution would permit. The creative mandate had been the leaven in the human lump working toward the recognition of the inherent equality of the sexes, the two halves of the generic man, made in the image of God, and set to work out his divine inheritance of dominion.

Mrs. Stanton was not the first woman to see that the right of suffrage was needed to secure and protect all other rights. Here and there throughout the ages prophetic souls had made a kindred claim, and in modern times our own land had had Abigail Adams and others of the foremothers of this Republic urging that the principles that "Governments derive their just powers from the consent of the governed" and "Taxation without representation is tyranny" should be adopted as our basis of national independence and should be applied to women. Margaret Fuller had demanded all that has ever been asked by anybody—absolute equality for women. The seed thoughts of such far seeing patriots took root and blossomed into the woman suffrage movement as we know it. The age and the conditions were ready for one who should be endowed with the necessary gifts for leadership.

In Mrs. Stanton the "woman movement" took the definite form of specific and organized demand. Her happy circumstances, her forceful and charming personality, her undaunted courage and suavity, her keen logic tempered with a merry heart and a quick wit, won for woman's cause the ear of the world. She was ably supplemented by a host of other great souls who suddenly sprang up not only here but in England. Perhaps—who knows?—they may have been the reincarnation of the Immortals who have stood for Liberty and fought its battles in ages past. We can fancy that they may have held a conclave on the shining shore and decided that the reason the freedom of the race had not been won by the blood that had been shed for it since Time began was because the blow had not been struck at the root of tyranny, which, fastening round the heart of the mother and holding close her life, made her bring forth new generations of slaves, with new fetters as firmly fixed as those that had been stricken off the generations before. "We must free women," they cry; "and only as women can we do it!" And so there were born Elizabeth Cady Stanton, Susan B. Anthony, Lucy Stone, and Matilda Joslyn Gage; and in England Mrs. John Stuart Mill, John Bright's sisters, Mrs. Wolstonholme-Elmy [*sic*], and a multitude of noble souls on both sides of the sea who set flying the banner of "Equality before the law," which stands for woman's educational, industrial, professional, legal, and political rights.[11] . . .

The story of Mrs. Stanton's life and work is familiar to the public, or may be learned from her autobiography, "Eighty Years and More," . . . I shall, therefore, only record some personal recollections, showing her as she appeared to one of her "suffrage daughters," as she loved to call the young women who rallied round her in the eighties.

I saw her first on the train, and was much struck with the conscious dignity and self-possession that every movement showed as, during a period of waiting, she paced up and down the car. It was so unusual a proceeding in those days for a woman to infringe on the monopoly of air and exercise enjoyed by the male traveler that it made an impression on me. We went our separate ways and she never knew that in that simple act she had taught a lesson of self-respect.

My first word with her was a welcome to the Western town where, as a member of the lecture committee, I had been instrumental in securing her to give her famous lecture, "Our Girls." There was some delay in the arrival of the gentleman who was to introduce her to her audience, and she said to me: "You will introduce me, of course." I was much astonished that she could be satisfied to be presented by a woman, and it seemed hardly to show her proper respect. However, her tone and manner convinced me of her sincerity and gave me the courage to obey. We are so accustomed now to women presiding that it is hard to conceive what a step this was at that time. It identified me in the public thought with the woman suffrage movement and it was in reality a crossing of the Rubicon for me. In this way and in the multitude of ways that her rare faculty of reading human nature suggested, she made friends and converted friends into adherents. . . .

It was extremely felicitous for the woman's rights movement, at a time when by press and pulpit it was denounced as all that was unholy and especially intended as a subversion of all woman's duties as wife and mother, that its head was so marked an example of the domestic virtues. Then there were no magazines devoted to home science. Sanitation and other modern helps to hygiene had not when she was a young mother been reduced to rules, so she had to think everything out for herself. "The puzzling questions of theology and the causes of poverty," she says, "now gave place to the practical one, 'What to do with a baby?'" Having directed all the powers of her mind to this subject, the conclusions she came to could not be shaken by protests of physicians, nurses, or fond friends. An instance showing the method with which her household was governed was related to me by herself and is not found in her reminiscences. Her baby was trained to sleep by the clock, and during his slumber no soul might enter the room. A carpenter, having neglected to make some repairs in the bedroom, at the designated time, came when the baby was asleep and was informed that he could not enter. He testily inquired when he could do the work, and Mrs. Stanton took out her watch and told him when the baby would be awake.

How well her wisdom served her family may be judged from the fact that all her seven children came to a strong and vigorous maturity. The knowledge gained by experience she sought to impart to others, not only on the lecture platform but on all occasions where it was possible. Especially was this the case when she saw children suffering through the ignorance of the mother. A crying baby was always an appeal to her for help. She soon had it in her arms, and, by giving it a drink, loosening its clothes, or changing its position, invariably quieted it. How thoroughly unconventional and natural she was in all this may be judged from the following incident:

On a hot day Mrs. Stanton entered a crowded car and took the only vacant seat beside a gentleman who almost immediately said: "Mother, do you know anything about babies?" She replied that this was a department of knowledge that she particularly prided herself upon. The gentleman then asked her what could be the matter with a child on the train who had cried most of the time for the preceding twenty-four hours. Mrs. Stanton, of course, knew nothing about this particular case, so she promptly suggested her favorite prescription—a bath. To her surprise the gentleman said if she would give the bath he would provide the necessary means. He forthwith produced an india-rubber bowl, a towel and a sponge. Mrs. Stanton, easily gaining the tired mother's consent, gave the baby a drink and a bath. The child enjoyed the treatment and was sound asleep before it could be dressed and Mrs. Stanton left it thus when two hours later she arrived at the point where she was to lecture.

A young man who got off at the same station accosted her and begged her to go and see *his* baby, which he said had cried almost continuously since it was born, and the doctors could not tell what was the matter with it. Mrs. Stanton went home with the father and soon discovered that the difficulty was tight bandaging, according to the instructions of an ignorant nurse. She remained a long time with the parents, telling them everything she could think of about clothes, diet and pure air. The next day, after she had reached another town, it occurred to her that she had said nothing about giving the baby water; so she telegraphed back: "Give the baby water six times a day." Her message probably was carried into many homes, for the father was a telegrapher, and for years his fellow operators along the line would occasionally call him up and say, "Give the baby water six times a day." . . .

In religion, as in philosophy, Mrs. Stanton was universal. A person said to me the other day, "But the Freethinkers claim her." I replied, "Let them claim her; there is enough of her to go round." . . .

Other questions, too, concerned her greatly. . . . Populism, Socialism, and other Reform political movements were subjects of serious attention.

I quote from her letters: "I rejoice in them all; they are the first bugle notes of the coming revolution of 'equal rights to all.' The report of that —— wedding should rouse us all from our apathy and indifference to the corruption that gives millions to the few while the many suffer for shelter, food, and clothes, denied all the good things of life. . . . When the rich young man asked Jesus, 'What shall I do to be saved?' Jesus said, 'Go sell all that thou hast and give to the poor.'[12] This text should be echoed round the globe, in all our pulpits, until those pretending to be Christians should be ashamed rather than proud of their millions." . . .

In the ages to come a free and exalted humanity will think of Mrs. Stanton as one of the world's greatest benefactors. Wives having risen to the full stature of human beings in personal and property rights will loyally remember her efforts, which first loosed the fetters in which the common law held women in this relationship. Mothers will clasp their babes in their arms and thank God that she lived to plead for their legal right to their offspring. Children better born and nurtured than their ancestors, will be taught how her voice was raised in their behalf. College maidens will recall her hard lot, denied admission to schools of higher learning because of her sex, and how earnestly she fought to open their doors to women, and will be grateful that they live when *all* educational opportunities are open to them. Women of all lands and climes will reverence her memory as they join hands in work for the good of the world, for they will then have the power to embody their behests in law. Men will realize that the word of Freedom was not spoken by her for women only but for them also; for—

> "If *she* be small, slight-natured, miserable,
> How can men grow?"[13]

NOTES

1. Gardener willed her own brain to Cornell (Miller, "Gardener, Helen Hamilton").

2. Quoted in Ginzberg, *Elizabeth Cady Stanton*, 185; *San Francisco Chronicle*, "Professor Wants a Woman's Brain"; "The Journal of Comparative Neurology, July," 528.

3. Dubois, *Harriot Stanton Blatch*, 86.

4. Bloomberg, "Cultural Critique and Consciousness Raising," 36.

5. Sneider, "Sewall, Mary Eliza Wright."

6. May Wright Sewall, "Tribute of May Wright Sewall. President International Council of Women," *Woman's Tribune*, 22 November 1902.

7. Helen H. Gardener [Alice Chenoweth], "Elizabeth Cady Stanton," *Free Thought Magazine* 21, no. 1 (January 1903): 3–10.

8. Stanton's first article on divorce, "How Shall We Solve the Divorce Problem? A Symposium: Article I," appeared in the *New York American and Journal* on 13 October 1902, the first in a series of articles by notables who had been asked to supply a symposium on the country's "divorce problem." The second of her pieces, "Mrs. Stanton's Article on Divorce: An Answer to Bishop Stevens," appeared on 27 October, a response to an argument by Bishop Peter Fayssoux Stevens—"How Shall We Solve the Divorce Problem: Article XV." Appended to Stevens's piece is an editorial note suggesting that a third Stanton essay would follow, having been penned two days before death. On 29 October the paper printed the third article (which Stanton had submitted at the same time as the piece published on the 27th), "Elizabeth Cady Stanton's Last Plea for Women: Article XVII," with a contradictory claim that it had been composed three days before she died. In her own prefatory remarks to this last piece, Stanton maintained that, having read the other offerings to the symposium, she "disagree[d] most heartily with most of the eminent churchmen who have stated their views" (*SP* 6:441–446, 452–453; Stevens, "How Shall We Solve the Divorce Problem: Article XV"; Stanton, "Mrs. Stanton's Article on Divorce: An Answer to Bishop Stevens"; Stanton, "Elizabeth Cady Stanton's Last Plea for Women: Article XVII").

9. The British author and politician William Ewart Gladstone (1809–1898) was prime minister from 1868 to 1874.

10. Clara Bewick Colby, "Elizabeth Cady Stanton," *Woman's Tribune*, 17 October 1903.

11. British woman's suffrage activist and writer Elizabeth Wolstenholme Elmy (1833–1918) was particularly instrumental in petitioning for acts supporting civil equality for wives. For "John Bright's sisters," Colby likely refers to British woman's rights reformers Priscilla Bright McLaren (1815–1906), the sister of politicians Jacob (1821–1899) and John Bright (1811–1889), and Ursula Mellor Bright (1835–1915), Jacob Bright's wife. Both women served on the revising committee for *The Woman's Bible* (Milligan, "McLaren, Priscilla Bright [1815–1906]"; Crawford, "Bright, Ursula Mellor [1835–1915]").

12. Matthew 19:21.

13. From the poet Alfred, Lord Tennyson's *The Princess* (1847).

Permissions

Emily Blackwell to Elizabeth Blackwell, 11 October 1869, Blackwell Family Papers, MC 411, Box 11, Folder 164, courtesy of the Schlesinger Library, Radcliffe Institute, Harvard University, Cambridge, MA.

Henry B. Blackwell to Isabella Beecher Hooker, 1 December 1869, ALS 4 pp. New York, NY, Isabella Beecher Hooker Collection, courtesy of the Harriet Beecher Stowe Center, Hartford, CT.

A. E. [Anna Elizabeth] Henion, "Elizabeth Cady Stanton. Some Reminiscences of Her Family Life, at Seneca Falls, N.Y., by an Old Acquaintance," typescript, n.d., Collection 37, Box 38, Folder 6, courtesy of the archives of the Seneca Falls Historical Society, Seneca Falls, NY.

Isabella Beecher Hooker to Susan Howard, 2 January 1870, ALI 18 pp., Hartford, Isabella Beecher Hooker Collection, courtesy of the Harriet Beecher Stowe Center, Hartford, CT.

Adelaide Johnson, Excelsior Journal 1902, Adelaide Johnson Papers, MSS 27821, Box 2, courtesy of the Manuscript Division, Library of Congress, Washington, DC.

Adelaide Johnson, Record of Portrait Sittings, Adelaide Johnson Papers, MSS27821, Box 71, courtesy of the Manuscript Division, Library of Congress, Washington, DC.

Margaret Stanton Lawrence, "Who Was Elizabeth Cady Stanton? My Mother," Parts I and III, Elizabeth Cady Stanton Papers, 4.5 and 4.7, Archives and Special Collections, Vassar College Libraries, Poughkeepsie, NY. Courtesy of Coline Jenkins, Greenwich, CT.

Caroline Severance, Speech on Elizabeth Cady Stanton, n.d., Caroline M. Seymour Severance Papers, mssSeverance, Box 5, Folder 36, courtesy of the Huntington Library, San Marino, CA.

Elizabeth Cady Stanton Autograph and Commonplace Book, Ms. P. 84.848, Thirza Lee, March 1831, courtesy of the Trustees of the Boston Public Library/Rare Books, Boston, MA.

Gordon, Ann D., ed. *The Selected Papers of Elizabeth Cady Stanton and Susan B. Anthony. Volume VI: An Awful Hush 1895 to 1906.* Copyright ©2013 by

Bibliography

Abarbanell, Jacob R. "The 'Thirteen' Superstition among the Fair Sex." *Belford's Magazine* 6, no. 36 (May 1891): 801–816.

Abbeville Meridional. National News Section. 9 May 1891.

Anthony, Susan B. "Tribute from Miss Anthony." *New York Times*, 27 October 1902.

Applegate, Debby. *The Most Famous Man in America: The Biography of Henry Ward Beecher*. New York: Three Leaves Press Doubleday, 2006.

Banner, Lois W. *Elizabeth Cady Stanton: A Radical for Woman's Rights*. Glenview, IL: Scott, Foresman, 1980.

Barker, Theo. "Train, George Francis (1829–1904)." In *Oxford Dictionary of National Biography*. New York: Oxford University Press, 2004. Online edition. October 2007. Accessed 5 October 2015. http://www.oxforddnb.com/view/article/49513.

Barrett, Faith, and Cristanne Miller, eds. *"Words for the Hour": A New Anthology of American Civil War Poetry*. Amherst: University of Massachusetts Press, 2005.

Barry, Kathleen. *Susan B. Anthony: A Biography of a Singular Feminist*. New York: Ballantine Books, 1988.

Baxter, Maurice G. "Webster, Daniel." In *American National Biography Online*. February 2000. Accessed 16 October 2015. http://www.anb.org/articles/03/03-00525.html.

Bitton, Davis. "George Francis Train and Brigham Young." *Brigham Young University Studies* 18, no. 3 (1978): 410–427.

Blackwell Family Papers. Schlesinger Library, Radcliffe Institute. Harvard University, Cambridge, MA.

Blackwell, Marilyn S., and Kristen T. Oertel. *Frontier Feminist: Clarina Howard Nichols and the Politics of Motherhood*. Lawrence: University Press of Kansas, 2010.

Blatt, Martin Henry. *Free Love & Anarchism: The Biography of Ezra Heywood*. Urbana: University of Illinois Press, 1989.

Bloomberg, Kristin Mapel. "Cultural Critique and Consciousness Raising: Clara Bewick Colby's *Woman's Tribune* and Late-Nineteenth-Century Radical Feminism." In *Women in Print: Essays on the Print Culture of American Women from the Nineteenth and Twentieth Centuries*. Edited by James P. Danky and Wayne A. Wiegand. Foreword by Elizabeth Long. 27–63. Madison: University of Wisconsin Press, 2006.

Bordin, Ruth. *Frances Willard: A Biography*. Chapel Hill: University of North Carolina Press, 1986.

Bowden, Henry Warner. "Parker, Theodore." In *American National Biography Online*. February 2000. Accessed 29 August 2015. http://www.anb.org/articles/08/08-01925.html.

Brandt, Patricia. "Free Thought in Oregon: The Oregon State Secular Union." *Oregon Historical Quarterly* 87, no. 2 (1986): 167–204.

Brodie, Janet Farrell. *Contraception and Abortion in 19th-Century America*. Ithaca: Cornell University Press, 1994.

Bullard, Laura Curtis. "Elizabeth Cady Stanton." In *Our Famous Women. An Authorized and Complete Record of the Lives and Deeds of Eminent Women of Our Times*. Edited by Alfred S. Worthington. 602–623. Hartford, CT: Hartford Publishing, 1888.

Burns, Sarah. "Yankee Romance: The Comic Courtship Scene in Nineteenth-Century American Art." *American Art Journal* 18, no. 4 (1986): 51–75.

Burton, Shirley J. *Adelaide Johnson: To Make Immortal Their Adventurous Will*. Macomb: Western Illinois University, 1986.

Campbell, Gordon. "Milton, John (1608–1674)." In *Oxford Dictionary of National Biography*. New York: Oxford University Press, 2004. Online edition, January 2009. Accessed 26 October 2015. http://www.oxforddnb.com/view/article/18800.

Campbell, Susan. *Tempest-Tossed: The Spirit of Isabella Beecher Hooker*. Middleton, CT: Wesleyan University Press, 2014.

Chicago Daily Tribune. "Free Thinker and Wife Are Suffocated in Bed." 31 October 1903.

———. "Pendleton's Presidential Pilgrimage." 23 December 1875.

———. "A Statue to Giordano Bruno." 10 June 1889.

Child, Hamilton, comp. *Gazetteer and Business Directory of Seneca County, N.Y. for 1867-8*. Syracuse: Hamilton Child, 1867.

———. *Reference Business Directory of Seneca County, N.Y. 1894-'95. With Map*. Syracuse: E. M. Child, 1894.

Closz, Harriet M. "Stanton, Austin, Craddock, the Humanitarian Trinity." *Blue Grass Blade*, 30 November 1902.

Cody, Loretta, with Sarah Barber-Braun. *A Mighty Social Force: Phebe Ann Coffin Hanaford, 1829–1921*. Introduction by Alan Seaburg. Privately printed by Loretta Cody, 2009.

Cole, Phyllis. "The Nineteenth-Century Women's Rights Movement and the Canonization of Margaret Fuller." *ESQ* 44, nos. 1–2 (1998): 1–33.

———. "Stanton, Fuller, and the Grammar of Romanticism." *New England Quarterly* 73, no. 4 (December 2000): 533–559.

Collins, Paul. "How to Pitch a Magazine (in 1888)." *New Yorker Online*. 2 September 2014. Accessed 19 October 2015. http://www.newyorker.com/books/page-turner/how-pitch-magazine-1888.

Collison, Gary L. "Theodore Parker." In *The Transcendentalists: A Review of Research and Criticism*. Edited by Joel Myerson. 216–232. New York: Modern Language Association of America, 1984.

Cooper, George. *Lost Love: A True Story of Passion, Murder, and Justice in Old New York*. New York: Pantheon, 1994.

Cott, Nancy F. *The Grounding of Modern Feminism*. New Haven: Yale University Press, 1987.

Crawford, Elizabeth. "Bright, Ursula Mellor (1835–1915)." In *Oxford Dictionary of National Biography*. New York: Oxford University Press, 2004. Accessed 3 October 2015. http://www.oxforddnb.com/view/article/41340.

Crawley, Laura. "Smith, Elizabeth Oakes." In *American National Biography Online*. October 2008. Accessed 16 October 2015. http://www.anb.org/articles/15/15–00625.html.

Davis, Sue. *The Political Thought of Elizabeth Cady Stanton: Women's Rights and the American Political Traditions*. New York: New York University Press, 2008.

"Death of Mrs. C. K. Smith." *Humanitarian Review* 9, no. 10 (1911): 624–626.

Densmore, Christopher. "Colman, Lucy Newhall." In *American National Biography Online*. February 2000. Accessed 27 October 2015. http://www.anb.org/articles/15/15–00141.html.

Dixon, Suzanne. "Cornelia." In *The Oxford Encyclopedia of Ancient Greece and Rome*. Edited by Michael Gagarin. New York: Oxford University Press, 2010. Online edition 2010. Accessed 16 October 2015. http://www.oxfordreference.com/view/10.1093/acref/9780195170726.001.0001/acref-9780195170726-e-311.

Donegan, Jane P. *"Hydropathic Highway to Health": Women and Water-Cure in Antebellum America*. New York: Greenwood, 1986.

DuBois, Ellen Carol. *Feminism and Suffrage: The Emergence of an Independent Women's Movement in America, 1848–1869*. Ithaca: Cornell University Press, 1978.

————. *Harriot Stanton Blatch and the Winning of Woman Suffrage*. New Haven: Yale University Press, 1997.

————, ed. "On Labor and Free Love: Two Unpublished Speeches of Elizabeth Cady Stanton." *Signs* 1, no. 1 (1975): 257–268.

————. "Part Three: 1874–1906: Introduction." In *The Elizabeth Cady Stanton–Susan B. Anthony Reader: Correspondence, Writings, Speeches*. Edited and with a Critical Commentary by Ellen Carol DuBois. Foreword by Gerda Lerner. Rev. ed. 172–200. Boston: Northeastern University Press, 1992.

————. "Woman Suffrage and the Left: An International Socialist-Feminist Perspective." *New Left Review* 1, no. 186 (March/April 1991): 20–45.

————. *Woman Suffrage & Women's Rights*. New York: New York University Press, 1998.

DuBois, Ellen Carol, and Richard Cándida Smith, eds. *Elizabeth Cady Stanton: Feminist as Thinker*. New York: New York University Press, 2007.

Dudden, Faye E. *Fighting Chance: The Struggle over Woman Suffrage and Black Suffrage in Reconstruction America*. Oxford: Oxford University Press, 2011.

Duluth News-Tribune. "News and Comment." 22 November 1902.

Dunfey, Julie. "'Living the Principle' of Plural Marriage: Mormon Women, Utopia, and Female Sexuality in the Nineteenth Century." *Feminist Studies* 10, no. 3 (Autumn 1984): 523–536.

Eller, Cynthia. *The Myth of Matriarchal Prehistory: Why an Invented Past Won't Give Women a Future*. Boston: Beacon, 2000.

Elliot, Reverend H. B. "Woman as Physician." In *Eminent Women of the Age*. Edited by S. M. Betts. 513–550. Hartford, CT: S. M. Betts, 1868.

Elwood-Akers, Virginia. *Caroline Severance*. New York: iUniverse, 2010.

Evans, William W., and Wesley W. Crofoot. *Seneca Falls and Waterloo Village Directory, 1874–5*. Syracuse: Evans and Crofoot, 1874.

Fairbanks, Mrs. A. W., ed. *Emma Willard and Her Pupils; Or Fifty Years of Troy Female Seminary, 1822–1872*. New York: Mrs. Russell Sage, 1898.

Faulkner, Carol. *Lucretia Mott's Heresy: Abolition and Women's Rights in Nineteenth-Century America*. Philadelphia: University of Pennsylvania Press, 2011.

Fischer, Gayle V. *Pantaloons and Power: A Nineteenth-Century Dress Reform in the United States*. Kent, OH: Kent State University Press, 2001.

Fisher, Sydney George. *The True Daniel Webster*. Philadelphia: J. B. Lippincott, 1911.

Frisken, Amanda. *Victoria Woodhull's Sexual Revolution: Political Theater and the Popular Press in Nineteenth-Century America*. Philadelphia: University of Pennsylvania Press, 2004.

Fuller, Margaret. *Woman in the Nineteenth Century.* In *The Essential Margaret Fuller.* Edited and introduction by Jeffrey Steele. 247–378. New Brunswick, NJ: Rutgers University Press, 1995.

Gac, Scott. *Singing for Freedom: The Hutchinson Family Singers and the Nineteenth-Century Culture of Antebellum Reform.* New Haven: Yale University Press, 2007.

Gallman, J. Matthew. *America's Joan of Arc: The Life of Anna Elizabeth Dickinson.* Oxford: Oxford University Press, 2006.

Gamber, Wendy. "Miller, Elizabeth Smith." In *American National Biography Online.* February 2000. Accessed 22 August 2015. http://www.anb.org/articles/15/15–00841.html.

Garrison, Marie H. "Michelet's Motto for Elizabeth Cady Stanton." *Free Thought Magazine* 21, no. 1 (January 1903): 22–24.

Garrison, William Lloyd, and Elizabeth Cady Stanton [E.C.S.]. "William Lloyd Garrison Crucifies Democrats, Train, and the Women of 'The Revolution.'" *Revolution,* 29 January 1868.

Ginzberg, Lori D. *Elizabeth Cady Stanton: An American Life.* New York: Hill and Wang, 2009.

———. "'The Hearts of Your Readers Will Shudder': Fanny Wright, Infidelity, and American Freethought." *American Quarterly* 46, no. 2 (1994): 195–226.

———. *Untidy Origins: A Story of Woman's Rights in Antebellum New York.* Chapel Hill: University of North Carolina Press, 2005.

Good, Jane E. "America and the Russian Revolutionary Movement, 1888–1905." *Russian Review* 41, no. 3 (1982): 273–287.

Gordon, Ann D. Afterword. In *Eighty Years and More: Reminiscences 1815–1897.* Introduction by Ellen Carol DuBois. 469–483. Boston: Northeastern University Press, 1993.

———. "Stanton and the Right to Vote: On Account of Race or Sex." In DuBois and Smith, *Elizabeth Cady Stanton: Feminist as Thinker,* 111–127.

Gordon, Ann D., and Bettye Collier-Thomas, eds. *African American Women and the Vote, 1837–1965.* Amherst: University of Massachusetts Press, 1997.

Gordon, Linda. "Voluntary Motherhood: The Beginnings of Feminist Birth Control Ideas in the United States." In *Women and Health in America: Historical Readings.* Edited by Judith Walzer Leavitt. 2nd ed. 253–268. Madison: University of Wisconsin Press, 1999.

———. *Woman's Body, Woman's Right: Birth Control in America.* Rev. ed. New York: Penguin, 1990.

Gordon, Sarah Barringer. "The Liberty of Self-Degradation: Polygamy, Woman Suffrage, and Consent in Nineteenth-Century America." *Journal of American History* 83, no. 3 (December 1996): 815–847.

Greeley, Horace. "The Educational Problem." *Independent*, 24 September 1863.

———. *Recollections of a Busy Life*. New York: J. B. Ford, 1868.

Greeley, Horace, and Robert Dale Owen. *Divorce: Being a Correspondence between Horace Greeley and Robert Dale Owen. Originally Published in the "New York Daily Tribune."* New York: De Witt, 1860.

Greenwood, Grace. "The National Women's Suffrage Convention at Washington." *Philadelphia Press*, 20 January 1869.

Griffith, Elisabeth. *In Her Own Right: The Life of Elizabeth Cady Stanton*. Oxford: Oxford University Press, 1984.

Griswold, Hattie Tyng. "Elizabeth Cady Stanton." *Unity* 50, no. 10 (November 1902): 149–150.

Grodzins, Dean. *American Heretic: Theodore Parker and Transcendentalism*. Chapel Hill: University of North Carolina Press, 2002.

Groseclose, Barbara. "Hosmer, Harriet Goodhue." In *American National Biography Online*. February 2000. Accessed 27 October 2015. http://www.anb.org/articles/17/17–00425.html.

Guarneri, Carl J. *The Utopian Alternative: Fourierism in Nineteenth-Century America*. Ithaca: Cornell University Press, 1991.

Gunter, Susan E. "Tilton, Theodore." In *American National Biography Online*. February 2000. Accessed 10 October 2015. http://www.anb.org/articles/16/16–01645.html.

Haber, Carole. *The Trials of Laura Fair: Sex, Murder, and Insanity in the Victorian West*. Chapel Hill: University of North Carolina Press, 2013.

Hardy, B. Carmon. "Lords of Creation: Polygamy, the Abrahamic Household, and Mormon Patriarchy." *Journal of Mormon History* 20, no. 1 (Spring 1994): 119–152.

Harper, Ida Husted. *The Life and Work of Susan B. Anthony*. 2 vols. Indianapolis: Bowen-Merrill, 1898.

Harris, Sharon M. *Dr. Mary Walker: An American Radical, 1832–1919*. New Brunswick, NJ: Rutgers University Press, 2009.

Hedrick, Joan D. *Harriet Beecher Stowe: A Life*. New York: Oxford University Press, 1994.

Henry, Josephine K. "Tribute to Elizabeth Cady Stanton." *Blue Grass Blade*, 9 November 1902.

Henry, Nancy. *The Life of George Eliot: A Critical Biography*. Malden, MA: Wiley-Blackwell, 2012.

Hogan, Lisa S., and J. Michael Hogan. "Feminine Virtue and Practical Wisdom: Elizabeth Cady Stanton's 'Our Boys.'" *Rhetoric & Public Affairs* 6, no. 3 (2003): 415–435.

Holton, Sandra Stanley. "'To Educate Women into Rebellion': Elizabeth Cady Stanton and the Creation of a Transatlantic Network of Radical Suffragists." *American Historical Review* 99, no. 4 (October 1994): 1112–1136.

Horowitz, Murray M. "Pratt, Daniel." In *American National Biography Online.* February 2000. Accessed 25 March 2016. http://www.anb.org/articles/20/20–00817.html.

Isenberg, Nancy. *Sex & Citizenship in Antebellum America.* Chapel Hill: University of North Carolina Press, 1998.

Jacoby, Susan. *The Great Agnostic: Robert Ingersoll and American Freethought.* New Haven: Yale University Press, 2013.

James, J. A. *The Christian Father's Present to His Children.* 2 vols. New York: Jonathan Leavitt; Boston: Crocker and Brewster, 1827. 4th American ed.

Jerry, E. Claire. "Colby, Clara Dorothy Bewick." In *American National Biography Online.* February 2000. Accessed 20 October 2015. http://www.anb.org/articles/15/15–00802.html.

Johnson, Adelaide, Papers. Library of Congress.

Jones, Martha S. *All Bound Up Together: The Woman Question in African American Public Culture, 1830–1900.* Chapel Hill: University of North Carolina Press, 2007.

———. "The Journal of Comparative Neurology, July." *Science,* 18 October 1895, 528.

Kern, Kathi. "'Free Woman Is a Divine Being, the Savior of Mankind': Stanton's Exploration of Religion and Gender." In DuBois and Smith, *Elizabeth Cady Stanton, Feminist as Thinker,* 93–110.

———. *Mrs. Stanton's Bible.* Ithaca: Cornell University Press, 2001.

Kerr, Andrea Moore. *Lucy Stone: Speaking Out for Equality.* New Brunswick, NJ: Rutgers University Press, 1995.

Kessler, Carol Farley, ed. *Daring to Dream: Utopian Fiction by United States Women before 1950.* 2nd ed. New York: Syracuse University Press, 1995.

King, Charles. "Notes from Washington." *Zion's Herald* 54, no. 5 (1 February 1877): 40.

Kohn, Denise M. Introduction. In *Christine; Or Woman's Trials & Triumphs,* by Laura Curtis Bullard. Edited by Denise M. Kohn. ix–xlv. Lincoln: University of Nebraska Press, 2010.

Kujawa, Sheryl A. "Brown, Olympia." In *American National Biography Online.* February 2000. Accessed 15 October 2015. http://www.anb.org/articles/15/15–00097.html.

Larned, Augusta. "The Woman's Congress." *Christian Union* 8, no. 19 (5 November 1873): 362–363.

Lawrence, Margaret Stanton. "As a Mother." *New Era* 1, no. 11 (November 1885): 322–323.

———. "Who Was Elizabeth Cady Stanton? My Mother." Elizabeth Cady Stanton Papers, Archives and Special Collections, Vassar College Libraries, Poughkeepsie, NY.

Leavitt, Judith Walzer. *Brought to Bed: Childbearing in America, 1750–1950.* New York: Oxford University Press, 1986.

Lederman, Sarah Henry. "Davis, Paulina Kellogg Wright." In *American National Biography Online.* February 2000. Accessed 10 August 2015. http://www.anb.org/articles/15/15-00166.html.

Locke, Mamie E. "Harper, Frances Ellen Watkins." In *American National Biography Online.* February 2000. Accessed 26 October 2015. http://www.anb.org/articles/15/15-00304.html.

———. "Howland, Emily." In *American National Biography Online.* February 2000. Accessed 22 August 2015. http://www.anb.org/articles/15/15-00350.html.

Lutz, Alma. *Created Equal: A Biography of Elizabeth Cady Stanton, 1815–1902.* New York: John Day, 1940.

Lynch, Robert Lee. "Bunner, Henry Cuyler." In *American National Biography Online.* February 2000. Accessed 18 October 2015. http://www.anb.org/articles/16/16-00219.html.

Mantell, Deborah Byrd. "*The Princess*: Tennyson's Eminently Shakespearian Poem." *Texas Studies in Literature and Language* 20, no. 1 (1978): 48–67.

Mayer, Henry. *All on Fire: William Lloyd Garrison and the Abolition of Slavery.* New York: W. W. Norton, 1998.

McArthur, Benjamin. "Jefferson, Joseph, III." In *American National Biography Online.* February 2000. Accessed 19 October 2015. http://www.anb.org/articles/18/18-00629.html.

McDaneld, Jen. "White Suffragist Dis/Entitlement: The *Revolution* and the Rhetoric of Racism." *Legacy* 30, no. 2 (2013): 243–264.

McFeely, William S. *Frederick Douglass.* New York: Norton, 1991.

McKivigan, John R. "Smith, Gerrit." In *American National Biography Online.* October 2008. Accessed 23 March 2016. http://www.anb.org/articles/15/15-00627.html.

McMillen, Sally G. *Lucy Stone: An Unapologetic Life.* Oxford: Oxford University Press, 2015.

Miller, Elisa. "Gardener, Helen Hamilton." In *American National Biography Online.* February 2000. Accessed 20 October 2015. http://www.anb.org/articles/15/15-00252.html.

———. "Rose, Ernestine." In *American National Biography Online*. February 2000. Accessed 27 October 2015. http://www.anb.org/articles/15/15-00581.html.

Miller, Howard S. "Kate Austin: A Feminist-Anarchist on the Farmer's Last Frontier." *Nature, Society, and Thought: A Journal of Dialectical and Historical Materialism* 9, no. 2 (April 1996, special issue): 189–209. From the University of Minnesota Digital Conservancy. http://purl.umn.edu/149963.

Milligan, Edward H. "McLaren, Priscilla Bright (1815–1906)." In *Oxford Dictionary of National Biography*. New York: Oxford University Press, 2004. Accessed 3 October 2015. http://www.oxforddnb.com/view/article/47643.

Million, Joelle. *Woman's Voice, Woman's Place: Lucy Stone and the Birth of the Woman's Rights Movement*. Westport, CT: Praeger, 2003.

Moore, James Ross. "Kemble, Fanny." In *American National Biography Online*. February 2000. Accessed 16 October 2015. http://www.anb.org/articles/18/18–00666.html.

"Mrs. Stanton on the Wheel." *Free Thought Magazine* 13, no. 9 (September 1895): 525.

Myerson, Joel, ed. *Transcendentalism: A Reader*. Oxford: Oxford University Press, 2000.

New York Daily Times. "New-England Anti-Slavery Convention." 2 June 1855.

New York Times. "In Memory of Bruno." 21 February 1889.

———. "Pankhurst Speech Opens Pocketbooks." 6 January 1912.

New York Tribune. "G. F. Train—C. M. Clay." 5 November 1862.

Nichols, M. S. [Mary Sargeant] Gove. "Water-Cure in Childbirth—Again." *Water-Cure Journal* 9, no. 4 (April 1850): 117.

Nichols, T. L. [Thomas Low]. "The Curse Removed." *Water-Cure Journal* 10, no. 5 (November 1850): 167–173.

Opdycke, Sandra. "Harper, Ida Husted." In *American National Biography Online*. February 2000. Accessed 17 September 2015. http://www.anb.org/articles/15/15–00305.html.

Owen, John. *The Skeptics of the Italian Renaissance*. 2nd ed. New York: Macmillan, 1893.

The Oxford Dictionary of Reference and Allusion. Edited by Andrew Delahunty and Sheila Dignen. Oxford: Oxford University Press, 2010. Online edition 2015. Accessed 16 October 2015. http://www.oxfordreference.com/view/10.1093/acref/9780199567454.001.0001/acref-9780199567454-e-348.

The Oxford Dictionary of the Christian Church. Edited by F. L. Cross and E. A. Livingstone. New York: Oxford University Press, 2005. Online edition 2009. Accessed 29 August 2015. http://www.oxfordreference.com/view/10.1093/acref/9780192802903.001.0001/acref-9780192802903-e-1024.

Painter, Nell Irvin. *Sojourner Truth: A Life, a Symbol*. New York: Norton, 1996.

Palmer, Beverly Wilson, ed. *Selected Letters of Lucretia Coffin Mott*. Urbana: University of Illinois Press, 2002.

Parker, Theodore. *The Relation of Jesus to His Age and the Ages. A Sermon Preached at the Thursday Lecture, in Boston. December 26, 1844*. Boston: Charles C. Little and James Brown, 1845.

Passet, Joanne E. *Sex Radicals and the Quest for Women's Equality*. Urbana: University of Illinois Press, 2003.

Penney, Sherry H., and James D. Livingston. *A Very Dangerous Woman: Martha Wright and Women's Rights*. Amherst: University of Massachusetts Press, 2004.

Perry, Marilyn Elizabeth. "Blatch, Harriot Stanton." In *American National Biography Online*. February 2000. Accessed 3 October 2015. http://www.anb.org/articles/15/15-00068.html.

———. "Livermore, Mary." In *American National Biography Online*. February 2000. Accessed 16 October 2015. http://www.anb.org/articles/15/15-00415.html.

Plummer, Mark A. "Pomeroy, Samuel Clarke." In *American National Biography Online*. February 2000. Accessed 13 September 2015. http://www.anb.org/articles/04/04-00799.html.

Potter, Helen. *Helen Potter's Impersonations*. New York: Edgar S. Werner, 1891.

———. "Reminiscences of the Lyceum: VIII—Susan Brownell Anthony." *Lyceumite and Talent*, no. 19 (December 1908): 14–15, 26.

Prieto, Laura R. *At Home in the Studio: The Professionalization of Women Artists in America*. Cambridge: Harvard University Press, 2001.

Rawley, James A. "Robinson, Charles." In *American National Biography Online*. February 2000. Accessed 17 March 2016. http://www.anb.org/articles/04/04-00859.html.

Remini, Robert V. *Daniel Webster: The Man and His Time*. New York: Norton, 1997.

———. *Henry Clay: Statesman for the Union*. New York: Norton, 1991.

Revolution. "The Revolution; The Organ of the National Party of New America." 15 January 1868.

———. "What the Press Says." 24 June 1869.

———. "Woman's Right to Cook." 7 October 1869.

Reynolds, David S. *John Brown, Abolitionist: The Man Who Killed Slavery, Sparked the Civil War, and Seeded Civil Rights*. New York: Knopf, 2005.

Robertson, Stacey M. *Parker Pillsbury: Radical Abolitionist, Male Feminist.* Ithaca: Cornell University Press, 2000.

Ruchames, Louis, ed. *The Letters of William Lloyd Garrison, Volume II: A House Dividing against Itself, 1836–1840.* Cambridge: Belknap Press of Harvard University Press, 1971.

San Francisco Chronicle. "Professor Wants a Woman's Brain." 17 November 1902.

Schmidt, Leigh Eric. *Heaven's Bride: The Unprintable Life of Ida C. Craddock, American Mystic, Scholar, Sexologist, Martyr and Madwoman.* New York: Basic Books, 2010.

Scott, Franklin William. *Newspapers and Periodicals of Illinois, 1814–1879.* Rev. and enlarged ed. Springfield: Trustees of the Illinois State Historical Library, 1910.

Severance, Caroline. *The Mother of Clubs: Caroline M. Seymour Severance—an Estimate and an Appreciation.* Edited by Ella Giles Ruddy. Los Angeles: Baumgardt, 1906.

———. Caroline M. Seymour Severance Papers. Huntington Library, San Marino, CA.

Sewell, Stacy Kinlock. "Remond, Charles Lenox." In *American National Biography Online.* February 2000. Accessed 16 October 2015. http://www.anb.org/articles/15/15-00568.html.

Sigerman, Harriet. "Gage, Frances Dana Barker." In *American National Biography Online.* February 2000. Accessed 16 October 2015. http://www.anb.org/articles/15/15-00247.html.

Silver-Isenstadt, Jean L. *Shameless: The Visionary Life of Mary Gove Nichols.* Baltimore: Johns Hopkins University Press, 2002.

Sneider, Allison L. "Sewall, May Eliza Wright." In *American National Biography Online.* February 2000. Accessed 22 October 2015. http://www.anb.org.colby.idm.oclc.org/articles/15/15-00612.html.

Spurlock, John. "The Free Love Network in America, 1850 to 1860." *Journal of Social History* 21, no. 4 (1988): 765–779.

Stanton, Elizabeth Cady. "Closing Address." In *Report of the International Council of Women.* 431–438. Washington, DC: Rufus H. Darby, 1888.

——— [E.C.S.]. "The Devil Again." *Lily* 3, no. 8 (August 1851): 63.

———. *Eighty Years and More: Reminiscences 1815–1897.* 1898. Introduction by Ellen Carol DuBois. Afterword by Ann D. Gordon. Boston: Northeastern University Press, 1993.

———. "Elizabeth Cady Stanton's Last Plea for Women: Article XVII." *New York American and Journal,* 29 October 1902.

———— [E.C.C.] [*sic*]. "For the Lily. The Devil." *Lily* 3, no. 1 (July 1851): 51.

———— [E.C.S.]. "Hester Vaughan." *Revolution*, 19 November 1868.

————. "How Shall We Solve the Divorce Problem? A Symposium: Article I." *New York American and Journal*, 13 October 1902.

———— [E.C.S.]. "Letters to Mothers. No. 1. The Boys of Our Village." *Lily* 3, no. 9 (September 1851): 66.

————. "The Matriarchate, or Mother-Age." In DuBois and Smith, *Elizabeth Cady Stanton, Feminist as Thinker*, 264–275.

————. "Mrs. Stanton's Article on Divorce: An Answer to Bishop Stevens." *New York American and Journal*, 27 October 1902.

———— [E.C.S.]. "My Bouquet." *Lily* 4, no. 6 (June 1852): 52.

————. "The Need of Liberal Divorce Laws." *North American Review* 139, no. 334 (September 1884): 234–245.

————. "Overland Letters." *Revolution*, 20 July 1871.

————. *The Selected Papers of Elizabeth Cady Stanton and Susan B. Anthony.* Edited by Ann D. Gordon et al. 6 vols. New Brunswick, NJ: Rutgers University Press, 1997–2013.

———— [E.C.S.]. "Sobriny Jane." *Lily* 3, no. 3 (March 1851): 23.

————. "The True Republic." In *The Papers of Elizabeth Cady Stanton and Susan B. Anthony: Microfilm Edition.* Edited by Patricia G. Holland and Ann D. Gordon. 45 reels. 15:1–83. Wilmington, DE: Scholarly Resources, 1992.

————. "The Woman's Rights Movement and Its Champions in the United States." In *Eminent Women of the Age.* Edited by S. M. Betts. 362–404. Hartford, CT: S. M. Betts, 1868.

Stanton, Elizabeth Cady, Susan B. Anthony, and Matilda Joslyn Gage, eds. *History of Woman Suffrage: 1848–1861, Vol. 1.* New York: Fowler & Wells, 1881.

————. *History of Woman Suffrage: 1861–1876, Vol. 2.* New York: Fowler & Wells, 1882.

Stanton, Elizabeth Cady, and the Revising Committee. *The Woman's Bible, Parts I and II.* New York: European Publishing, 1895, 1898. Rpt. New York: Arno, 1972.

Stanton, Henry B. *Random Recollections.* New York: Harper & Brothers, 1887.

Stanton, Theodore, and Harriot Stanton Blatch, eds. *Elizabeth Cady Stanton as Revealed in Her Letters, Diary, and Reminiscences.* 2 vols. New York: Harper & Brothers, 1922.

Stevens, Peter Fayssoux. "How Shall We Solve the Divorce Problem: Article XV." *New York American and Journal*, 27 October 1902.

Stewart, James Brewer. "Garrison, William Lloyd." In *American National*

Biography Online. February 2000. Accessed 18 October 2015. http://www
.anb.org/articles/15/15-00256.html.

Taylor, Clare, ed. *British and American Abolitionists: An Episode in Transatlantic Understanding*. Edinburgh: Edinburgh University Press, 1974.

Terborg-Penn, Rosalyn. *African American Women in the Struggle for the Vote,
1850–1920*. Bloomington: Indiana University Press, 1998.

Tetrault, Lisa. "The Incorporation of American Feminism: Suffragists and
the Postbellum Lyceum." *Journal of American History* 96, no. 4 (2010):
1027–1056.

———. *The Myth of Seneca Falls: Memory and the Women's Suffrage Movement,
1848–1898*. Chapel Hill: University of North Carolina Press, 2014.

Thomas, Tracey A. "Elizabeth Cady Stanton and the Notion of a Legal Class
of Gender." In *Feminist Legal History: Essays on Women and Law*. Edited
by Thomas Boisseau and Tracey Jean Boisseau. 139–155. New York: New
York University Press, 2011.

Thoreau, Henry D. *The Writings of Henry D. Thoreau: Journal Volume 1:
1837–1844*. Edited by John C. Broderick et al. Princeton: Princeton University Press, 1981.

[Tilton, Theodore]. "Mrs. Elizabeth Cady Stanton." In *Eminent Women of the
Age*. Edited by S. M. Betts. 332–361. Hartford, CT: S. M. Betts, 1868.

———. "Notes about Women." *Revolution*, 6 July 1871.

Tone, Andrea. "Black Market Birth Control: Contraceptive Entrepreneurship
and Criminality in the Gilded Age." *Journal of American History* 87, no. 2
(September 2000): 435–459.

Train, George Francis. "Letter from Geo. Francis Train." *Revolution*, 22 April
1869.

Tuchinsky, Adam. *Horace Greeley's "New-York Tribune": Civil War–Era Socialism and the Crisis of Free Labor*. Ithaca: Cornell University Press, 2009.

United States Census, 1860. New England Historic Genealogical Society Online Database. AmericanAncestors.org.

United States Census, 1880. New England Historic Genealogical Society Online Database. AmericanAncestors.org.

Van Voris, Jacqueline. *Carrie Chapman Catt: A Public Life*. New York: Feminist Press at the City University of New York, 1987.

Voss, Arthur W. M. "The Evolution of Lowell's 'The Courtin'.'" *American
Literature* 15, no. 1 (1943): 42–50.

Weiss, John. *Life and Correspondence of Theodore Parker*. 2 vols. New York:
Appleton, 1864.

Wellman, Judith. *The Road to Seneca Falls: Elizabeth Cady Stanton and the*

First Woman's Rights Convention. Chicago: University of Illinois Press, 2004.

Wertz, Richard W., and Dorothy C. Wertz. *Lying-In: A History of Childbirth in America*. New York: Free Press, 1977.

West, Richard Samuel. *Satire on Stone: The Political Cartoons of Joseph Keppler*. Urbana: University of Illinois Press, 1988.

Wheeler, Leslie, ed. *Loving Warriors: Selected Letters of Lucy Stone and Henry B. Blackwell, 1853–1893*. Introduction by Leslie Wheeler. New York: Dial Press, 1981.

White, Barbara A. *The Beecher Sisters*. New Haven: Yale University Press, 2003.

Who's Who in New York City and State. New York: L. R. Hamersly, 1904.

Williams, Edwin. *The New-York Annual Register for the Year of Our Lord 1830*. New York: J. Leavitt, 1830.

———. *The New-York Annual Register for the Year of Our Lord 1831*. New York: Jonathan Leavitt and Collins & Hannay, 1831.

———. *The New-York Annual Register for the Year of Our Lord 1832*. New York: J. Seymour, 1832.

———. *The New-York Annual Register for the Year of Our Lord 1833*. New York: Peter Hill, 1833.

Winter, Thomas. "Swinton, John." In *American National Biography Online*. February 2000. Accessed 14 July 2015. http://www.anb.org/articles/15/15-00677.html.

Index